Discoursing Minority

Discoursing Minority

In-Text and Co-Text

Edited by

Anisur Rahman
Supriya Agarwal
Bhumika Sharma

RAWAT PUBLICATIONS

Jaipur • New Delhi • Bangalore • Hyderabad • Guwahati • Kolkata

ISBN 978-81-316-0640-7

Published by
Prem Rawat for **Rawat Publications**
Satyam Apartments, Sector 3, Jawahar Nagar, Jaipur 302 004 (India)
Phone: 0141 265 1748 / 7006 Fax: 0141 265 1748
E-mail: info@rawatbooks.com
Website: www.rawatbooks.com

New Delhi Office
4858/24, Ansari Road, Daryaganj, New Delhi 110 002
Phone: 011 2326 3290

Also at *Bangalore, Hyderabad, Guwahati* and *Kolkata*

Typeset by Calidad, Pondicherry
Printed at Chaman Enterprises, New Delhi

Dedicated
to the growing perseverance of
Comparative Studies

Contents

Acknowledgment x

Preface xi

***Section 1* Discoursing Minority**

1 Minorities across Cultures 3
Keki N. Daruwalla

2 Spokespersonship in Literary Theory: The Act of Elites Speaking for Minorities 12
Dorothy Figueira

3 The Parameters of "Minority Discourse": Attempting an Identification for Literary Historiography 23
Ipshita Chanda

4 Genre and Genus as Minority Discourse: Rethinking the Categories of Dalit Literature 34
Christi A. Merrill

5 The Sacred Writings of the Minorities 45
Gurbhagat Singh

6 Discoursing Minority: Twentieth-Century Constructions of Indian Muslims 53
Anisur Rahman

7 Violence that Dare Not Speak Its Name: Construing and De-construing Minority Men 78
Mashrur Shahid Hossain and Kazi Asraf Uddin

8 Negotiating Difference: Minority Discourse and Translation 100
Assumpta Camps

Section 2 **In-Text**

9 Redefining the Secular and the Modern: The Politics of Identity and the Minority Discourse in Contemporary India 115
E. V. Ramakrishna

10 The Artiste as Woman: The Seeking Spirit of Vidya Rao and Tulsi Badrinath 127
Laxmi Kannan

11 Alternative Discourses of Power: A Comparative Reading of Select Muslim Asian Texts 142
Ameena Kazi Ansari

12 The Spiritual Economy of Caste and the Politics of Inversion: A Theme-Based Study of Three Dalit Narratives from Bangla 153
Sayantan Dasgupta

13 *L' Ecriture feminine*: Writing from the Margins 161
Rachel Bari

14 Political Intervention in Minority Discourse: *Storm in Chandigarh* and *India: A Million Mutinies Now* 171
Maninder Pal Kaur Sidhu

15 Subaltern Voices in Indian Epic Recitals 182
Rashmi Mathur

16 Of Possession and Dispossession: Narayan's *Kocharethi: The Araya Woman* and Mohanty's *Paraja* 193
Charu Mathur

17 History of Race: Islands in the Nation 203
S. Asha

Section 3 **Co-Text**

18 Marginalizing Rural Life: Tolstoy and the World Literature Anthologies 219
John Burt Foster, Jr

19 Communist Autobiographies and Minority Discourses: Leon Trotsky and Alexandra Kollontai 233
Kunal Chattopadhyay

20 Diasbled but Beautiful and Proudly Resistant: Applied Theatre for the Disabled as Minority Discourse 255
Nehemiah Chivandikwa and Owen Seda

21 Blurring the Boundaries of the Canon: Place and Performance as Alternative Practice in the Townships of Colonial Rhodesia 278
Owen Seda

22 Re-claiming the Mammy: Racial, Sexual and Class Politics Behind "Mammification" of Black Women 291
Shaweta Nanda

23 Voices of Silence: The Case of Women Musicians 305
Bandana Chakrabarty

24 Minority Discourse through Bioscope: *Fire* and *Between Two Women* 315
Pragati Sobti and Amit Joshi

Contributors 326

Index 328

Acknowledgement

The editors thank the following for their support and cooperation towards organizing the conference on *Minority Discourses Across Cultures* of which this volume is an outcome: Comparative Literature Association of India, Central University of Rajasthan, University Grants Commission, Indian Council for Cultural Relations, contributors to this volume, and Rawat Publications.

Editors

Preface

As history writes itself in different ways, certain concerns acquire greater visibility at certain points of time, compared with others. In our times, it is the turn of Minority Discourse to share centre stage with some other concerns of the postcolonial era. Broadly speaking, "minority" has been used primarily as a term of reference for communities of people that have suffered marginalization, neglect, threat, loss, and such other predicaments in varying degrees. With the growing academic and socio-political concerns for minorities, several significant questions could be posed to initiate a debate with clinical detachment. These could include whether minorities can be classified in terms of their numerical strength or whether it is a condition of mind for the minorities to think of themselves as the other. Also, whether it is a self-defeating exercise for them to vociferously protest against the treatment meted out to them or whether they should strike a compromise with their precarious existence at the secondary and even at the tertiary level. Further, it could be worth asking whether it is a matter of some political design on the part of their others to construct stereotypes regarding them or whether the panacea of the minorities lies in firmly denying all such socio-political constructs that consign them to a perennial state of non-existence. All these could lead to another set of questions which include if minorities are self-obsessed groups of people, incompatible with the majority, posing social problems of very isolated nature or if they constitute a critical segment in the larger political design of a nation.

It could be equally pertinent to ask if their being culturally different is a point of their strength or of their weakness. One could further interrogate why the minorities have come to be debated upon only in our times and why they were not so focussed upon earlier. From yet another position and perspective, it could be possible to assert that "minority" is a relative term; it is neither static nor given and keeps on shifting perennially with time, place, and the determining conditions of human life and survival. Extending such logic further, it could be posited that it does not necessarily refer to a people; it could also refer to institutions and traditions, as well as smaller minorities and bigger minorities, minorities within minorities, and even majorities within minorities, which may be illustrated incessantly through real-life situations.

It may be deduced from what has been posited above that an effort to develop a discourse on the minorities could be both frustrating and promising. It could be frustrating because conflicting and irreconcilable responses to the possible questions posed above are bound to appear and lead to a melee of opinions, and promising because the diversity of positions taken might contribute towards the emergence of a wholesome discourse. The important question at this moment of time is: how can we possibly problematize minority which is being so widely discussed now in the domains of literature, history, politics, society, art, culture, and theory. Also, it would be pertinent to answer as to how important it would be to establish the parameters of minority historiography, the logic of their categorization if so required, the genuineness of their representation in the broader scheme of life and times, and the importance of marking their genealogy if that might help in identifying and contextualizing them in a larger perspective of the modern nation-state. Yet another question to address would be if this phenomenon of minority may be understood necessarily in terms of majority–minority framework and if this may relate to the binary of the powerful and the powerless. It must be noted that with the progress of civilizations and the construction of new knowledge systems, it is now possible to engage with these issues more critically and purposefully in order to give minorities their individual identity and their space to establish their mark in all domains of existence.

A plethora of issues concerning the minorities that could engage the attention of academics led to the idea of holding an international conference on *Minority Discourses Across Cultures*. This conference was organized by the Comparative Literature Association of India (CLAI) at the Central University of Rajasthan in February 2012. Apart from taking note of the striking diversity in perception about the minorities and their representation in literatures and art forms, the conference addressed several seminal issues as to how and why minority writing had emerged as such a strong site to interrogate the ostentatious constructions by centres of hegemonic knowledge. It was quite clearly noticeable that while emerging distinctly within the broad category of the so-called "World Literature", minority writing had made efforts to engage with the ignored histories and neglected perceptions of marginalized people. In fact, the expression of minority experiences showed that there were very close and subtle associations between art and society which deserved further exploration. This made way for demonstrating how literature could become a major instrument towards giving voice to those relegated to the background. It also took into consideration the intricate arguments championed in dominant discourses in contrast to the complex representations of alterity. The larger understanding of minority as a site for new poetics within the vast complex of world literatures facilitated an engagement with basic questions concerning the presumptuousness of elitist authorship. It addressed the question as to what role could literature play in deconstructing negative stereotypes and constructing positive identities in diverse cultural contexts. It also interrogated if the artistic articulation of minority experiences could make way for the rejection of heavy political denominators that reiterate the element of "difference" to perpetuate control and authority.

The essays included in this volume address a large variety of issues. Apart from theorization on minority, there are studies that focus on various other aspects like race, ethnicity, caste, class, gender, literature, and visual and performing arts representing diverse locations and contexts. There are discussions on minority communities like those of the Muslims, Christians, Sikhs, Parsis, Anglo-Indians, Jews, Dalits, Blacks, and African Americans. Furthermore, the volume has essays on select writings on minorities available in Bangla, English,

Malayalam, Oriya, and Russian. It also examines the representation of minorities in literary forms like fiction and epics and art forms like film, theatre, and music. It would be interesting to note that these essays are linked together in one major way in that they underscore the power of resistance and make space for a larger minority discourse. In all, the contributions to this volume bring out how the concept of minority is understood, defined, contested, and represented in its varied narratives in order to construct realities and deconstruct myths. In fact, minority discourse aims at creating the narratives of hope, faith, and belonging rather than of obliteration, segregation, and denial. By affirming the policy of inclusion and denying the politics of exclusion, it develops its narratives born out of lived experiences. It does so only to underline what is left unheard, even though that is sometimes overtly stated and sometimes covertly suggested. The aesthetic transformation of these experiences has created its own paradigms of meaning and its unique traditions in history and society, economy and politics, culture and literature, arts and artefacts.

Looking forward, it could be suggested that minority discourse may not mature as an alternative hegemonic discourse; it may rather be inclusive and objective by incorporating the richness and diversity of its constituents. It does not have to remain enslaved in the complex of minorityism; it may negate it to its benefit. Instead of being obsessed with the self, it has to engage with its other to evolve its own narratives of liberal belonging. This book makes an attempt to bring out the richness and variety of minority discourse across histories, cultures, and spaces. It engages with the notion(s) of minority to interrogate stereotypes and draws upon verbal and cultural texts to define and develop a larger discourse that underlines the major markers of our postcolonial world. It examines literary testimonies and art forms, both classical and modern, to explore broader areas of contestation among peoples and communities. To meet its greater aim, it develops theoretical parameters and puts them to test in critical practice. The book is dialogic in nature and comparative in approach as it makes way for Minority Studies in and outside India to raise questions and seek possible answers.

Anisur Rahman

Section 1

Discoursing Minority

1

Minorities across Cultures

Keki N. Daruwalla

I

The subject of minorities is becoming more complex by the day. In a globe where endless migration trails are crossing each other, every diaspora is a minority. The Chinese, Japanese, Koreans, and Indians are minorities in America. The Hispanics are a major minority there, and I found in Texas and other places great efforts in hospitals and public institutions to become bi-lingual. The Baluch and the Sindhis, and certainly the Muhajirs, consider themselves minorities in Pakistan. The Shias who get bombed in their mosques once a week in the Land of the Pure, meaning Pakistan, are definitely a minority. Santhals are a minority in Assam; the Marwaris may be a majority in Marwar, but not in the North East, or even Kolkata. Kanyakubj Brahmins have a right to think of themselves as a minority where they are, in and around Kanauj, and the Sarju Parin Brahmins have the right to consider themselves a minority even on the banks of the Sarju river, which always belonged to the Sarju Parin. And poets have a right to feel they are a bloody minority. (Which would be a fallacy, because poetry readers and buyers are a minority, while poets are dime-a-dozen.) Wonder of wonders, cuckolded husbands have started feeling they are a minority. The right to feel like a minority is guaranteed in the Bill of Human Consciousness.

The complexity doesn't end here, especially for a sub-continent where religious and political polarizations go hand in hand.

But we'll come to our little patch later. A global outlook is very slowly taking over the planet, all for the better, I thought. The ideal of a universal citizenship has taken root in our consciousness. This ideal itself is linked to the emancipation of victimized minorities. It has provided momentum to modern political thought and also to the way we live. As an example, just see how the status and lives of Afro-Americans and American Indians have changed over the last half a century. The transformation in nomenclature itself tells a tale – from Negro to Black, then Afro-Caribbean, and now Afro-American. Indian caste names have also travelled the same way. We are in an era which is trying hard to apply balm, and play down sobriquets. Remember the old ones? *Kyke* for Jew (and Joseph Brodsky tells us the Russian word for Jew is *yevrei*), *katwa* or circumcized for the Muslim, in Pakistan idolater or *buth parast* for the Hindu. Once upon a time, the term for Zoroastrians in the entire Middle East was *Gabr*, that is, Zoroastrian. To quote Jalaludin Rumi:

> What is to be done, O Moslems? For I do not recognize myself.
>
> I am neither Christian nor Jew, nor Gabr, nor Moslem
>
> I am not of earth, nor of water, nor of air, nor of fire;
>
> I am not of the empyrean, nor of dust, nor of existence, nor of entity.
>
> I am not of India, nor of China, nor of Bulgaria, nor of Saqsin.

But unlike Rumi, most of us, fashioned out of common clay, are of entity and existence and do belong to a race, a religion, and a land.

II

I don't know what I am about to say has much to do with minorities. But the last century saw some great divides between peoples: Turks and Azerbaijanis, Nazis and Jews, Arab and Jew, Serb and Croat, Tutu and Huti, Hindu and Muslim – you name it. It was as if a barbed wire had been laid between races. And there were terrible wars. There was also freedom from colonialism, human rights coming to the fore, and those of course included minority rights.

I would first like to say that I am against minorityism as a creed, for it goes against the grain of a wide "commonality of our shared humanity". Citizenship status rises above ethnic or religious barriers. Where is the scope for particularity and difference? The world believes in equal moral worth for all, also equal rights and opportunities. There is inbuilt equality in the concept of citizenship – the laws are the same for all. Then we may ask why do people feel excluded and disadvantaged? The crucial question is: are they being treated like the "other"?

Equal laws may not always translate into equal treatment. One reason is that law enforcers carry their baggage of religious and caste prejudice and are not impartial. Problems also lie with the minorities – their group specificity and resistance to assimilation. Political theorists call this the "solitarist" approach to identity. People belonging to all other denominations are known to the Parsis as "*Parjat*", that is, other religions, other castes, other people. There is a tremendous prejudice against mixed marriages in my community. Minorities don't merge. The question I would like to pose is: "why should they assimilate?" An overarching collective identity should not obscure individual traits and patters of behaviour. Benjamin Barker in his book *Strong Democracy* admits that citizenship does not exhaust a person's social identities, but it takes a moral priority over all else. But we need to remember that particular interests and claims should take place within a community, a common vision established by the public realm.

There is a question we will have to pose to ourselves: Is the public sphere of general interest and well-being in opposition to a private sphere of particular interest and affiliation? The focus of the minority problem is identity. If identity was inconsequential, minority problems would also be less evident. If religious and racial identities are vague, the issues regarding minorities would recede in the background. But with the slow erosion of faith, religious identities have got entrenched. Actually, one should have started with identity, more so after the encouragement to Jihad by the CIA in the aftermath of the Brezhnev invasion of Afghanistan. Since then, the emphasis on solitary identity has tended to submerge the plurality of identities we all possess. There are things other than mere adherence to one group. Moreover, adherence to one group should not automatically mean a freeze on, or distance from, other groups. We don't have to see minorities exclusively in their ethnic or religious garb, or persona. Moreover, there can be upward mobility in class, but mobility in terms of identity is difficult in the sub-continent. A cobbler remains a cobbler, no matter how high he rises economically. To an extent, in the social scale also he or she remains more or less the same.

When we talk of minorities we need to look beyond numbers at times. The majority–minority binary is to be reckoned in terms of power as well. Power would mean majority. Empowerment is a basic component of how a group feels, how confident it is, and how self-assured. This is very evident in the Middle East. The Shiahs are a majority in Bahrain, but look at how they were treated? Till the fall of Saddam, they had got an equally shabby deal in Iraq. The Alawis have ruled Syria since the rise of Hafez al Assad and the Ba'ath party. They formed just 12% of the population once, though now they are said to be 20%. They were not even considered Muslims till the Mufti of Damascus pronounced them as Muslim at the start of the twentieth century. But they hold all the levers of power in the country, and in the case of a regime change, there could be a blood bath of the Alawites. None of the paradigms applied to the subjection of minorities could be applied to them in Syria. We must not forget that the state is always the majority.

Deconstructing a Stalinist or a Leninist dictatorship is easy. Even a fanatical Islamist one as we had in Taliban-ruled Afghanistan run by Muhammad Umar, or by Zia-ul-Haq in Pakistan, could offer easier unravelling. But de-constructing the treatment of minorities in a liberal democracy such as ours is much more complicated. Rousseau's General Will has pitfalls for the minorities, unless safeguards for them are in-built in the system, that is, the legal framework and the constitution. The problem becomes inextricably political. We are not at all sure if it was the General will that ruled in both these countries or was it merely the power of the Ak 47? Surely a majority of the Afghans did not want women to be treated the way they were.

Surely, there is a big enlightened lobby in Pakistan who do not want the Blasphemy Law. Still they murdered the governor who espoused opposition to it. And the entire Jehadist section in the country treated the murderer like a hero. His images were all over the TV. It is sad that extremists come to the top in Asia and Africa. This doesn't do the Muslim community any good globally.

Political theorists are talking of the right to forbearance. Negative responsibility of individuals and groups is being discussed, which reflects upon the responsibility or the guilt about what one fails to prevent. We must be very clear about two things. *First*, federalism by its very definition accommodates national diversity. Without this element, federalism becomes meaningless. *Second*, democracy and secularism go hand in hand with minority rights. There can be no democracy without a safeguard for minority rights and *vice versa*.

III

To properly understand the situation on the sub-continent, Western critics have to go back to political theory. While Western thought is all about individual rights, we are concentrating on group rights. We need to start thinking in terms of group duties as well, but we haven't come to that stage. Emphasis on individual rights seems to us atomistic, perhaps selfish and materialistic. Further, capitalism can never be a panacea in the East, in the land of Buddha and Gandhi. Admitted, many of our capitalists will be greedier than those in the West. They will fudge taxes and bribe and make unaccounted money. They may even stuff their bank notes in Geneva and Zurich, not forgetting the Channel Islands. A visit to the Channel Islands by me in 1989 or 1990 to lecture on a harmless subject like the Commonwealth caused quite a scare in NRI circles in London. I got invited to exclusive homes for dinner by people who were about seventeen economic strata above me. But here's the rub: however greedy some of us may be, the accretion of capital can never become a value in India or Burma, or Nepal and Bangladesh. We in India remember Gandhiji's well-known saying, "There is enough for everyone's need on the planet, but not enough for everyone's greed".

Amartya Sen in one of his books has quoted Stephen Leacock, who takes on Adam Smith, the father of modern economics.

Adam Smith, Adam Smith
Listen what I charge you with!
Didn't you say
In class one day
That selfishness was bound to pay?
Of all the doctrines that was the pith.
Wasn't it, wasn't it, wasn't it Smith?

(Leacock, apart from being a humorist, was also an economist. As a college student, I had read his book *Laugh with Leacock.*)

Muslims in India have a cross to carry. The first charge they have to face is the breaking up of India in 1947. This is aggravated by the new images of *Bharat Mata*. A bleeding anthropomorphic Mother India cut into half makes the matter quite emotional for some. There are sections which never let the masses forget this. The cry before Partition was "*akhand rahega Hindustan/nahin banega Pakistan*". Moreover, there are close to 140 million of them, 99.9 % harmless decent citizens. A handful of Jehadis, planting bombs in busy streets have given the community a distorted image. Ask the rightist sections among the majority and you'll get a litany of accusations. Similarly, one *fatwa* by some obscurantist seminary should not be allowed to taint the community with a belligerent identity. A protest against a writer like Salman Rushdie by a small section who have most probably not read him should not be exploited to question the tolerance level of an entire community. There is no end to stereotyping Muslims – their growth in numbers is exponential because of their four wives and that kind of nonsense. One in 10,000 may be having four wives. They are far behind in education, especially education of the girl child. Job-wise and housing-wise they lag behind. I don't think there is a single Muslim in my whole colony. Thirty years ago I asked my daughter how many Muslims there were in her class. One, she answered, in a class of 40.

Our minorities are huge; they form 18.4% of the population, numbering 189.5 million. Muslims are 72.8 % of the minority population, 13.4 % of the total population according to the 2001 Census. They number 140 million. And they lag behind in employment. It is not that they are making no efforts to learn regional languages. In Maharashtra, I am told, Marathi is made so difficult that no Muslim can get through in an interview. In the police, they are less than 3% in Maharashtra.

When people talk of fanaticism, we need to remember the Crusades. When Ferdinand and Isabella drove the Jews out of Spain and Portugal (it was they who pressured Portugal to follow suit – a month after Columbus set sail for America), it was the countries of Islam which gave Jews shelter, the great Maimonides among them.

Here it needs to be said that India has one of the most tolerant majorities in the world. Look how favourably India compares with the Middle East. You can't construct a Hindu temple or a Sikh Gurudwara anywhere in West Asia. Hindus, I am told, cannot take out a funeral procession in Pakistan chanting *Ram nam satya hai.* And look at what we have incorporated in our constitution. Six Articles in the constitution, from 25 to 30, are devoted to the rights of minorities and the courts also keep a vigilant eye over how they are treated. We also have considerable reservations in our government services for the scheduled and the backward classes, though none for religious minorities.

The Zoroastrians left Iran and got shelter in Gujarat. Various sects have got sanctuary here. The Qadianis are much safer in India than in Pakistan, where about 5000 were slaughtered in the early 1970s. Our national reality is quite complex. Much of the Khalistan trouble started with an attack on a Nirankari procession. So, there you have it – minorities considering their sub-sects as adherents of heretic cults and attacking them. The so-called Heretics have been the most vulnerable since the days of Manichaeus. During a year in Oxford, I lived on St. Giles Street where Latimer and Ridley were burnt at the stake on the charge of heresy on 6 October 1555, in the reign of Bloody Mary. There is a plaque commemorating this. A word about victimhood: minorities are apt to fall prey to this. Remember Sir Mohammad Iqbal's rather well-known couplet:

Rehmaten hain teri ghairo ke kashanon par

Barq girti hai tho bechare Musalmano par.

To which my crude riposte (in the only verse I have ever written in Urdu) is:

Barq ham pe bhi giri gyarah sau salon se

Par hamne nahin kiya shikwa upar walon say.

But this complex of victimhood is not confined to religious minorities. The Irish had the same feeling a century ago. Let me quote here lines from Domhnall MacNeachtain's "Fragments from an Epic" included in an anthology compiled by Daiken, Leslie H. and Harry A. Kernoff:

We have no ships to send the negroes Yeats,

We have no ships to come to outer races

To breed with them and Gaelicize their faces

To show Paul Henry in the no Paul Henry places;

The world has seen us beggars at the gates

With 'Made in England' on our very faces.

What are we but a dresserful of plates?

I haven't touched upon women as yet. We saw what happened in Kolkata quite recently. A lady was ridiculed by the police as well as a lady chief minister for reporting a rape case. A rape victim becomes an accused in our country. The first thing she is asked is what she was wearing and what did she do to invite rape. Though they are half of humankind, they are the most vulnerable minority, never mind their numbers. I am not apologizing for using the term "minority" as an across-the-board metaphor for vulnerable sections. The prejudice against women goes back to thousands of years. Rousseau "excluded women from the public realm of citizenship because they were the caretakers of affectivity, desire and the body." He thought that "their dangerous heterogeneous sexuality must be kept in check, chaste and confined to marriage. Enforcing chastity on women will keep each family a separated unity, preventing the chaos and blood-mingling that would be produced by illegitimate children."

Let me conclude now. Let me revert to what I said earlier about universal citizenship. There is a possibility of error in balancing the idea of universal citizenship with special minority rights. In India, we have given ourselves a fine constitution, guaranteeing safeguards for minorities. But the constitution is not a Procrustes bed which can fit in all crises that may arise between our diverse elements into its particular sized frame.

REFERENCES

Kritzeek, James. "Rumi: Love Poems from Diwan-i-Shams-i-Tabriz" (Poems of Shams of Tabriz) in *Anthology of Islamic Literature*. p. 254, Pelican, 1964.

Daiken, Leslie H. and Harry A. Kernoff (compilers). *Goodbye Twilight: Songs of the Struggle in Ireland*, London: R.H.A. Publishers Lawrence and Wishart, 1936.

2

Spokespersonship in Literary Theory: The Act of Elites Speaking for Minorities

Dorothy Figueira

In a recent article published in *The Comparatist*, the Cuban-American critic, Alfred Lopez, discussed Jose Martí's reading of Walt Whitman. From this article, I learned that Whitman was a cursory reader, perusing a dozen books at any time, reading a few pages here and there, seldom getting sufficiently interested in any volume to read it in its entirety, dipping into various genres and reading no language but English. Although he never traveled beyond North America, it did not prevent him from envisioning the many places he evokes in "Salut au Monde" though, as Lopez notes "his own mystical, abstracted vision of an America is at once generalized and exceptional" (Lopez 2011:5). The world Whitman presented in this poem was populated by undifferentiated Others "facilely reduced to 'Camarados' in turn subsumed into his Hegelian vision of America as an ever-expanding end-of-History" (Lopez 2011:6).

Lopez compares the American poet to the Cuban Martí and speculates on their possible encounter at a reception following a lecture on Abraham Lincoln by Whitman at Madison Square Theater in 1887. If Martí and Whitman did, in fact, speak, it would have been in English, although Martí could have dialogued in Spanish and French. Martí might have broached any number of interesting topics, since he was learned in the classics and had advanced degrees in law and philosophy, was a renowned journalist, editor, novelist, and playwright. One does not want to belittle Whitman, but Martí's considerably larger intellectual scope was grounded, as Lopez notes, in "a keen awareness of cultural and material difference" (Lopez 2011:7). While Whitman did not possess expertise in a broad range of subjects and disciplines, one certainly would not guess it from his poetry, or its expansive and expansionist claims. Whitman had no scruples regarding his parochial vision or his provincial experience of the world. Certainly, none surface in poems such as "Starting from Paumanok", where the American poet imagines himself "sailing to other shores to annex the same, yet welcoming/every new brother. Coming among the new Ones myself to be their companion/and equal" without stopping to wonder how he proposes to accomplish this encounter in English. One might even question how his prospective new "brothers" might feel about being "welcomed" in their own homeland by some interloper (Lopez 2011:10).

Perhaps, by now, you suspect where I am going with this train of thought. Whitman's inverted logic of welcoming new brothers as long as they speak English presents a crystallization of American exceptionalism that serves as an apt metaphor for what I see at work in recent formulations of World Literature. Martí's interdisciplinarity, in-depth knowledge of other cultures and languages, and awareness of cultural difference calls to mind Comparative Literature at its disciplinary best. I fear that Whitman's claims to annex the world reflect far more World Literature's rather imperialistic vision of a world to be consumed in English, the new academic hegemonic language. It is ironic that one model was, and is practised in America, by mainstream figures and the other model, by Hispanic renegades like Martí, Lopez, and myself.

It is my thesis that in World Literature, just as in Whitman's poem, it is not imperative to respect the intellectual history of a given population or its literature. Sometimes it is merely enough to evoke their existence (as Whitman did) and offer nominal representation and a selectively partial exploration (as we do in World Literature anthologies today). As we saw in the case of Whitman, there is considerable hubris involved when one speaks for the *Other*.

So too for World Literature. Although it affects a respect for the *Other* as a reified object of cultural difference, world literature only delivers a superficial and unidirectional overview, with Anglophone culture as the one recognizing the non-Anglophone and (often) non-white culture. In order "to be" or "speak out," the non-white and/or non-Anglophone culture must seek the legitimacy and recognition from white culture and use the language of white culture to produce itself (Rizvi 1994:63). Institutionalizing the study of the other in such a format promotes assimilation with domesticating egalitarian demands attached. A pedagogy such as World Literature obscures issues of power and privilege, by rendering the other tokenistic (Chow 2002:113).

World Literature is indebted to theories and pedagogies that have arisen in the past thirty years. For example, it shares multiculturalism's mission to recognize the contributions of neglected groups and offer a reform project heralding diversity and promoting a progressive politics. Like postcolonial criticism, it pretends to uncover occluded and submerged identities and to liberate the oppressed. Yet, the samples of under-represented and repressed literatures offered by World Literature do not in any way problematize a Euro-Amero-centric perspective. World Literature promotes an ethos of recognition without adequately questioning Euro-centric definitions of knowledge. Like other pedagogies of alterity before it, World Literature ultimately delivers stasis and consolidates control. The worldly collaborators in World Literature anthologies resemble Ashis Nandy's depiction of postcolonial criticism's gladiators saluting the Caesars of Western academe.

As I have noted elsewhere, it is quite possible that the resurgence of interest in World Literature betokens an effort on the part of scholars to refashion themselves now that other theories and pedagogies of alterity have proven themselves to be bankrupt. The World Literature scholar whose formation has been almost exclusively in English literature can reinvent the wheel; do what the comparatist has been doing for decades and claim, in the process, to be non-elitist because he or she does not bother to learn foreign languages. But, I ask you, what is more elitist than practising a brand of criticism that claims to champion a voiceless and under-represented world but does so only in the English language? Since when does the imposition of Western ways of thinking on the non-West make us non-elite? There is a simple lesson to be learned here: We should not take at face value academic projects that blithely claim to engage in a reform process. World Literature claims that the standards of cultural and linguistic specificity to the discipline of Comparative Literature that have supposedly been lost. Have they, in fact, truly disappeared? Or are certain critics just saying that so they can sanction provincialism, reestablish the hegemony of the English language, and reinstall the monolingual, non-ethnic, and non-minority critic? I am very suspicious of solutions to the supposed death of our discipline when what certain critics propose is far less than what comparatists have delivered for decades without subtitles.

In my book, *Otherwise Occupied*, I make the case that academic theories and pedagogies of the Other (identity studies, multiculturalism, postcolonial criticism, and now we might add World Literature) were constructed and used in America to undermine Affirmative Action by influencing institutional policies for recruitment. I investigate how these various theoretical constructions of the *Other* have proliferated in direct proportion to the failure of statistical evidence to support the success claims of institutional diversity. I make the claim that they aid in masking the continued marginalization and containment of America's minorities within academe. I also show how they dovetail very nicely with university marketing concerns. I analyze how in the past, universities have occluded low numbers in diversity by establishing various ethnic studies programmes and peopling them with under-represented ethnics. Identity Studies have thus contributed to the balkanization of ethnics into fields for which they were deemed biologically and culturally suited. In other words, minorities can enter the ivory tower only if they are willing to settle for studying themselves. In America, postcolonial criticism served a demographic purpose. It allowed a privileged Asian and Middle Eastern diasporic professoriate to speak on behalf of their supposedly mute brethren. In the bureauctratic institutionalization of World Literature, we can now see a process of taking back the American university from both the minorities housed in identity studies and Third World model minorities supervising multicultural and postcolonial studies. We have come full circle back to Whitman. We too have learned to celebrate linguistic limitations and fragmentary knowledge. If we ascribe to recent pronouncements by David Damrosch, we too can now engage in a quasi-mystical endeavour that glorifies nothing but good old American exceptionalism. Whitman was able to indulge his fancies because he lived in an openly imperialistic age, in an America that reveled in its belief in white supremacy and gloried in an aura of rural utopianism. Our modern theorists of the world must be more subtle. And here, as in all scholarly justifications for shady political postures (from academic Marxism to the moral relativism of deconstruction), we call upon theory to assuage our consciences. In this particular instance, we rely on postmodernist views of a hybridized and syncretic world.

The work of Baudrillard has proven particularly influential in this regard, especially his notion that travel can be viewed as a spectacular form of amnesia. According to such a theory, any part of the world can be recreated or made to stand for another. In a world of third-order simulacra, encroaching pseudo-places merge to eliminate geographical or ethnic space entirely. This leveling out of the world has contributed in the last 30 years to the theoretical creation of metaphorical space in which critics might dwell that is separate from the real space they inhabit. In this metaphorical space, critics can voice ideologies of subversion and rebellion that are simply too unsettling, if voiced from their own actual space. Their delicate balancing acts stem from the paradox of their inhabiting a space of bourgeois comfort, while needing at the same time to distance themselves from global capitalism. When critics appropriate the metaphorical space of the *Other*, whether they be postcolonial, the nomad, the exile, the queer, or now even the entire world, they hope to exonerate themselves for all the benefits they receive from this same capitalism. In this process, we find the meeting of incommensurables, a deep-seated need for the experience of political engagement coming out of the 1960s meeting a 1990's need to be media savvy, to package and market intellectual capital. There is no small irony in how easily these two conceptual frameworks have melded. In American institutions today, the marketing concerns are, therefore, twofold. *First,* there is marketing to and through university administrators who buy into the idea that alterity initiatives are the most advanced and "logical" approach to the miasma of competing cultures and ethnicities. In such cases, engaging the other easily degenerates into the diversity promised by World Literature. Through such an initiative, institutions can recruit and pretend to "restructure" with supposedly radical responses to new socio-economic realities. Viewed in this light, World Literature is nothing but the latest *avatar* of earlier theories and pedagogies purporting to engage the *other* that have sprung up on American campuses in the last three decades.

Like the earlier fads in Multiculturalism and Postcolonial Studies, the newly-minted World Literature Programs are practical in that they are all are relatively easy "specializations", demanding no in-depth knowledge of another culture or foreign languages. As in Whitman's poetry, the *Other* preserves its own heritage, as long as it speaks English (Prashad 2000:112). These pedagogies all feed the same brand of American isolationism of which Whitman sings. Like Whitman, these pedagogies of alterity, World Literature included, claim to engage the world; they pretend to do the *other* "better" than Comparative Literature does. Damrosch even claims that World Literature, unlike the elitism of Comparative Literature, is democratizing. Students, who are not trained in elite American universities where you can study languages like Sanskrit and Nahuatl, can still partake of the world's literature. Students who have not even studied common foreign languages and their literatures due to their content-light training in non-elite universities in non-elite places can also do World Literature. It is the most practical pedagogy (and I quote Damrosch here) "for readers in a country such as India who have difficulty doing broad-based comparative study because they have long struggled against linguistic nationalisms and regionalisms."

I do not know about you, but I feel such formulations betray not only a sense of *noblesse oblige*, but seem to revel in American cultural provincialism and triumphalism. In the world of World Literature, it suffices to anthologize the world according to Western paradigms and preconceptions. World Literature's project pretends to redraw boundaries and claims to unmask inferential racism. However, its deficiencies merely highlight the hubris of those who speak for and hence co-opt the other. It deflects attention away from social issues such as discrimination, unequal access, and hierarchies of ethnic privilege that are far from being resolved (Huggan 2000:126) in academe today. Under the guise of promoting tolerance, World Literature, like the other pedagogies of alterity before it, enables academic elites to displace, diffuse, and thus intensify class, gender, and racial contradictions.

Such are the criticisms that I and other scholars have leveled against pedagogies of alterity. By now, some of my Indian colleagues must be tired of me coming to CLAI as I have done in the past and exposing the gimmickry of American academe. So, I will not waste your time any longer enumerating the solipsistic postures of the various actors forging brilliant careers showcasing such supposedly innovative pseudo-pedagogies. I will rather examine how such frighteningly exportable trends impact on the Indian stage. In recent Indian conferences and book exhibits I have attended, there is an interesting development worth noting. From my vantage point as an outsider, I have noticed a burgeoning interest in research on Dalit literature. Each year, there are more and more papers devoted to this topic. Moreover, this scholarship is often the work of non-Dalits. I was wondering whether the increased interest in Dalit literature might not play the same institutional role in India that pedagogies of the other have played in the US. Is there any chance that something called Dalit Studies will take root in India and, like multiculturalism in America, it will lead to the co-optation of India's minority voices by its non- minorities? If Dalit Studies flourishes as the various forms of Identity Studies have in the West, it could become India's means of marginalizing and containing minorities within academe without openly violating the mandates of the Mandal Commission.

At last year's CLAI, I tried to attend as many papers by young scholars as I could, especially those panels dealing with the Dalit experience. What I heard was very informative: many of the papers on Dalit literature mirrored the discourse of victimhood found in identity studies in America (among which I count Black Studies, Women's Studies, Multiculturalism, and Postcolonial Studies). By this I mean they followed a now standard script in which one first must point out unequal distribution of power. Then one naturally talks about under-representation and marginalization of the group in question. Finally, one claims to deconstruct repressive modes of thought (Lopez–Merzec 2011:683). Beyond following this master narrative to the letter, a number of the papers I heard compared a Dalit writer to another minority writer from another culture, such as a comparison of Urmila Pawar with Maya Angelou. It did not surprise me that the presenters would seek to compare Dalit authors with American Blacks, since the Dalits themselves sought inspiration in the Black poetry of the 1960s and modeled their political movements on the Black Liberation struggle, especially on the activities of the Black Panther Movement. I also noticed a clear sociological breakdown of these panels. They were for the most part segregated with some panels consisting entirely of Dalit scholars and others organized exclusively by non-Dalits. However, in one panel I attended where both groups participated, I distinctly remember the non-Dalit panelists speaking first and then leaving the room before the Dalit contingent even presented their papers! I say this in no way to be critical of the papers or the young scholars who might not have understood conference protocol. Rather, I bring up my impressions of last year's conference in order to draw a more fundamental concern regarding our discipline.

In literary studies today, we have become promiscuous spokespersons. Spivak muted the subalterns to make a place for the critic (herself) to speak on their behalf. She filtered Mahasweta Devi who herself was a high-caste spokesperson for tribals. It seems, Western readers can travel to India metaphorically but they should not drink anything unless it is filtered. This double filtration process was intended to market the *amrita* of Indian literature for consumption abroad. But such a filtration process involves co-optation and this problematic abuse of spokespersonship did not begin with Gayatri Spivak. In India, there is a long and distinguished history of non-untouchables speaking for untouchables dating back to the

Sant *parampara*. Literature offers fine examples of this trope. In addition to Mahasweta Devi and Spivak, we have Mulk Raj Anand who, because of his exemplary Communist credentials, was allowed to speak for the subaltern. We also have Premchand who represented the Untouchable other in ways that have not gone without criticism. Of course, the most distinguished modern case for such spokespersonship is that of Gandhi himself. Even the Mahatma was criticized for co-opting the voice of his "beloved" Harijans. The legitimacy of his position as their spokesperson was challenged by none other than Ambedkar. Along with his followers, he dared to assert that, as an eminent jurist, perhaps he should speak on his own peoples' behalf.

Jasbir Jain has, I think, drawn a fundamental distinction regarding this issue of spokespersonship when she compares what she has termed a "literature of empathy" to a "literature of experience." She bases her thesis on aesthetic concerns, when she asks how the privileged writer can represent the Dalit. Jain pinpoints a key problem with a literature of empathy. She asks, "Where is the lack in the privileged writer" that enables him, or her to speak about the suffering of others? In posing this question, I feel that Jain has cut to the heart of what is at issue in speaking for the victimized other. I would reply to her query that there is no lack in the privileged author or critic that ethically sanctions their utterances or renders them aesthetically legitimate. In academe, to quote Aijaz Ahmad, textual culture can only pretend to be activist culture. Theory and Criticism do not change the condition of the disenfranchised. Critics who claim otherwise are fooling themselves and others. When academics speak, they usually do so for personal gain. The lack experienced by the non-minority need not be existential; it can quite easily be selfish – simply the lack of a job or the lack of proper recognition. One speaks for the other to co-opt that other, to take his or her apportioned voice and sometimes, as a wonderful consequence, the place allotted for that other by the system that tries to or, more often, pretends to redress past discrimination. But my response is coloured by the hindsight of half a century of Affirmative Action in the US and the manner in which the ability to serve its initial population has been limited by institutions and the pedagogies they install. I have seen just too many privileged individuals – in both the East and the West – who resent the benefits ear-marked for minorities. They think why these others should get jobs and funding, when I feel I deserve them more. So you find in the US the tricks of non-minorities minoritizing themselves by extending the definition of discrimination to include the most comfortable groups imaginable, people who have never suffered the inequities experienced by the populations for whom these accommodations were created. In India, we have high-castes temporarily having themselves adopted by low-caste families to partake of reservation quotas.

In conclusion, we might want to think back to how Walt Whitman blithely welcomed his "camarados" in their own land. It is important to be wary of those who undertake the task of speaking for others and articulating their experience. The motivations behind such acts of comradery are not always noble. There is simply something unsavoury about middle class whites speaking for Blacks, Native Americans and Chicanos. There is something inappropriate about diasporic privileged Indians first muting and then speaking for Indian subalterns or even worse, standing up before a white audience in an elite American university and identifying their experience with that of poor American Blacks. And there is just something silly about monolingual World Literature scholars speaking for the world. So, in India, one should look with some scepticism on academic non-Dalits colonizing Dalit Studies, if such a field is ever created here. Because, if spokespersonship for the Dalit other is effectively co-opted by non-Dalit spokespersons, then universities might not need to hire Dalits at all in the future. What I fear is that, just as it has happened in the States, such a strategy is the whole purpose of the game.

REFERENCES

Chow, Rey. "Theory, Area Studies, Cultural Studies: Issues of Pedagogy in Multiculturalism." in *Learning Places: The Afterlives of Area Studies*, edited by Masao Miyoshi and H. D. Harootunian. Durham: Duke University Press, 2002, 103–18.

Huggan, Graham. "Exoticism, Ethnicity, and the Multicultural Fallacy." in *"New" Exoticism: Changing Patterns in the Construction of Otherness*, edited by Isabel Santaolalla. Amsterdam: Rodopi, 2000, 91–96.

Lopez, Alfred J. "Translating Interdisciplinarity: Reading Marti Reading Whitman." 35: 5–18. 2011.

Prashad, Vijay. *The Karma of Brown Folk*. Minneapolis: University of Minnesota Press, 2000.

Rizvi, Fazal. "The Arts, Education and the Politics of Multiculturalism." in *Culture, Difference and the Arts*, edited by Sneja Gunew and Fazal Rizvi. St, Leonards, Australia: Allen and Unwin, 1994, 54–68.

3

The Parameters of "Minority Discourse": Attempting an Identification for Literary Historiography

Ipshita Chanda

This is an effort to seek the parameters for defining "minority discourse" as a category for literary historiography. Our question is: can "minority" be a thematic kernel,[1] or a category providing coherence in writing a history of literature. It proceeds from the assumption that literary historiography must take as its foundation literary categories, an issue that has been engaged with in much of the seminal writing on the historiography of Indian literatures.[2] I will engage with the relationship between the aesthetic and the political, and ask whether it is adequate to define "minority" literature on the basis of its politics, and argue that the literary characteristics ascribed to "minority" discourse are in fact reflective of the politics of literary production, from which stems a located discourse which we term literature. At the most, we may say that minority cultural production is unashamed to claim its politics as a way of distinguishing itself from the more abstract (but still overtly political) stance taken by practitioners who believe in Art for Art's Sake. But how does this make minority discourse any different from those which testify to the social and political functions of cultural production? This question would naturally lead to the issue of identity and its role in cultural production. My purpose here is to take "minority" as a kernel around which a historical narrative may be structured. From this, it may be clear that I am proposing only to look at literary method, that is, how the student of Comparative Literature may identify "minority" as a structuring element in the cultural products that she studies, among them, literature. Then the expression of the human lives and experiences resulting from this idea – the modes of representation of "minority" as a thematic idea in literature, become available for the construction of a history of literature. Thus, the concept of "minority" requires a location and a name before it becomes a thematic element for any narrative.

For how else may we identify the literary discourse of the minority? Minority is a numerical term; hence there must be a number which involves actual evidence. But it is also a relative term – a minority cannot exist without a majority, and unless we allow this relationality into our definition, our attempt at categorization and labeling remains suspect. The discourses that stem from minority as an absolute category, without relation to its opposite, lead us to appreciate the extent to which politics is palpable in or may be read into self-expression and its analysis. For even the most rabid of non-theorists would agree that "self-expression" is an irreducible element of art, in addition to everything else we attribute to it. Given that, how does one define a minority in art? At most, we may define the location of the self that is expressed, and often not expressed, as anyone who has even approached the threshold of Women's Studies as a discipline will recognize. In this case, women are demographically a minority in societies where female infanticide is prevalent because male children are more welcome than female children. But does that mean that when the sex-ratio is evened out, patriarchal norms will be overturned and gender equality will be achieved only because of numerical change? Women's cultural production may not legitimately claim minority status then, but will it cease to be the discourse of the deprived, the oppressed and the marginalized? What then about the women who even within the larger group of women are discriminated against by virtue of class or caste?

Perhaps we can begin with the understanding that since it is the self that is put before us in the garb of artistic creation, that self forms the basis of what will define the minority. An immediate argument of bad faith would be that every man (and I use that word with full consciousness) is an island, and so we are all minorities of one. The discourse of Individualism from which this position stems culminated in the many declarations of individual rights of Man and Woman, finally spawning a repertoire of "civil" rights due to "free" men – who were in a minority in the land that they were forced to inhabit as slaves. Europe too had in every country the difference of race, but enslavement became America's history. The minority in this case were also the displaced, the disenfranchised, dispossessed on the basis of skin colour, and not only because they were few in number: there were groups which were fewer in number, yet infinitely more powerful. So the discourse of the "minority" is never only dependent upon numbers: besides the intersecting discourse of race, class, community, religion, and gender, the definition of the minority also requires spatial and geographical location to become a viable category.

So are we to conclude that minority discourse is based upon a numerical minority, or is there some characteristic that identifies a group of people as a minority – number may be part of its definition, but it is not confined to number alone? I pose this as a question at the outset because it seems to me that to conceptualize the minority is the first stage of entering the discourse – for comparative method would immediately lead us to ask – whose discourse? And where is it located?

Suppose we take the case of caste division in Indian society. This division is a form of living where too we may point to the relational nature of its operation. Caste practices in their survival form a documented history of the everyday. The caste hierarchy, peculiar to Indian society, has spawned a relational culture albeit of exclusion, rather than of community. When we seek to study this relational structure, we are faced with a set of what for want of a better word, I could call academic categories, with an emphasis on the word academic. Exclusion and inclusion are just two terms in which all these practices would fit – but could we fit minority, dependent on precise numbers, within either exclusion or inclusion? Because minorities are the "other" of both these categories: those who are excluded may be in either a minority or a majority, depending upon the grounds of exclusion or inclusion. How then do we theorize minorities apart from location, and without an understanding of the relational operation of those locations?

Relational operations except in their most stark manifestations do not make for effective "representational" or identity politics. The discourse of the minority is necessarily a cultural discourse predicated upon being identified as such. The construction of a self in relational terms does not preclude the possibility of using the idiom in which those relationships are structured in the social hierarchy. The language of caste, just like the language of gender has presented translators with innumerable ontological questions. In sum, the violence that we characterize as definitive to dalit writing, the aggression and the inversions that have been identified as generic markers of dalit literary language are simple consequences of the fact that language itself is located, that identity is the locus of many discourses, and is a discursive construction in itself. In pointing out this reality as represented in and through the language of "literature" and in producing literature which seeks to foreground human existence and experience from a "different", that is, hitherto silenced, unrepresented reality, those who inhabit this reality declare their understanding and rejection of the politics that had silenced them or usurped their voices. The history of the world shows at large that those who have been thus refused voice and representation, participation and rights, are more likely to be in a majority than in a minority. Thus to label it minority literature on the basis of numbers without taking cognizance of the aspects of location and relationality, which are the basic tools of a comparative analysis, appears puzzling.

It may perhaps be better to elicit the characteristics of literary texts rather than the caste or class of the author. We often characterize dalit literature with a specific form of language use. Our assumption is that there is some convention or norm that we credit the language of dalit writers with breaking. The taboo of "literary" or "standard" language as opposed to "common" or "local" usage, does exist, but is not a literary taboo; it is a social taboo that non-literary categories of analysis have grafted onto literature. Indeed, if the battle of Bhartendu Harishchandra for a purified, Sanskritized "Hindi" purged of Perso-Arabic words and expressions is a political agenda expressed in literary form, it is also a way of locating the literary event both in literary history and in the history of the society and the time of its production. The division of Hindi and Urdu is a consequence of this position that Bhartendu takes up, and the conflict between Hindi and Hindustani for endorsement as "national" language cannot be understood unless this identification is taken into account. This is simply to state that language is a literary, as well as, a social tool; it cannot be either one without being rooted in the other. The special characteristics of the language used by any writer or artist, whether belonging to a minority, a marginalized community, or an oppressed group, is located and realized in the location of the language user's daily life. Hence the language used by a minority is marked as much by the realities that the writer feels as part of a minority group as a writer belonging to the majority would. And the idea of a "standard" literary language becomes redundant, the moment we accept that language is a living social resource, and that no language is any better or worse than any other. If we take these two observations into account, we will see that there is no cause to point out "non-standard" or "non-literary" or "located" language existing in minority discourse alone; at the most, such an assertion would have the critical importance of alerting us to the located language use of all discourses, and compel us, as readers of literature, to pay attention to location as the fundamental shaping influence on the very medium of literature itself.

I have argued that "minority" status is a relative position but that seems to undercut the very logic of minority as an absolute category of identification. Separated from the larger number in respect of which it is a minority, the actual number of the minority may well be quite large in itself. From which position, then, should the self in this case be conceptualized? Surely, from both: a minority relative to the larger majority, and from within a group that is relatively "minor", but in its actual size large enough to be seen as a majority in a different location. Ultimately, the ground on which the expressive and experiential self is located in time and place, will underpin its final contours. Hence, a member of a minority may well feel marginalized in certain circumstances, but may itself be a cause for marginalization of other, smaller groups in other circumstances. African–American feminists[3] in the middle of the last century theorized their position as radically incommensurable. They were the "other" of the white men and white women because they were black; they were the "others" of black men and white men as they were women; and finally they could not feel solidarity with the white women, because though they were all women, race divided them and often undercut gender solidarity. They shared sexual oppression with white women, but were divided by race, and racial oppression with black men, from whom they were divided by gender. This fundamental difference based on an overlapping of multiple oppressions may be further complicated by unpacking "black" as a categorization for classifying cultural production. Are we then finally coming rather too close to the idea that we have dismissed earlier that every individual is an island unto herself, and hence in a minority of one?

The socio-political and the cultural are in a dialogic relationship shaping the forms of living and being in a particular time and place. They mutually inform expression and practices of human life and the idioms follow the structuring rules of separate domains. When we apply the categories forged by one disciplinary discourse to another, we open ourselves to the danger of starting with an acceptance of oppositions that are structured into one but not necessarily applicable to another. When the categories for understanding societies stratified in one way are applied to analysis of the phenomena manifest in another, then the need for retooling the categories and even discarding them must take precedence over the desire for fashionable (and often misplaced) theoretical formulations. Identity is a political agenda expressed sometimes in literary terms; we may treat it as such and proceed in the analysis of cultural production, but if we make this a defining characteristic of literary discourse, then we are simply confusing the location of the literary practitioner with literature itself.

The danger in using the value-free tools of Comparative Literature as a discipline for the reading of marginalized literatures, or minority discourses, reveals that both minority and margin are political counters, and cannot function as absolutes. What Ranciere[4] calls the "aesthetic regime" of a particular time and place forerounds its own definition of "literature" and those who resist this definition and work to reconceptualize literary practice are, as the *avant-garde*, the modern or the renaissant, often also the minority. Literature, unfortunately for the theoretician, exceeds theory and resists being pruned to fit into it. Sometimes, it even robs the critic of its own pleasures by haunting her with its political incorrectness. Since I have demarcated the extra-literary from the literary and argued for a set of concepts for reading literature wherever it is produced, rather than for attributing special characteristics to literatures produced by specific named groups, the reader may think that I am referring to an ideal designated as pure literature. In order to answer the question, is there a human core untouched by the subtle fingers of social and political conditions, or what we are neutrally calling location, what better strategy than to turn to literature itself?

> Deprived by destiny a *baamin* woman got married to a *jatiya*, a worker in leather. She began to be greatly disturbed to the point of suffocating due to the stench of the leather being cured in the pit. Her heart fluttered, she began to feel nauseous, her head reeled. She could not feel the pangs of hunger, nor could she sleep properly at night. Her eyes burned all the time. She would clutch a rag to her nose, moistened with itr, it's fragrance blocking the smell of leather, and put another cloth over her mouth.
>
> Days do not take years to pass.
>
> One day the *baamani* said to the *jatiy*a proudly, "Just see my miraculous powers. My coming has removed the stench from your house. This is the proof of the wondrous abilities of the upper castes."
>
> Her husband said, somewhat sardonically, "The stench remains as it was, it is you who have got used to it. I did not expect that the nerves in your nose would die such a quick death. Now please spend less on itr and fragrant oils."
>
> "Are you out to give me advice? I have decreased that expenditure long ago. After all, if I do not keep the good of my own household in mind, who will?"[5]

The title of this story is "The Delusion of Truth" by which is meant, as the story shows, that something is mistaken for the truth, not that "truth" itself deludes. Truth remains intransient. The reality of caste exists in the very language itself: the *baamani* is deprived by destiny, so she marries a *jaatiya;* she proclaims to her husband that she is blessed with the wondrous powers of the upper castes – but that does not prevent her from what we would so easily understand as "adjusting", except that this adjustment is set within a frame of virilocal social relations: if you are a woman, you live in your husband's house. How do you ease your way there? How do you balance the fact that deprived by destiny, you are an upper caste woman having to fulfill certain duties, both emotional and social, as dictated by your gender role in such a society? You are in a minority as a woman (given the sex ratio in Rajasthan and Haryana, this is a more grueling reality than is expressed in this story), but as a *baamin,* you may be socially above the *jatiya* – yet in a *jatiya* household, you remain a minority. The operative point is, how do you negotiate this relational location? Here we see that the *baamin* woman seeks her identity and then just lives it out within a web of social relations, knowing that a certain entrenched form of life alone is existence, and one may otherwise end up only with the bitterness of deprivation. Deprivation is the theme of much minority literature, since it is a fact that defines some minorities: but the struggle to negotiate a life which cannot be limited by deprivation despite being dogged by it is the mark of literature. Does the baamin's assertion and adjustment introduce us to a mode of negotiation? Is the function of this complex tale to unsettle our fixed securities about human life and living, however politically correct they may be? And do we also learn to wonder whether literature produced by minorities and about minorities, may be called "minority" literature for political rather than literary reasons?

> A horseman of the desert once, under the pretext of seeing the world, strayed onto the lush green frontiers of an oasis and the first thing that struck him with wonder was that the crows here were as black as anywhere else, but cawed so sweetly that you could just keep listening to them forever. When you desire water with such intense lack of restraint

even milk seems to be of no use at all. When he heard a clacking sound close by, he turned his horse towards it. Neither the horse nor it's master had seen such a sight before. Water dripped continuously into the tank through long earthen vessels. The horse neighed a couple of times, loudly. Perhaps it was very thirsty. The horseman tried to take it towards the water, drawing on the reins. But the horse would start and rear away from the water as soon as they drew close to the tank. What kind of water is this that drips with this constant sound? The clacking of the water seems to have taken a stubborn decision never to fall silent. Finally both the horse and the master both grew irritated with the clacking sound.

The horseman went to the peasant who was steering the waterwheel and said with great arrogance, Ey you rustic! Stop this clacking of yours. Can't you see my horse is starting and rearing away? If you can't understand even this without being told, how will you farm the land ?

The farmer said quite simply, I understand very well what I need for my own ends. It seems that you do not know that as long as this clacking continues, there will be water. If you want to make your horse drink, it will have to be in the midst of this clacking. If that stops, the water stops.

But my horse is rearing and starting.

So then, instead of asking the clacking to stop, get your horse to stop rearing. Only then can it drink water.[6]

The "relationality" of social existence is abused by its denial and misuse: if you do want the horse to drink, then you must accede to the conditions that can make it possible, rather than try to change them to suit yourself. Numbers, money, birth, or belief, whatever may be called upon to justify the abuse of relationality, force alone forms the final justification. And resistance to this force is the very basis of social justice. To reduce one's being in the world to a single strand is to violate oneself, and accept this violation by others. Thus, "minority" appears inadequate as a historical category unless it is located in time and place, and its relational dynamics become part of the narrative of history.

The purpose of a critical reading is to recognize the politics of literature – how the very regime of the literary configures the relation between the visible and the sayable. The regime of signification or "aesthetic" that decides what art is, regulates the shaping of literature. Critical activity has the responsibility to unveil this regime and lay bare its very construction to show how it has been shaped by the forces of power at a given time and place. The structuring of poetics around voicing/voiceless/silence characterize a political position, locating art within the hierarchy of a social order which is implicated in shaping modes of expression. Language or literature become, therefore, the objects of study inasmuch as they are deployed to function in accordance with a regime of signification derived from a definition of literature itself which privileges one form of language use and rejects another.

The task of a comparative historiography of literature is to trace the forces that shape this formation, not as literary art but as a formation that is christened literature by a specific time and place. Questioning the legislation for a particular kind of writing, a particular form of self-expression, using the language of certain social categories, whether they are gender, class or caste, in the definition of literature, is a political act which introduces the reader to the aesthetic of a time and place, shaped by human endeavour rather than received scripture. Literature written by minorities and majorities, just like any other art form practised by them is located in experience. They have available to them the same milieu, but this availability is underwritten by the dialectics of force deployed to undercut relationality. Locating identity rather than treating it as an absolute, and in the abstract, reveals the many ways in which a single human being exists in society. To fix her identity as part of a minority, serves only a limited purpose, while obfuscating the larger political responsibility of historically grounding the regime of signification which underlies the definition of literature as a discourse.

The ideology of Comparative Literature (and one would leave it to others to call it a philosophy, if it qualifies as such) demands relationality, rather than what is arrogantly called "acknowledgement" and the humility to listen rather than the exclusivity of categorization.

NOTES

1 Roland Barthes. "Introduction to the Structural Analysis of Narratives" in *Image Music Text*, trans. Stephen Heath, London: Macmillan, 1978.
2 See for instance, Sisir Kumar Das. *A History of Indian Literature* vol. viii, Amiya Dev "Writing Indian Literary History" in *Literary Historiography* ed I Chanda, *Literary Studies in India Series*, Kolkata: Jadavpur University, 2004.
3 See, for instance, Patricia Hill Collins, *Black Feminist Thought: Knowledge, Consciousness and the Politics of Empowerment.* Boston: Unwin Hyman, 1990.
4 Jacques Ranciere. *Aesthetics and Its Discontents.* trans. Steve Corcoran, London: Polity, 2009.
5 Vijaydan Detha, 'Sacchai ka bhram' in *Chaudhurain ki Chaturayi*, New Delhi: Vani Prakashan, 2010, p. 37. Translation mine.
6 Vijaydan Detha, 'Khatpat ki sadhana' in *Chaudhurain ki Chaturayi*, New Delhi: Vani Prakashan, p. 32. Translation mine.

REFERENCES

Barthes, Roland. "Introduction to the Structural Analysis of Narratives" in *Image Music Text*, trans. Stephen Heath. London: Macmillan. 1978.

Collins, Patricia Hill. *Black Feminist Thought: Knowledge, Consciousness, and the Politics of Empowerment.* Boston: Unwin Hyman, 1990.

Das, Sisir Kumar. *A History of Indian Literature* (volume viii) Amiya Dev " Writing Indian Literary History" in *Literary Historiography* ed. Chanda, *Literary Studies in India Series*, Kolkata: Jadavpur University. 2004.

Detha, Vijaydan. 'Sacchai ka bhram' in *Chaudhurain ki Chaturayi.* New Delhi: Vani Prakashan, 2010.

____ 'Khatpat ki sadhana' in *Chaudhurain ki Chaturayi.* New Delhi: Vani Prakashan, 2010.

Ranciere, Jacques. *Aesthetics and Its Discontents.* trans. Steve Corcoran, London: Polity, 2009.

4

Genre and Genus as Minority Discourse: Rethinking the Categories of Dalit Literature[1]

Christi A. Merrill

How ethical are comparisons between American slave narratives and Dalit autobiographies when reaching out to student audiences in America today? The very analogy – as popular as it is compelling – tends to reify simplistic narratives of strength in the face of adversity, leaving the impression that the outcome of the struggles today in India against caste-based discrimination will triumph eventually, following in the path of the already-successful nineteenth-century movement for emancipation from slavery in the United States. Such optimism is neither misplaced nor morally suspect, if balanced by attention to the particularities of each example in such a way that allows students to understand each history in its own terms. What critical skills are necessary for helping students work through these complicated issues of discrimination through literature?

I approach this question as a Hindi translator myself who has recently begun rendering Kausalya Baisantri's Dalit feminist *jivan ki katha* (as life narrative, or life story), *Dohara Abhishap [Doubly Cursed]*, from Hindi into English, and primarily as a literature professor who teaches a range of courses featuring Dalit autobiographies: in lower-level undergraduate surveys introducing students to South Asian culture, in upper-level undergraduate courses focusing on South Asian literature and human rights issues, as well as in graduate seminars reflecting on first-person, gendered accounts of discrimination and violence. What categories should be mobilized when including this type of literature in a syllabus? What is our role as academic translators and literature scholars in marketing difference? The question is two-fold: over genus (how can we compare race and caste?), and over genre (how is a nineteenth-century slave narrative like a late twentieth-century or early twenty-first-century Dalit autobiography?). In this study, I hope to suggest that the question of how to read genus against genre are interlinked beyond the etymological.

I understand from Arun Mukherjee's laments about the editorial and marketing decisions taken by the American publisher (Columbia University Press) of her English translation of Omprakash Valmiki's *Joothan* that a translator has very little control over the publicity materials that accompany the publication of a book. Nevertheless, as an instructor I frequently find students parroting the phrasing and perspectives of that very ad copy in classroom discussions and in written papers, and so in this article I will turn my attention to those materials as my primary site of investigation. I proceed under the conviction that the categories we employ as we approach these works have a profound effect on our individual reading experiences (especially students'), and that it is crucial that we think critically about the genus-based and genre-based comparisons used to market Dalit literature.[2] I acknowledge the many persuasive arguments that have been made in the past two decades of the dangers of making easy equivalences in translation exchanges, and I see my own investigation as an extension of those conversations.[3] In this paper, I will reflect on the comparisons American publishers make in online marketing materials for Dalit accounts in translation.

I would like to start with the promotional material published on the Powell's Books online, where Omprakash Valmiki's *Joothan: A Dalit's Life* (mentioned above) is compared explicitly with both slavery and apartheid:

> Valmiki tells a riveting story of growing up in a village in the newly independent India. It is a story of survival, of oppression as grievous as slavery or apartheid, and of victory as well, as the author manages to get an education and ultimately learns to embrace his identity and become a spokesman for his community.

Here and elsewhere on this site we are assured that Valmiki's personal story has something to teach us about the Dalit movement more generally, with the writer as "spokesman for his community." The emphasis on both "grievous...oppression" and on "victory as well" signals to readers that Valmiki's account will help them become familiar with the most horrific details of untouchability as it has been traditionally practised, and will also allow them to witness a historical transformation first-hand as the caste system is overthrown – thanks, in part, to the brave efforts of writer–activists such as Valmiki. Linking untouchability with "slavery or apartheid" locates the struggles in a specific point in the unfolding historical narrative, which is imminently repeatable, and hence where victory is inevitable.

The comparison has a respected genealogy. As a student at Columbia University in New York, Bhimrao Ambedkar himself noticed the similarities between the experiences of the American Negro (as African-Americans were called then) and untouchables in India, and his observations about the struggles of that minority group for equality in the United States post-slavery deeply influenced his own political strategies. Many years later, in the 1970s, this explicit comparison was revived when a group of Marathi writers and Dalit activists founded the Dalit Panthers, named self-consciously after the Black Panthers in America. In both cases, victory was sought but never assured. More recently, at the 2001 U.N. World Conference Against Racism held in Durban, South Africa, a group of Dalit activists proposed that the word "caste" be included in the anti-racism statement by the UN's Human Rights Council (which was later adopted.) This move sparked a public debate about the strategic uses of "race" that is helpful for us to think about in the context of the mutual and ongoing influences between academic and non-academic discourse.

In a 2001 article in *The Hindu* called "Race and Caste", the Indian academic and public intellectual Andre Beteille wrote about being "a student of anthropology in Calcutta in the 1950s" reading M.F. Ashley Montagu's (1942) "Man's Most Dangerous Myth: The Fallacy of Race" which contended that the widely-used concept of race was, as he puts it, "politically pernicious and scientifically anomalous." He contends that this critique of the notion of race was generally accepted by the mid-twentieth century, including, he adds, by Franz Boas in his book *Race, Language and Culture*. Beteille then complains:

> Despite all the hard work done by anthropologists from Boas onward, the idea of race dies hard in the popular imagination. That is understandable. What is neither understandable nor excusable is the attempt by the United Nations to revive and expand the idea of race, ostensibly to combat the many forms of social and political discrimination prevalent in the world. It is sad but true that many forms of invidious discrimination do prevail in the contemporary world. But to assimilate or even relate them all to 'racial discrimination' will be an act of political and moral irresponsibility.

Like those writing the ad copy for Valmiki's autobiography, the Dalit activists in Durban were insisting on this analogy between race and caste precisely to offer an equation between the two and thus to repeat the relative success story of African–Americans in the United States. A key part of their strategy was to link these two categories in the minds of people around the world and thus to put pressure on the dominant group in India, in a manner similar to first the legal and then social emancipation of African-Americans in the United States.[4] Beteille, however, is critical of such a move, claiming that its very premise is built on dubious scholarship:

> Not content with condemning racism and racial discrimination, the U.N. now wants to take on 'racism, racial discrimination, xenophobia and related intolerance'. It has in its wisdom decided to expand the meaning of racial discrimination to accommodate exclusion or preference 'based on race, colour, descent, or national or ethnic origin'. In doing so it is bound to give a new lease of life to the old and discredited notion of race current a hundred years ago. By flying in the face of the distinctions between race, language and culture, it is seeking to undo the conclusions reached by the researches of several generations of anthropologists.

The "old and discredited notion of race" he refers to is deeply implicated in colonial projects placing Western European man at the top of a moral and racial hierarchy whose invocation of scientific objectivity (authorized by scholars) renders the findings inevitable and neutral. Edward Said, most notably, has lambasted these classificatory systems for their Orientalist insistence on essentializing character types, ever since eighteenth-century scholars like Carl Linnaeus fit these racial types and characters into an interconnected system of stereotyping (what Said calls 'related generalizations') that have enjoyed enduring authority. (119)

How are these categories mobilized politically? Beteille is exercised by the notion of equating "caste" with "race" in the Human Rights Council statement, but notes a distinction between these taxonomies and the practice of discrimination based on it:

> Interested parties within and outside the U.N. would like to bring caste discrimination in general and the practice of untouchability in particular within the purview of racial discrimination. The practice of untouchability is indeed reprehensible and must be condemned by one and all; but that does not mean that we should now begin to regard it as a form of racial discrimination. The Scheduled Castes of India taken together are no more a race than are the Brahmins taken together. Every social group cannot be regarded as a race simply because we want to protect it against prejudice and discrimination.

His statements raise important issues about the ways academic classificatory systems are politicized (for purportedly different ends) in public discourse, which I will only touch on briefly here in order to note the similarity between the colonial and postcolonial contexts. In this particular example, for instance, Beteille himself went on to align himself with the upper-caste and right-wing elements of the Indian government who were resistant to including "caste" in the U.N. statement.

Kamala Visweswaran's work on this debate in particular is much more nuanced, and worth exploring here, especially for her insights about the importance of the perspective of those narrating the experience of discrimination. In a chapter in her book *Un/common Cultures: Racism and the Rearticulation of Cultural Difference* (Duke, 2010), she points out that Beteille failed to make a distinction between these categories as stereotypes and their underlying basis:

> In order to make his argument about established scientific opinion, Beteille invokes the names of two anthropologists, Ashley Montagu and Franz Boas, who in fact held two diametrically opposed views. Montagu, of course, was best known for his book *The Fallacy of Race,* while Boas in

> *Race, Language and Culture* went on to distinguish the biological basis of race from social groupings based on language or religion. Boas's intervention, as Beteille sympathetically notes, was to establish a clear distinction between 'race,' a biological category with physical markers, and other social groupings based on language, religion, nationality, style of life, or status....Yet, Beteille's reiteration of the Boasian position on race during the WCAR debates entails a misreading that has been as damaging historically for American anthropology as it has been for the emergence of a Dalit sociology. (148)

Her insight most relevant here is to distinguish between "race" (i.e., an ontology or essential category, that came into the scholarly discourse in the eighteenth century with Linnaeus and others) and "racism" (which she emphasizes is based on the experiences of those suffering the discrimination). She goes on to compare the writings of African-American activists like W.E.B. du Bois and Martin Luther King on racial discrimination with contemporary debates on caste, including their own questions about the comparison, as well as Ambedkar's correspondence with King and du Bois. She explains:

> If we recognize, as did Du Bois, that the experience (and indeed, the category) of race is produced, not by biology, but by the social experience of racism, and extend this understanding to the relationship between caste and casteism, then we can see that the daily experience of harassment, subordination, and subjugation; 'the social heritage of slavery; the discrimination and insult' [as Du Bois puts it]; the experiences of caste terror render the Dalit experience of casteism is very much like the experience of racism. Since caste is constructed through the social experience of casteism, it would thus seem that we have a socially constructed notion of caste that mirrors Du Bois's understanding of the caste-like nature of racism in the United States. Caste, like race, is not an essence or an identity, but a product of social forms of discrimination. As one Dalit activist put it, 'Caste is not something one is; it is something that is done to you.' (150)

How can one analyze caste as "a product of social forms of discrimination" in translation? If, as Scott suggests in her famous 1991 article "The Evidence of Experience", personal experience has little scholarly credibility in the field of history (or in any social science, she implies), what is its status in academic literary circles? That is, how might we incorporate these personal and exceedingly subjective encounters with these categories into our own theoretical approaches?

After all, in both the undergraduate classroom and in the non-academic public sphere, the rhetoric of social science still has utmost authority, as we see on the Powell's Books website promoting Valmiki's autobiography:

> Dalits today constitute about one sixth of India's population. Spread over the entire country, speaking many languages, and belonging to many religions, they have become a major political force. As a document of the long silenced and long denied sufferings of the Dalits, Joothan is not only a contribution to the archives of Dalit history, but a manifesto for the revolutionary transformation of society and human consciousness.

In part the publisher and the bookseller must offer credible background information about the Dalit movement, but they are also purveying a front-row seat in this "revolutionary transformation". The promise is that the reader is invited to be in league instead with a revolutionary, and thus to be on the right side of history. This is an entirely different kind of history than that which concerns Scott. In the case of Dalit autobiography, the writer and the reader are invited to be part of a shared history with the readers joining the writers in acting as agents of change rather than being treated as objects of study.

As it happens, Scott discusses an American example of autobiographical writing that aims to make visible "difference" (in this case, a gay, male writer as different from mainstream heterosexual society), to raise larger questions about what historical credibility autobiographical writing has. While the conceptual stakes for a literature scholar are different than those of a historian, her observations on the relationship of experience to genre are particularly relevant. She writes: "The project of making experience visible precludes analysis of the workings of this system and its historicity; instead it reproduces its terms" (779). Her concern is that autobiographical writing does not achieve the kinds of transformations it promises in theory. Her article thus introduces a quandary about what one publisher – as we shall soon see – has called "caste literature activism": since it relies on autobiographical work to make a claim for these experiences of discrimination, its authority is entirely based on personal identification between writer and reader. How might we as academic translators and literature scholars frame these personal encounters in such a way that avoids replicating and even reinforcing stereotypes?

In the promotional material for Urmila Pawar's *The Weave of My Life: A Dalit Woman's Memoir* that appears on the Columbia University Press, Wandana Somalkar also makes an analogy between slavery and the Dalit experience, and goes so far as to claim that the very act of writing – that, by implication, the reader endorses by buying the book for sale – is a step towards emancipation:

> The sufferings of the Dalit are, like those of the black slave in America, the sufferings of her community. Not only this, because the path to emancipation is also a social project rather than an individual one, the Dalit autobiography combines witnessing and experiencing in an act of sharing that gives it a political force.

The ad copy does not specify who exactly is considered part of this ongoing "social project" and what ethical responsibilities are attached to being included in this "act of sharing". More importantly, the copy does not specify what "political force" this genre of writing asks us to endorse. Certainly, those making the comparison between slave narratives and Dalit autobiography are mindful of the success of novels such as *Uncle Tom's Cabin* and slave narratives such as *The Narrative of the Life of Frederick Douglass* in winning over the sympathies of the dominant group. Rather than pursue this comparison in historical terms, a lineup of literature scholars are invoked to suggest that Pawar be read as both activist and as accomplished writer, a combination that is reported to enjoy noteworthy precedent in the genre of Dalit first-person writing:

> We can make a comparison here with what M. S. S. Pandian says about two recent Dalit autobiographical texts, *Karukku* and *Vadu*, originally written in Tamil. 'The everyday, the ordinary, a temporality that is not teleological, and a language of affect and incomprehension invest caste with certain presentness and immediacy and opens up a space for moral and political appeal to the upper castes. The burden of caste is thus returned to the upper castes.'…Urmila Pawar's memoir follows in this genre; what is different is that, unlike her predecessors, she approaches

her subject both as a writer with some literary achievement already under her belt and as an activist who has tried to organize Dalit women and has a specific stance on Dalit feminism. It seems that her objective is to document both caste and patriarchy in the lives that enter into the weave of her memoir. 'The language of affect and of incomprehension' that Pandian writes of are somewhat toned down as compared to some of the earlier Dalit autobiographies.

That Somalkar calls the genre variously "autobiographical texts" and "memoir" seems significant, for it suggests that this literary category itself is undergoing transformation simultaneous with the social and political category of caste. By celebrating Pawar's "literary achievement" as well as her ability to "document both caste and patriarchy", she is suggesting that this genre might appeal to both social scientists and humanists, and have both artistic as well as political value. Or even, that its artistic value can be understood politically, and its political value artistically, if we can avail ourselves of an appropriately interdisciplinary scholarly perspective. What might that be?

On the Oxford University Press website Lakshmi Holmstrom's English translation of Bama's *Karukku* (classified as an "autobiography") is called "a classic of subaltern writing", thus bringing together the humanist idea of classic literature with the social scientific concern with subalternity. They call Bama herself a "caste literature activist", thus collapsing any distinction between the writer's political commitments and her creative endeavours. In an excerpt published in *Outlook India* of Lakshmi Holmstrom's introduction to the Indian edition (published by Macmillan), Holmstrom insists:

> The events of Bama's life are not arranged according to a simple, linear or chronological order, as with most autobiographies, but rather, reflected upon in different ways, repeated from different perspectives, grouped under different themes, for example, Work, Games and Recreation, Education, Belief, etc. The argument of the book is to do with the arc of the narrator's spiritual development both through the nurturing of her belief as a Catholic, and her gradual realization of herself as a Dalit.

Here too this Dalit autobiography is being celebrated in ways that might appeal both to one's literary sensibilities (as ground-breaking and exceptional) and to one's training in social science (as offering an alternative, self-generated classification system). It is significant too that Holmstrom uses terms like "argument" and narrative "arc" that mix disciplinary terms. We might even read Holmstrom's celebration of Bama's thematic groupings, and the different perspectives they reveal, as leading to a more complex analysis of what Scott calls "the workings of this system and its historicity", one that does not reproduce received terms (Said's "related generalizations") but instead calls the entire system of classification into question – of both genus and of genre at once – because her work has literary merit and is also credible from a social scientific point of view. An accomplished translator and literary critic such as Holmstrom is thus able to finesse our most unproductive disciplinary expectations by suggesting that Bama herself has been effective at doing so all along.

NOTES

1. This article is part of a larger project I am currently researching on genres of literary non-fiction focused on human rights. A senior fellowship from the American Institute of Indian Studies and the National Endowment for the Humanities has afforded me time to devote to this project; I gratefully acknowledge this support, along with the University of Michigan for allowing me a year of leave from teaching and Jamia Millia Islamia University for what has been an exceedingly productive and lively affiliation. I would also like to thank Professor Anisur Rahman for creating an opportunity for my recent work to be included in this volume.
2 Katherine Wilson makes a similar point about what she calls "atrocity literature" whereby the memoir about the genocide in Cambodia by writer Chanrithy Him, for example, was compared to Anne Frank's testimony about the Holocaust in Europe, and she was introduced to her American audience as "the Cambodian Anne Frank". (33)
3 Most notably in the context of translating human rights, see Lydia Liu, "Legislating the Universal: The Circulation of International Law in the Nineteenth Century".
4 In an introductory chapter to the two-volume collection, *Translating Slavery: Gender and Race in French Abolitionist Writing, 1780–1830,* Françoise Massardier-Kenney shows how crucial international pressure was on changing the minds of American citizens about the immorality of slavery. She also argues that this identification was gendered.

REFERENCES

Print Sources

Baisantri, Kausalya. *Dohara Abhishap.* Delhi: Parameshwari Prakashan, 1999.

Massardier-Kenney, Françoise. Dorish Y. Kadish and Françoise Massardier-Kenney, eds. *Translating Slavery: Gender and Race in French Abolitionist Writing, 1780-1830.* Kent, Ohio: Kent State University Press, 2009. Vol. I: 3–18.

Liu, Lydia H. 'Legislating the Universal: The Circulation of International Law in the Nineteenth Century.' In *Tokens of Exchange: The Problem of Translation in Global Circulations,* edited by Lydia Liu (Durham, NC: Duke University Press, 1999): 127–64.

Mukherjee, Arun, Alok Mukherjee, and Barbara Godard. 'Translating Minoritized Cultures: Issues of Caste, Class and Gender.' *Postcolonial Text* 2.3 (2008): 1–23.

Said, Edward. *Orientalism.* New York: Vintage, 1979.

Scott, Joan W. 'The Evidence of Experience,' *Critical Inquiry,* Vol. 17, No. 4 (Summer, 1991), pp. 773–797.

Visweswaran, Kamala. *Un/common Cultures: Racism and the Rearticulation of Cultural Difference.* Durham, North Carolina: Duke University Press, 2010.

Wilson, Katherine. 'Anne Frank Abroad: The Emergence of World Atrocity Literature,' *World Literature Today,* May-June 2013, 28–33.

Online Sources

Beteille, Andre. 'Race and Caste.' *The Hindu.* 10 March 2001. http://www.hindu.com/thehindu/2001/03/10/stories/05102523.htm Accessed 12 July 2012.

Holmstrom, Lakshmi. 'Introduction to Karukku,' (excerpted from the book courtesy Macmillan India Limited) *Outlook India.com.* Web 23 April 2001. http://www.outlookindia.com/article.aspx?211413 Accessed 15 July 2012.

Sonalkar, Wandana. 'Foreword' to *The Weave of My Life: A Dalit Woman's Memoirs* by Urmila Pawar. Columbia University Press. http://cup.columbia.edu/book/978-0-231-14900-6/the-weave-of-my-life/excerpt. Accessed 14 July 2012.

'Joothan: A Dalit's Life.' Powell's Books. http://www.powells.com/biblio/9780231129725. Accessed 12 October 2009.

'Karukku: Lakshmi Holmstrom and Bama. Oxford University Press. http://ukcatalogue.oup.com/product/9780198078302.do Accessed 15 July 2012.

5

The Sacred Writings of the Minorities

Gurbhagat Singh

Minority refers to a group that is discriminated against and subjected to injustice in practice by a majority and enjoys less power. Deleuze, A modern theorist of minority, mentions three major characteristics of minority and its articulatory systems: (i) deterritorialization, (ii) connection of its individual members to a political programme, and (iii) collective assemblage of its enunciations (Deleuze 1993:154). By deterritorialization Deleuze means the creative endeavour of a minority to get out of the constrained space of the oppressive majority through construction of a nomadic space of freedom. The construction of a political programme means that whatever is thought or expressed by a minority addresses the political questions confronted in its historical-existential situation. The third characteristic suggests that a minority enunciation or expression is not individual; it represents the entire group with its angst and aspirations.

It would be quite appropriate to advance Deleuze's theory and say that a minority is overloaded, embattled, and explosive. It is a group of Excess, to use an expression of Bataille. Giving a very original insight, Deleuze has also said that a minority is always in a state of becoming. In simple words, a minority is ceaselessly creative. Since it is oppressed, for its freedom it continously thinks of a free space, creatively destroys and de-constructs to re-territorialize. This creative re-territorialization means developing a new mythic or symbolic framework to see things afresh. But what Deleuze, Geertz, or even

Lenin and Stalin, have theorized about the minorities/small cultures, emphasizing their differences, is a product of the situation arisen after Nietzsche and the "death of God". Minorities have existed even in earlier times. The Jews, Buddhists, Jains, Zoroastrians, and other ethnic groups of the Americas have asserted their very vital and autonomous presences.

Before the advent of our modern/postmodern and Marxist revolutionary paradigms, the sacred was also employed as a deterritorializing and liberative medium by the minorities to de-constrain themselves. The dominant majority used the idea of sacred, and constructed its discourse around it, whether written or oral. The whole system was developed to organize politics, society, individuals, and their relationships accordingly. Therefore, to de-condition or deterritorialize meant to re-invent/re-construct the matter of the sacred. That could initiate re-organization of the entire life of a society. We can also say that the earlier forms of radicalism were the endeavours of re-rendering the entire matter or content of the sacred through writing or orality. In India, two major re-renderings were done. First by the Buddhists in the *Dhammapada* and some *Sahajyani* poetry of the monk-poets, later done by the Sikh Gurus and Bhagats in Sri Guru Granth Sahib and the Dasam Granth. The re-renderings clearly point out the crises of their contemporary societies. The re-renderings thus become vital efforts to tide over the crises.

The pre-Buddhist crisis was related to the homogenization of Indian society according to the Brahmanical system of four castes and the primacy of *Atma-Brahman* identity ("Thou art that"). The realization of *Atma-Brahman* identity was possible through elaborate ceremonies. According to Radha krishnan, "As a matter of fact, the Buddha was more definitely opposed to Vedic orthodoxy and ceremonialism" (Radhakrishnan1977:15). The *Dhammapada* which consists of the utterances of the Buddha, approved by the First Council of Buddhist scholars, reduces the whole matter of the sacred to ethics and the moral law. If the humans follow the moral law, suffering can cease and *Nirvana* can be attained. Radhakrishnan mentions two positions regarding the Buddhism's relationship with the Brahmanical system of the Upanishads. He calls Buddha's teaching as both "derived" from, and at variance with, the Upanishads (29). At variance in the belief in change, through ethical practice, they become rather than remain static. Now we know that any recommendation for stasis is motivated by homogenization. We grow only by not clinging to the kind of identity between *Atma* and *Brahman*. But this becoming is not ordinary motion; it is "above" the normal stasis and motion. In Chapter IV of the *Dhammapada* it is said about a sage: "Even as a bee gathers honey from a flower and departs without injuring the flower or its colour or scent, so let a sage dwell in this village" (75). The notion of fragrance-like non-injuring dwelling is the Buddha's *Anatta* (not-self) or transindividuation that relates to the total universe, the wholeness of life; it cuts through alienation, or conditioning done by the *Atma-Brahman-like* doctrine elaborated through the caste system. Rather than relating the human to the unitive *Brahman* that may result in egoism, the *Dhammapada* relates to the wholeness of reality through virtual or moral practice. The *Atma-Brahman* doctrine has been substituted with the *Anatta*-Moral Law doctrine to block the possibility of homogenizing unity that later on resulted into violent confrontations between Hinduism and Buddhism. In Chapter XIV of the *Dhammapada*, *Nirvana* is not stated just as a negative idea: "The awakened declare *Nirvana* to be the highest (of things). He verily is not an anachronite who opposes (others), he is not an ascetic who causes grief to another" (121). In Chapter XV, happiness or *Sukh* has been related to the giving up of both victory and defeat.

The matters related to grief, victory, and defeat indicate the presence of some angst-ridden and injured groups of the society that were subordinated by the homogenizing dominant majority. The categories and expression system of the *Dhammapada* make us think of that society which was also ordered by bloodshed and violence. This ordering is not only a modernist phenomenon. A twentieth-century culture theorist Walter Benjamin, with the Jewish fascist conflict in the background, has told us that cultures are organized by the dominant majority with its imposing paradigm. The *Dhammapada* as a sacred text, understandably, becomes a weapon to resist and counter the homogenization of a subordinated group although the *nirvanic* way out suggested transcends all group limits.

Medieval Buddhism, between the eighth and eighteenth centuries, faced two kinds of homogenization. One was *Vedantic,* championed by Shankaracharya and articulated in his classic work *Brahmsutrabhashya.* The other one was advocated and used by the Mughal State for its own political and social hegemony. Citing the Chandogya *Upanishad* (vii:16), Shankara establishes that *Brahman* is unitive: "Unity is the true existence while manifoldness is evolved out of false knowledge" (Deutsch and Van Buitenen (eds.) 1971,182). For that reason, the highest *Brahman* cannot possess double characteristics" (192).

The fast spreading Islam and later the Mughal state were unitarian in their thrust. The *Allah*-sign that they were asserting was inspired by the Suras of *Quran* emphasizing absolute unity. Sura 3:1 says: "*Allah*! there is no God! the Living! The Self-Subsisting Eternal" (1981:71) Sura 37:4 says: "Verily, Verily your God is one" (*ibid.*:1136). Thus, in the Shankaracharya's text and in the Mughal State's practice of the Revelations, the emphasis was on absolute un it y and singular interpretation that could result in the subordination of other groups. Their pressured otherness creatively exploded into differential, emancipative sacred discourses which brought some distinct world views and expression systems.

In the tensorial process and interaction with the *Atma-Brahman* identity doctrine of homogenization, between the eighth and twelfth centuries, Buddhist poets of the monasteries of Midnapore in West Bengal, known as *Sahajyanis,* further evolved the *Thathata* or Suchness doctrine. The *Sahajyanis* believed in awakening the lotus-plexes or higher nerve centres through four *Kayas* or subtle bodies. Those were *Dharm Kaya, Nirman Kaya, Sambhog Kaya, Sahaj Kaya.* The fourth, *Sahaj Kaya,* was the *Sahajyani* innovation. It aimed at combining in *Chitta,* or Consciousness *Shunyata* (void) and *Karuna* (Compassion). The innovative *Sahajyan* emerged from the down-trodden. The monk-poets talked of realizing the *Sahaj-tattva* or Suchness as a fully lotus-centred *kundalini,* the effeminate energy called *Nairatma* or Dombi. Dombi was a low and untouchable caste. In a *Sahajyani* song the poet Kanha-pada addresses the *yogini* Dombi: "......I embrace the yogini... O yogini... I shall not live even for a moment… I shall kiss thy life and drink the lotus-juice" (Dasgupta 1969: 103). The marginalized *Sahajyani* monk-poets have not only made a major semiotic intervention by naming the higher *Niravanic* energy as the low-caste Dombi who is effeminate and a *yogini*.

The Buddhists were striking at the superstructures of the society dominated by the Brahmanical and Ismalic male-feudalisms. The *Sahajyanis* have assigned the liberative responsibility to woman. This emancipative work was begun by the Buddha himself. He permitted women to enter the highest Buddhist order, even though he thought the permission would shorten the life of the order. In the *Mahaparinibban Sutta* (Radhakrishnan 1977:14), the Buddha is recorded having said while answering a question of the disciple Ananda: "If Ananda, women had not received permission to enter the Order, the pure religion would have lasted long, the good law would have stood fast a thousand years. But since they have received that permission, it will now stand fast only five hundred years" (V: 3).

The process of making primary, holistic, and semiotic subversion by substituting the *Atma-Brahman* identity doctrine with the *Anatta*-Moral Law doctrine and by emphasizing the cosmic, creative realization through the effeminate *Sahaj-yogini,* peaked in the Sikh sacred texts *Sri Guru Granth Sahib* complied in 1604 A.D. and The *Dasam Granth* compiled in the early eighteenth century A.D. The *Guru Granth* consists of the hymns composed in *Ragas* and *Desi* music by the Gurus and the Bhagats who belonged to the down-trodden sections of different cultural regions of the Indian subcontinent. The major sign of *Sri Guru Granth Sahib* that becomes an alternative to the *Vedantic* Unitive sign Brahman, is "*Wahiguru*," which literally means the Guru of Wonder. His very significant signified or attribute is seeing with the simultaneity of unity and diversity. *Wahiguru* causes *Vismad*, or Joyous Wonder, not homogenization or caste-hierarchization. Guru Nanak says in *Rag* Asa: *Vismad* beings, *Vismad* diversity/*Vismad* forms, *Vismad* colours (SGGS:463). The presence of *Wahiguru* creates *Sahaj*-ecstasy in Kabir, a prominent Bhagat poet of the Guru Granth. He experiences a reversal, that is, transformation from the oppression of existence to the ecstasy of *Sahaj*, which is cosmic equilibrium. Kabir was a weaver by caste.

He constructs a vital transformational metaphor from his weaverly existence when he says: "In this reversal/are forgotten both family and caste. We are now weaved in Sunna-Sahaj" (SGGS: 1158). Bhagat Ravidas who was a shoe-mender, constructs the sign of *Begumpura* or utopian city in which none will pay the taxes (of the homogenizer).

A very significant characteristic of *Wahiguru* is that He has no single name. As has become clear in the post-Nietzschean "death of God" debate, it is the obsession with, or clinging to a particular name that causes the hegemonic intention to subordinate groups to fall in line with an Order, Order in the sense of Foucault. Assigning a single name to the Divine, or any Utopia, certainly creates an obsessive situation to obliterate differences. The Guru Granth, as if anticipating our present problematics and its postmodern solutions, accepts multiple names of the Utopia/Divine: like *Allah, Brahman, Parbrahman, Ram, Rahim, Karim, Gossain, Akal Purakh, Ek Onkar, Bhagwan*, and many more. *Wahiguru* is the umbrella name that constitutes the wide multiplicity of names and creates a sense of wonder and awe. In the semiotic idiom, we can say that the *wahiguru* of the Guru Granth has many signifieds. In fact, in the rich mosaic of multi-roots and multi-cultural connections, *wahiguru* becomes a ceaseless signifier. It forms itself in the endless chain of signifiers, the chain and the base repertoire of signifiers in the sense of Derrida and Benjamin. The *Wahiguru* of the *Guru Granth*, thus, is an ever-becoming signifier, never freezing to stasis.

The multi-rooted and multi-lingual model of the *Guru Granth* for elaborating the Divine has also been employed by Guru Gobind Singh in the creations of *The Dasam Granth*. Most of these creations belong to the late seventeenth and early eighteenth centuries. In the *Akal Ustat* and *Jap Sahib,* the Divine/*Akal* Purakh has been elaborated both negatively and positively. The addresses to Him of various cultural, religious, ethnic groups have been acknowledged as valid. In *Akal Ustat* it is said: "The Arabs of Arabia revere Your Name. The Firangis of France revere You. The Quraishis of Kandhar know You. The Westerners of the West revere You in their faith" (1973: 48). The reverence of the Red Indians living near San Francisco and the reverence of the Tibetans have also been acknowledged as right (48:52).

According to the tradition, the *Jap Sahib* and some portions of the *Akal Ustat*, in which the multi-cultural and multi-rooted model of the Divine appears, were read out to the Sikhs baptized by Guru Gobind Singh in 1699 A.D. at Anandpur *Sahib*.

Another creative advance or act of becoming manifested in Sri Guru Granth Sāhib is that the whole mystery of the Divine and the abundance of life can be appropriately realized through *Mahala*-spirituality. All the *banis*/revealed words of the Gurus have been presented in the *Guru Granth* as realizations of *Mahala*-spirituality. *Mahala* literally means woman. Although scholars differ on the interpretation of *Mahala*, yet the metaphoric structure and experiential component of the *banis* reveal that the Gurus considered the woman's responses and endowment far more alive to higher energies. Guru Nanak Dev's creation *Barah Mah* is an evidence of this consideration. The Gurus conferred the greatest honour upon woman for her wholesome and holistic creative realization. This hour is historic and very richly *avant-gardist*.

In the process of ceaseless becoming, as elaborated above, the *Guru Granth* has also given the idea of "Hari Dhan," the Divine as *Vismadic* (Wondrous) capital. If worked out in all its possibilities this idea of capital is an advance on the prevalent idea of just, competitive, market capital that runs our socio-economic systems, whether socialist or capitalistic. *Vismadic* capital will be non-exploitive, counter-hegemonic. It will preserve the wondrous diversity of the world. In *Rag* Suhi-Guru Ram Das says: "Oh brother! Cumulate Hari as capital. It helps here and ahead. Hari Dhan is obtained from. The community of the True" (SGGS:734). As elaborated by me elsewhere, the idea of *Vismadic* capital is different from the socialist and capitalistic capitals. It is a step forward to found a society of gift and dignity replacing the interest-based growth and profit-driven society, not free from exploitation and group conflicts.

In this brief study, based on the Indian experience, I have suggested that even before the advent of modern and postmodern liberative paradigms, the minorities had existed with their emancipative programmes. They had employed the sacred discourse for political and social freedom. In their ceaseless becoming, stimulated by consciousness, oppression, zestful striving, they had gone beyond reaction and creatively, and explored some new dimensions of reality to bring about holistic change.

REFERENCES

Dasgupta, Sashibhushan. *Obscure Religious Cults*. Calcutta: Firma K. L. M. 1969.

Deleuze, Gilles. *The Deleuze Reader.* Ed. Constantin V. Boundas. New York: Columbia University Press, 1993.

Deutsch, Eliot and J. A. R. Van Buitenen. *A Source Book of Advaita Vedanta.* Includes Shankara's Brahmsutrabhashya Translated by Eliot Deutsch. Honolulu: The University of Honolulu Press, 1971.

Radhakrishnan, S. ed. and trans. *The Dhammapada*. Madras: Oxford University Press, 1977

Singh, Gurbhagat. "The Difference of Small Cultures and their Global Significance." *Literature of Small Cultures: An Assertion of Difference.* Edited by Deepinder Jeet Randhawa. Patiala: G.S.S.D.G.S. Khalsa College, 2010.

Sri Guru Granth Sahib. Amritsar: Shiromani Gurdwara Parbandhak Committee.

The Dasam Granth. Patiala: Punjabi University, 1973.

The Holy Quran. Translated by Abdulla Young. Brentwood: Amana Corporation, 1981.

6

Discoursing Minority: Twentieth-Century Constructions of Indian Muslims

Anisur Rahman

A METAPHOR FOR AN ARGUMENT

Dair naheen, haram naheen, dar naheen, aasatan naheen
Baithhey hain rahguzar pe hum, ghair hamein uthhai kyun

—*Ghalib*

I do not intend to translate this Urdu *shair* by Mirza Asadullah Khan Ghalib; I rather choose to engage with what he intends to state in as defiant a term as is characteristic of his poetry. Literally, he means that he neither has a temple nor a mosque; neither a threshold nor a shrine, where he could presumably seek his solace, and since he has none of the four, he sits with pride on the pathway and daringly questions as to why should anyone remove him from there. Metaphorically, Ghalib is trying to suggest that it matters little even if those four sources of his sustenance are not available to him, as he has already claimed an open space for himself and feels better rewarded in a state of dispossession than in that of possession of the traditionally powerful sites of belonging. I allude to Ghalib not because he belonged to a community that is designated now as a "minority", nor do I refer to him because he wrote in a language that is associated with the Muslim minority today, but more significantly for the fact that he constructs his "self" in relation to the "other" and inhabits a free space that may not be usurped. Instead of lamenting over his deprivations, he gathers courage and seeks a secular space as a site of his belonging. Ghalib could not have guessed how this stance could bear upon the larger minority discourse today, and how it could serve as a metaphor for a people, oddly labeled as "minority". In his audacious step to secure a place on the pathway without blocking the passage for others, he underlines the need to carve a space and an identity for the dispossessed, and also the necessity to ensure their individual liberty and the power of self-determination. Drawing upon this metaphoric frame of reference that offers an occasion to examine the larger predicament of a people, I would like to engage with some issues relating to the Muslim minority that constitutes a major part of the modern Indian discourse on individual, society, culture, and politics.

PARAMETERS

As a race and a people, Muslims have been a curious phenomenon of history. In India, they form the largest numerical minority today. They have presented themselves, and have been represented by others, in diverse ways. The racially conscious twentieth century has had a plethora of Indian intellectuals, littérateurs, historians, social thinkers, politicians, and others (belonging to non-defined categories), who have found it perennially obligatory to develop their loose or structured discourses on this hugely contested community of people. In the complex web of narratives developed on Muslims in relation to their faith, culture, education, economic status, social assimilation, and political affiliations, there are significant issues that concern their lives, their vulnerability, the broader conditions of their survival, and more importantly their individual, communal, and national identities. In the melee of widely different constructions, the Muslim community in the multi-religious and multi-cultural

India is considered now a cultural boon, now a social bane; and now the nation's self, now the nation's other. While the points and counterpoints of reference have differed consistently, the community has been unwittingly projected in this process as an enigma, defying an easy definition or classification.

To put the argument in context, I should like to divide the modern Indian discourse on Muslims into two broad categories and identify them as *exclusivist discourse* and *inclusivist discourse*. While the exclusivist discourse is too clearly marked by its tenacity, the inclusivist one is characterized by a liberal tone and tenor emphasizing on resolution and reconciliation, understanding and indulgence. As the exclusivists and the inclusivists have represented two different mindsets, they have written two widely disparate texts, created two incompatible structures of meaning, and disseminated two irreconcilable kinds of messages. They might further be identified as creating the *discourse of divergence* and the *discourse of convergence* in their own rights. The exclusivists, representing the discourse of divergence, have projected the rightist understanding of society, while the inclusivists, representing the discourse of convergence, have configured the largely-looming-other, identified as minority, in a concurrent, sometimes even conflicting, relationship with the majority. In sum, the two discourses have been distinguishable for their sharp differences with each other, even as they have negotiated and mediated with myriad socio-political realities and pursued their own commitments towards contextualizing and relocating their two-pronged projects of exclusion and inclusion with respect to the Muslims.

To enlarge the argument further, I might posit that the champions of exclusivist discourse have marked the inherent discrepancies between the minority and the majority communities, and registered their disagreement with the Muslim minority in particular, especially with reference to their religious faith and culture. They have insisted on their arrival in India as "invaders" who encroached upon the space of the Hindu natives and have made a case, therefore, that they must belong to this land only on their own terms and conditions. They have evolved their own notions of cultural nationalism along the lines carved by the philosophy of Hindutva and have projected their own principles of universality, power, and dominance. As their perceptions turned into stubborn ideologies, they perceived religion as the foundation stone of the state and became the committed ideologues of Hindu revivalism, reiterating the supremacy of the Hindu race, Hindu nation, and Hindu nationalism with great obstinacy. These exclusivist ideas have been developed and disseminated by ideologues like B. S. Moonje, Bhai Parmanand, V. D. Savarkar, M. S. Golwalker, K. B. Hedgewar, and their descendants like K. S. Sudershan, Praveen Togadia, and Subramanian Swamy, to name only a few of them. Their ideologies have come to be implemented in practical terms in the succeeding generations by the Sangh Parivar, broadly aligning with the Rashtriya Swayam Sevak Sangh, Vishwa Hindu Parishad, Bajrang Dal, Bharatiya Janata Party, and Shiv Sena, apart from a plethora of other social and political organizations. It might be quite possible to mark that while the spirit of intellectual engagement and restrained rhetoric declined after Savarkar, the activities of the political parties to realize the ideologies propounded earlier gathered greater momentum. All their efforts, in totality, have been political in nature and have been aimed at rewriting the nation, both in literal and metaphorical terms, by gaining political control at the centre.

It may be marked further that while the Hindutva ideologues have problemtized the Muslim minority, they have made themselves susceptible to contestations, in turn. In engaging with the Muslim issue, they have operated as agents of image-making who have developed their own instruments in terms of their own logic and language. While they have emerged as the defining agencies of the Muslim community, they have typified and characterized their own insular function, rather unwittingly. They have contested their own cases, developed their own discourses of difference, and become, in turn, yet another site of contestation themselves. As they have problematized the minorities, they have also problematized the so-called "majority", and the two taken together have projected a larger collection of people living in a complex social matrix. In this intricate process of marking the other, and being marked as a defining agency in consequence, these ideologues and their followers have reiterated a self-constructed gospel that the Hindus alone have constituted the nation ever since, and shall do so ever after. This has amounted to denying space and identity to the Muslims which could be given to them, as they argued, only if they relinquished their religious and cultural identity and joined the exclusivist bogey which defined nation, nationalism, and nationhood in insular terms.

As against this, the inclusivist discourse has negated the monolithic notion of a nation constituted of a people following a single faith and culture. Instead of limiting the nation and the people to a certain race and a religion, it has tried to delimit its boundaries to welcome multiplicities of all kinds – social, cultural, religious, and political. It has set aside the coercive principles of universality and the rule of unilateral power and dominance. It has looked for points of convergence and has projected the eminent possibilities of union between the majority and the minority communities, as it has created space for cordiality, mutuality, and unity. This has been reflected in a rich variety of writings by statesmen and politicians, writers and historians, social thinkers and commentators. There is, however, an interesting point to note that while the exclusivists have put forth their ideas as agenda, the inclusivists have left their ideas open to contestations even within themselves. Their varied stances might be seen in the works of writers and reformers like Sir Syed Ahmed Khan and Altaf Hussain Hali, iconic nationalists like M. K. Gandhi, Jawaharlal Nehru, and Abul Kalam Azad, proponents of Muslim cause like Mohammad Ali Jinnah and Mohammad Iqbal, historians like Mohammad Mujeeb and Ramachandra Guha, social commentators like Rafiq Zakaria and Asghar Ali Engineer, liberals like Khushwant Singh and Kuldip Nayar, and a host of others representing various other shades of opinion. These diverse groups of inclusivist authors and intellectuals have represented the dynamics of a vibrant civil society, underlined its priorities, and made a case for the homogeneity of a people and the sanctity of their nation.

This is precisely the point where I should like to make a few propositions. *First*, while the exclusivists, in representing the types and stereotypes of the Muslim minority, have indirectly represented the articles of their religious faith and reflected upon their politics, the inclusivists have represented their notions of the secular and reflected upon themselves as secularists. *Second*, while the exclusivists have created a sacrosanct notion of the majority, necessarily representing the mainstay of power, the inclusivists have constructed a larger paradigm of the Indian people constituted of the majority and the minority together. *Third*, while the exclusivists have been driven by their well-defined motives to exercise their socio-political control over the minorities, the inclusivists have not been necessarily moved by any condition of complete control. *Fourth*, while the exclusivists have constructed the Muslim minority as the silent recipients of their dispensations, the inclusivists have allowed them occasions to speak and take part in the larger scheme of the nation as a secular space. *Fifth*, while the exclusivists have represented a narrow psychic condition nurtured over the ages, the inclusivists have represented broader mindsets nursed to negotiate with multiplicities of faith and culture. As both the exclusivists and the inclusivists have kept playing their given roles in relation to the Muslim minority, both have been engaged in image-making of distinct kinds. In understanding and problematizing the Muslim minority, both have pursued their well-defined policies. However, I would posit that it is in this persistent and divergent representation of the types and stereotypes of the Muslim minority that the parameters for the existence and survival of this community of people can be found. Let us now look at the two broad paradigms that the exclusivists and the inclusivists have represented and the oppositional discourses they have put forward during the twentieth century.

Paradigm 1: Exclusivist Discourse

Let us begin by examining the exclusivist stances evolved and reiterated by at least two major organizations, Akhil Bharatiya Hindu Mahasabha and Rashtriya Swayam Sevak Sangh, which paved the way, in the coming decades, for the emergence of the Sangh Parivar, a conglomerate of like-minded right wing political parties and organizations. Apart from individual variations with respect to their subsidiary aims, all of them stood committed essentially to Hindu revivalism. This being their basic aim, they presupposed the exclusion of all other races, religions, and cultures from the domain of the Hindu. The manner in which they constructed the Muslims can only be understood with the help of their essential predilections in which Muslims remained a constant obsession for them ever since the founding of the Hindu Mahasabha in 1914 and that of the RSS in 1925. B. S. Moonje and Bhai Parmanand, the two presidents of the Hindu Mahasabha and the two Hindu ideologues of the earlier days, adopted a stance against the policies of the Congress party, Gandhi's principle of non-violence, as well the Muslims who, they thought, were unduly favoured. Their ideologies found full flowering in V. D. Savarkar, an agnostic, a littérateur, an advocate of militarism, a critic of the Congress party, and a president of the Hindu Mahasabha, who emerged as the most influential figure towards propagating a religio-political philosophy which he chose to call "Hindutva". In his famous-infamous treatise called *Hindutva*,[1] he engaged with some seminal issues that he projected as the keystone of his thesis. He defined the "Hindu" as one who considered Bharatvarsha, spread from the Indus to the Seas, as his Father-Land and the Holy-Land, which also empowered him with a religious faith. Keeping close to this, he evolved the philosophy of "Hindutva" which embraced the perceptions and aspirations of all the Hindus and was different from "Hinduism" in its reach and sweep. Further, he perceived the Hindus both as a nation and a race that had the blood of the Aryans, the Kolorians, and the Dravidians in them, and "Sindhusthan", not "Aryavarta", as their home. He obviously disparaged the Muslims and labeled them as invaders, an expression that has carried on ever since. Developing a larger picture of his people, their religious faith, and their land of belonging, he considered "civilization" to be a cumulative heritage of the Hindu race spread over a vast span of time and space. Savarkar expressed his views as a creed, a credo, and a philosophy drawn basically upon history and religious faith. He influenced the like-minded Hindu nationalists and brought about a climactic change in favour of his philosophy which was well appreciated by his contemporary and subsequent followers. Savarkar's Hindutva denied space to the Muslim and Christian minorities as he thought that taking them into the fold would amount to putting the Hindu majority to disadvantage. He was unable to reconcile with Muslim presence and believed that the Muslims could pose a danger to the nation because they still dreamt of re-establishing their rule in India. He turned naturally against the Congress, Gandhi, and Jinnah and thought that all their acts, directed towards Muslims, were acts of appeasement. The two phrases – "Hindutva" and "Appeasement" – that have been at the core of recent Hindu discourse in India hark back to Savarkar's philosophy of exclusive Hindu *rashtra* (nation) with no space for the minorities of any origin.

Savarkar's legacy was ably carried forward by Hedgewar and Golwalkar who exerted their personal conviction with official sanction given to them by the Rashtriya Swayam Sevak Sangh. Hedgewar was the founder and the first *sarasanghachalak*[2] (supreme head) of RSS. He kept the Muslim factor outside the domain of his consideration, criticized the Congress party for Muslim appeasement, and promoted Hindu nationalism along the lines laid out by Savarkar. Golwalker succeeded Hedgewar as the second *sarasanghchalak* of RSS. He was opposed to the idea of a secular Indian state as he drew upon the logic of exclusion whereby the non-Hindus could be taken into the fold only if they held the Hindu religion in reverence, embraced the Hindu culture, and became a part and parcel of the *rashtra*, as a native rather than a foreigner. He was much too vituperative against the Muslims and offered them too stringent a condition for living in this country.[3] He took his argument to the extreme right which led the future commentators to call him and his followers the advocates of fascism and anti-Semitism. His plea for the maintenance of racial and cultural purity by drawing upon the German example with reference to the Jews gave him a unique logic to deal with the Muslim factor in India.[4] He thought that the Hindus, the Muslims, and the British were the three parties involved, and the Hindus had to fight and establish their power over them, especially over the Muslims. *Rashtra*, according to him, was composed of five elements: a geographical area, a race, a religion, a culture, and language, and India was "the noblest in the world" as a *rashtra* in spite of its "degenerating contact with the debased 'civilization' of the

Musalmans and the Europeans for the last ten centuries" (41). The descendants of Savarkar and Golwalkar carried these fundamental arguments further with individual variations. K. S. Sudershan and his successor, Mohan Bhagwat, kept the logic alive with the same conviction after them.

With Bal Thackeray, the supreme commander of the Shiv Sena, a right wing party with ethnocentric bias, a different note was struck. Like the earlier ideologues, he too equated Islam with violence and considered its followers as the perpetrators of the wrong. As such, he went in consonance with the exclusivists but added yet another dimension to their argument by imparting a sectarian touch to it. Although it might appear a minor change of little consequence, the re-naming of Bombay as Mumbai was a symbolic pronouncement of a different kind which transformed the secular nature of the city in a palpable way. Similarly, the slogan of Mumbai for Mumbaikars was yet another step towards the same end of segregating a space in exclusive terms for its own people. These steps were both concrete and symbolic as they placed a premium on the local against the national. The logic of Hindu *rashtra*, thus, shrunk to the logic of a region for the regionalists. Shiv Sena's mouthpiece, *Saamna*,[5] struck the notes of dissidence rather strongly which went in tune with the rhetoric of defiance developed after Savarkar. The Mumbai riots of 1992–93 gave him an opening to reiterate his stance against the Muslims with greater intensity. It also gave him an opportunity to strengthen his argument for the regional against the national. With these riots, another exclusivist, Subramanian Swamy, also got an opportunity to appropriate the old logic of extreme disaffection and express himself in an idiom of hatred and with gestures of militancy. He set up a blatant agenda on how to deal with the Muslim factor. He propagated terrorism in open terms and made a retrograde case by suggesting that Hindus should now do serious soul searching as they can no longer be killed in "halal fashion" and bleed till the nation met its end. Following Savarkar, he created a dangerous hiatus when he said that the fanatic Muslims considered the Hindu-dominated India as an "unfinished chapter of Islamic conquest". Like the propagators of hate, he blatantly asserted that every Hindu–Muslim riot in India since 1947 had been started by Muslim fanatics. He echoed the stereotypical stance of the Hindu ideologues, especially Golwalkar, when he asserted that the Muslims will have to accept the Hindu religio-cultural legacy in order to be accepted as a part of the larger Hindu society. He came up with his suggestions, typical of his retrograde mindset, that the Hindus must develop a pure Hindu outlook. Rightly claiming that the Hindus must not bow down to terrorists' demands, he wrongly advised that they must retaliate at every terrorist attack, as if terrorism could be contained by terrorism. He came up with several strategies which included the removal of Article 370, demolition of the mosque at Kashi Vishwanath along with three hundred such other mosques elsewhere, implementation of a Uniform Civil Code, making the learning of Sanskrit and the singing of *Vande Mataram* compulsory. Echoing Golwalkar's extremism, he demanded that India be declared a Hindu *Rashtra* where only those could have a voting right who acknowledged that their ancestors were Hindus. He further advocated for a law that allowed people from other faiths to convert to Hinduism, but he argued that this law must prohibit the Hindus to convert to other faiths. While he declared that caste could not be decided by birth, he also argued that land from Bangladesh could be annexed to make space for the migrants from there.[6] It would not take much effort to establish that Swamy was only falling in line with the hard-core exclusivists as he shared his views with Savarkar and his rhetoric with Golwalkar. Swamy defied all sense of balance and proportion and spread the worst kind of hatred. He rode the exclusivist bogey and used a blasphemous diction only to reiterate an already defeated thesis. This mindset has often been reflected in inflammatory addresses of Praveen Togadia. Commenting on him, Rafiq Zakaria wrote:

> The spokesman of Vishwa Hindu Parishad, Praveen Togadia, has publicly approved of the massacre of Muslims in Gujarat. He told Time magazine: "Things will get more and more violent. You can impose a curfew in one place, but there will be an incident somewhere else. When you control that, there will be a third place". Told about it, a Muslim woman in Ahmedabad said: "I know we are all going to be killed. I will ask my sons to escape and be terrorists" (344).

The stances of Swamy and Togadia have many a point of intersection in how they construct Muslims and how they create a case for an *akhanda Bharat* (indivisible India). The inability of one to live with the other was well diagnosed by M. N. Roy who said, "Indeed, there is no other example of two communities living together in the same country for so many hundred years and yet having so little appreciation for each other's culture. No civilized group of people in the world is so ignorant of Islamic history and contemptuous of the Mohammedan religion as the Hindus".[7]

Paradigm 2: Inclusivist Discourse

Alongside the narrow and negative exclusivist constructions of the Muslims, the intellectually tempered and rationally justifiable inclusivist projections have always been making their way at the same pace. We have had a number of inclusivists to strongly interrogate the exclusivists and project a holistic view of Indian history and Indian Muslims. One might go back in history and begin this account with Sir Syed, a judicial officer in the British East India Company, who was the first philosopher, reformer, and educator to place Muslims in a modernist context. His anxiety regarding the status of his people and their co-existence with other communities, led him to make a big case for their educational and political empowerment. It also led him to develop a holistic view of modern India and the modern Indian. His friend and biographer, Hali, who distinguished himself as a littérateur and a reformer, carried forward his concern for the community in yet another direction. He became more concerned with the problem of social and moral degradation of his people, in general, and the condition of women, in particular. Both Syed and Hali shared their anxiety about the Muslim community, not as political leaders but as intellectuals with acute social concern. Taking the discourse about the Muslims still further, one might also refer to Jinnah and Iqbal. Jinnah, who took the line of a nationalist and argued for Hindu–Muslim unity in the early phase of his political career, got disappointed with the Congress and the growing Hindu communalism and moved ultimately towards championing the Muslim cause exclusively. He grew from a nationalist to a sectarian and from sectarian to a separatist during the hectic phase of his political career. He found in the Muslim League a platform for championing his cause for Muslim representation and ultimately a separate land for them. This was clearly borne out by the passing of the Lahore Resolution in March 1940 whereby the case for the Muslims to claim a separate state for themselves found its way. This logic went in line with those of the Hindu nationalists who too had been making a case for India as *Hindu rashtra*. Iqbal, a philosopher-poet, not quite in tune with the Muslim leaders and the Congress party, also believed in the political empowerment of Muslims. He evolved a way to combine the social and the political with the religious and tried to develop a modernist context for the survival of the Muslims. Both Jinnah and Iqbal came to flag the case of the Muslims – Jinnah with his demand for a separate Muslim state and Iqbal with his desire for a safe space for Muslims in the dominion of India. However, none of the two nursed views that could be called communal, although they expressed their dissatisfaction with the order of the day and sought their own ways of resolution.

The case of Gandhi and Nehru falls in an entirely different category. With Truth and Non-violence, being the two cardinal principles of his philosophy, Gandhi evolved a completely different modus operandi to earn India's independence and keep it united. These principles also served him as the bases of his religious doctrine and political ideology to bring Hindus and Muslims together. He firmly believed that both the communities had equal privileges to share, equal rights to exercise, and equal duties to perform. The fasts that he observed to stop the Hindu–Muslim riots, and the position he took to protect the Muslims, stand testimony to his comparative understanding of religions, especially Hinduism and the Abrahamic religions. In bringing truth, politics, and religion to bear upon one another, he made an extremely catholic and philosophically charged comment on those who held narrow views on these three and thought of the land as divided along narrow lines.[8] Keeping close to Gandhi's ideology, Nehru, who distinguished himself as a statesman, a liberal democrat, and an architect of modern India, developed a clinical view on the Hindu–Muslim issue. He was against communalism quite clearly, and he did not hesitate in identifying the communalists even if they belonged to the Congress. "Many a congressman was a communalist under his national cloak," (136) he wrote while assessing the worsening communal situation in the country. He held both the Muslim and the Hindu communalists responsible for inculcating an insular view of Indian nationalism.[9] Through their writings and speeches, both Gandhi and Nehru developed a perspective that was political in appearance but intellectual in reality. Both of them maintained their disapproval of the communalists, irrespective of their political affiliations and socio-cultural upbringing. They could not have, thus, appreciated the stances of the likes of Bal Gangadhar Tilak, Sri Aurobindo Ghosh, and Lala Lajpat Rai who brought in religion to define the contour of the nation to be.

A larger discourse on Muslims was, however, best developed in Azad who stood apart from Jinnah and Iqbal and who combined the best qualities of a nationalist, a secularist, and a democrat. On the questions concerning nationalism, human brotherhood, minority, Hindu–Muslim/Hinduism–Islam dichotomy, and a deep commitment to India as a nation, Azad emerged as the most seminal of all the thinkers. As a committed nationalist, he shunned the Hindu–Muslim divide on religious and communal terms. In his Congress Address of 1923, he came out in quite clear terms: "Instead of Swaraj and Khilafat, slogans of *Shuddhi* are being raised. 'Save the Hindus from Muslims,' says one group, 'Save Islam from Hinduism', says another. When the order of the day is, 'Protect Hindus' and 'Protect Muslims', who cares about protecting the nation?" (145). Another facet of this very problem got manifested in yet another address about two decades later, in 1940, when he expressed himself in much more biting terms and said

> If there are any Hindus among us who desire to bring back the Hindu life of a thousand years ago and more, they are just dreaming and such dreams cannot become real. Likewise, if there are any Muslims who wish to revive their past civilization and culture, which they brought a thousand years ago from Iran and Central Asia, they too, dream and the sooner they wake up the better (162).

Azad dug at both the Hindu and Muslim ideologues and defined nationalism in terms of "man's collective consciousness and a notion of social order" (51). Clearly striking a note of difference as compared to Golwalkar, he identified race, country, colour, and language as the four major hindrances in the way of human brotherhood and suggested that Islam rejected all the four in favour of healthy universalism. Significantly, therefore, Azad did not consider Muslims as a minority because numbers, he thought, did not decide a community's status as a minority or majority group of people. He rather believed in the validity of the shared heritage when he categorically proclaimed in his Congress Address of 1940: "Our shared life of a thousand years has forged a common nationality. Such moulds cannot be artificially constructed. Nature's anvils shape them over the centuries. The mould has now been cast and destiny has set her seal upon it" (162). Azad did not consider Muslims a minority and foretold categorically that whatever be the constitution of India like in the future, it would surely be a democratic one, and that there should be no misgivings about the minority and the majority classification. As a great advocate of India's indivisibility, a great opponent of India's Partition, and a great supporter of Hindu–Muslim unity, he said that he would like to go for their unity if he were to choose between swaraj and Hindu–Muslim unity.[10] He emphasized upon the claim of Hinduism on the Indian soil in the same measure as he emphasized upon the claim of Islam on this land.[11] This came out clearly in the way he exhorted the Muslims of Delhi against migrating to Pakistan in one of his most passionate speeches he delivered from the ramparts of Jama Masjid in Delhi. Âzad was a liberal political visionary of the first order who proposed a case diametrically opposed to those of the exclusivists.

One of Azad's close associates, Humayun Kabir, a thinker and a politician in his own right, extended Azad's logic in yet another direction when he engaged with the question of the minority and argued that there could be no democracy without a minority and that the minority communities were the "problem" of the modern age only, as the earlier ages were essentially monarchic in nature and spirit.

He defined this category of the minority in a more scientific manner five years after the death of Azad in his Srinivas Sastry lecture at the University of Madras in 1963, by developing a psychological angle. He said,

> Every minority is in a sense a protestant group, a dissident group. Every minority is a heretical group when compared to the majority. It is not an exaggeration to say that the dissidents are the salt of the earth, provided that they remember that they are dissidents in terms of quality and not dissidents merely because of birth (18).

He considered minorities to be a necessary part of a democratic setup who represented themselves as religious, economic, political, linguistic, tribal, racial, or linguistic groups. He considered Indian Muslims to be a part of the universal brotherhood, and more pertinently, as a part and parcel of the broader Indian socio-political complex. As such, he assigned them a place of parity with others.[12] Both Azad and Kabir seem to join hands on one essential point that it is the worth of a people that distinguishes them rather than their birth or numerical value, which are of no consequence. Kabir came up with an enlightened argument that an informed minority could be more powerful than the uninformed majority.

It should be in place to refer here to Mohammad Mujeeb who developed a detailed historical-cum-philosophical discourse on Indian Muslims. His single-line explanation that "All human history is a complicated process of self-expression and self-realization" (555) holds good and makes the Indian Muslim retain himself with remarkable confidence. As a historian who considered history to be a complicated process of self-realization and self-expression, he contextualized Indian Muslims in a larger perspective. He proposed that there can be no generalization about Indian Muslims as it is likely to mislead and represent the truth only partially. He underlined the duality of Hindu–Muslim perception in an objective fashion in saying that "The Indian Muslims are judged by non-Muslims and, vice versa, the non-Muslims by Muslims, as if the historical record of one party could be separated from the record of the other ..." (555). Regarding how the Muslims have conducted themselves, Mujeeb developed a perspective which was as applicable to the reading of the past as it is to the reading of the present. He wrote:

> Indian Muslims lived their own life, according to their lights, that everything which might be considered as achievement was a part of the process of their self-expression and self-realization, and that the evils we see in their actions were, like all the evils we generally see in human actions and their results, due to diverse causes, of which the fact of their being Indian Muslims may or may not have been one (556).

He separated popular bias from objective reality and suggested that personal choices and dispositions of individuals may not be taken for the testimonies of a community. While Mujeeb developed a theoretical and rationalistic perspective on Indian Muslims, there are others who approached this subject with entirely different tools in hand which include the signs and symbols of the time, as also the facts and figures to substantiate their readings. One might refer to historians like Ramachandra Guha who constructed the Hindus and Muslims in a socio-political framework and projected a point of view that combined the richness of personal observation, the rigour of research, and the power of drawing substantiated academic conclusions, even at the cost of being abused.[13] A succinct study of how Hindus and Muslims operated and interacted, and how some of the more prominent Muslims from the late nineteenth century to the mid twentieth century, have constructed themselves and, in turn, constructed their community may be seen in Rajmohan Gandhi with great profit.[14]

It would also be in place to refer here to Rafiq Zakaria whose concern with the plight of the Indian Muslims was expressed in the way he diagnosed and commented on their predicament in general. He mentioned ten notions prevalent among Hindus regarding Muslims, namely: (a) Islam discourages destruction of idols, (b) the Quran permits destruction of places of worship, (c) Islam does not allow freedom of worship, (d) Islam believes only in Muslims instead of universal brotherhood, (e) Quran doesn't recognize the great savants born in India, (f) Islam does not encourage Muslims to be patriotic wherever they are in a numerical minority, (g) Islam treats Hindus as *kafirs*, (h) Quran asks for perpetual jihad (war) against *kafirs*, (i) Muslims and non-Muslims are not to be treated equally by the state as per Islam, and finally (j) Islam permits polygamy (349). He was clearly diagnostic when he mentioned the following: If Indian Muslims have to preserve their identity, there are five factors they must concentrate on: (a) education, (b) employment, (c) social adjustment with Hindus, (d) family planning, and (e) political realism (332). He referred to William Muir's defamatory book, *Life of Mahomet* written in four volumes, and the writing of the blasphemous book, *Rangila Rasul*, which resulted into Muslim fury, and a Muslim fanatic killing the publisher (364). Zakaria's reading might further be related with the interpretation of history and historiography of communalism that has shown a phenomenal growth in our times and has been dealt with serious academic rigour for at least one simple reason that communalism has been a major threat to Indian democracy, which has called for detailed academic examination.[15] The concerns of journalists like Khushwant Singh and Kuldip Nayar, who shared many of Zakaria's comments in their own ways, are too well known to be discussed in any detail here. It would, however, be pertinent to bring this argument to a close by referring to a more recent intervention by a literary writer and academic like Tabish Khair who has chosen to live abroad and yet remain connected with the land of his birth, as one who is born here remains connected. "There is much I am proud of in India, and there is much I am ashamed of," he wrote, and continued further "…I am not a nationalist in the sense in which parties like the Shiva Sena define nation … (25–26) And so, I hang on to my passport. For, I was born in India. If I were to relinquish my passport, I would do so in favour of a country that I found superior to India" (28). It may be posited that Khair's is the voice of the modern Indian Muslim who takes pride in being what he is and does not either need to offer excuses for being so or defend himself against any charge made on the basis of subscribing to a religious faith or culture.

The dichotomy between the two ways of approaching the Hindu Muslim factor has resulted in some Hindus believing that the Muslims are a potential threat, they are terrorists, they owe allegiance to Pakistan, they cannot live at peace with others, and they do all that the Hindu society disapproves of. Similarly, there is a section among Muslims who believe that Hindus are the perpetrators of hatred, they are fascists, and that they would never accept Muslims as fellow countrymen. The number on both the sides is small, which is why such hideously diabolic perceptions have not yet succeeded in taking from India its deep faith in democratic principles of existence, although India has kept itself perennially engaged in negotiating with those forces to keep the existence of Muslims from hanging precariously.

PREDICAMENT

Moving away from the two diametrically opposed constructions of Muslims in India, let me now consider the broader Muslim predicament caught in the melee of opinions, arguments, and debates. While minorities may share certain common traits, they are also different in a variety of ways, not only from each other but even within themselves. If the members of a minority community are marked for sharing a history and a culture, for identifying with their community, and for sustaining stereotypical prejudices against themselves, the Muslims in India may not be necessarily judged as a minority with these traditional and constraining parameters. Indian Muslims embody multiple identities as a religious, a cultural, a linguistic, a political, an economic, and an educational minority. This gets all the more complicated when we consider the fact that as the largest minority in India, they have presented themselves as variously, as they have been represented by the exclusivist, the inclusivist, and the intercessionist groups of scholars and activists. This also explains why Muslims as a minority have emerged as a non-negligible-major in a country that rightly seeks its pride in taking its minorities – the Sikhs, the Christians, the Parsis – together with the Hindus in a secular frame of survival.

Let me posit further that no study of Muslim minority in India may be possible in isolation without reference to history's consequential players, right from the seventh to the eighteenth century as traders, rulers, infamous invaders, and finally the Sufi saints. All of them, with their aims well defined, worked differently from each other. The traders worked for good will to earn their profit, the rulers ensured peace and stability to be in power, the invaders used aggression to subjugate and gain control, and the Sufi saints worked for the fusion of cultures to create a composite society. To this remarkable variety of approaches to the Indian land and the people, comprising essentially of Hindus and Muslims, may be added the examples of the dynasties like the Mamluks, the Khaljis, the Tughlaqs, the Syeds, the Lodhis, the Mughals, and the Surs, as also the regional Muslim kingdoms of the Qutub Shahis and the Adil Shahis who succeeded in their own ways by promoting local cultures, and working for the local good. An entirely new socio-political dynamics emerged with the advent of the British who were committed to finding roots for the British Empire on the Indian soil and devising their policies accordingly. In fact, the plot of the British intervention thickened rather ominously, as they realized soon that their panacea lay in dividing the Muslims and the Hindus as two communities opposed to each other. It may be worthwhile to note that the post-Partition phase saw yet another departure in this complex plot when the Muslims came to be taken as a distinct minority, even though they had started showing fissures in their relationship with the Hindus during the independence movement itself.

The variegated patterns of the Hindu–Muslim relationship and the emergence of the Muslims as a minority project many questions deserving critical attention, both for a comprehensive understanding of the community as also of the nation. Thinking of Muslims as a minority in post-independence India, one needs to consider first if Muslims, as a minority, can ever be fully and satisfactorily defined. The question as to who is a Muslim is as difficult to answer as it is to define who is an Indian, mainly because the idea of India and that of the Indian is too complicated and, therefore, too contested. Justifiably enough, it must evade even a workable answer. Even if one develops a view on their identity and their possible definition, one also needs to answer whether or not the nomenclature of the "Indian Muslim" would be more appropriate than that of the "Muslim Indian". Both these nomenclatures do not only carry different shades of meaning embodied in the prioritization of the "Muslim" over "Indian" and "Indian" over "Muslim", they also define them distinctly and differently from each other with respect to their affiliations, motives, and manners. At yet another remove, there are more complicated questions to answer which include questions like whether the Indian Muslims are a homogenous group of people or whether they necessarily subscribe to the Quranic figure of the Muslim. Similarly, one could also ask if they could be taken as representing a certain cultural pattern symbolized by a worn out *tehmad* and a soiled skull cap, or is it that their identity is to be determined mainly by their economic status marked by deprivation, or their political commitment characterized by adherence to a given political party. One also needs to answer whether they invariably venerate the space offered by the madrasa that has been much-maligned in the recent past or whether they keep themselves confined only to the holy precincts of the mosque. These images of the Muslim minority are projected more prominently than the ones where they are seen as highly educated, completely secular, culturally refined, remarkably affluent individuals and groups, representing the modern Indian milieu and taking part in realizing the nationalist aspirations.

It would appear from a closer analysis that Muslims live many lives in India today. In each of the six domains of polity, economy, society, culture, education, and nation, they are distinguishable for the great variety they represent in their apprehension and action. In each of these domains, they project themselves both as retrograde and modern, fettered and liberated, economically deprived and remarkably affluent, and marginally educated and highly accomplished in modern knowledge. It is futile to look for any uniformity in the way they render themselves. It would be interesting to note that the heterogeneous nature of Muslim existence denies their stock image even though it is the reiteration of stock images that has caught greater attention. These stock perceptions have been reiterated by diverse agencies of which the more important ones are the ideologues of the political parties, exclusivist forums, and a section of the press which again is marked by regional, national, and linguistic differences. To counter the dominant discourse based on stereotyping of the community, it may be argued that the Muslim minority represents images of the grotesque and ironic, comic and tragic, pathetic and pliable. Muslims in the post-independence and the postcolonial India are the non-negligible-major; they constitute a part of the main and stand for the whole.

It would also appear from a broader analysis of the present responses to the Muslims and the Muslim predicament that there are at least three banes that have contributed towards their stereotyping to a large extent. These include three largely misconceived notions about *jihad*, *kufr*, and fundamentalism. Gandhi's notion of *jihad* as *dharma yuddh* stands completely marginalized in comparison to *jihad* as an act of sheer militancy, just as *kufr* is totally misrepresented as blasphemy rather than a state of unbelief. Similarly, fundamentalism is taken as an attribute of the retrograde rather than a way to reach the spirit of the matter. In the same category of misrepresentation falls an expression like "secularism", which is repeatedly used as a false refuge rather than a genuine way of life and living. Other incorrect notions reiterated over a long period of time include: Islam breeds destructive tendencies, it shuns other religions, it discourages patriotism, and it perpetuates polygamy. These are the misleading parts of the construction that challenge the exclusivist discourse. I should like to posit here that this huge map of misreading is made of scandalous readings of religion and socio-cultural practices of the Muslims. As the truth lies on the other side of the argument, it must be said that there are significant cohesive forces that integrate and distinguish the people in the Indian subcontinent, more than they do anywhere else, but they are not as easily marked as the outrageous constructions are. I would assert further that these texts or metaphors of disaffection are rooted in a historical moment of time in the Indian subcontinent which is, ironically enough, the moment of India's freedom and also of its partition in terms of people, and all their resources by which they lived. The year 1947, as I have argued elsewhere, is our "intersection time"[16] that has shaped our consciousness and set us apart in many ways.

Conditions of belonging in a majority–minority state may not remain perennially stable. They cannot ever be so. Predicaments can only alter, history can only re-configure itself. Life has to remain in a constant state of flux, now coursing well, now moving with jerks, now pacing precariously, but always confirming to what Ghalib had said:

Dil hi to hai, na sang-o-khisht, dard se bhar na aaye kyun
Roengey hum hazar baar, koi hamein sataaye kyun

For those who wish to connect, Ghalib says that what I have in my chest is a heart, not a piece of stone or brick; it must be moved by pain; and that I will weep a thousand times, but then why should anyone coerce me at all.

NOTES

1 *Hindutva: Who is a Hindu?* (1928) was originally published as *Essentials of Hindutva* in 1923. It is the first comprehensive treatise that made way for the future right wing political parties, their votaries of various social and professional affiliations, broadly called Hindu revivalists/nationalists. The book has a comprehensive thesis divided into thirty-one sections that develop discourses one a number of issues; some of the important ones being his discourses on Hindu, Hindutva, Hinduism, Hindu Nation, Sindhusthan, Buddhism, Arya, Hindusthani Language, Foreign Invaders, and Civilization. Savarkar sounds scholarly, logical, and definitive in the way he builds his argument in favour of a people and their land.

2 A *sarasanghchalak* is the philosopher and guide of the organization and contributes towards character building and maintaining order and discipline which is the credo of the organization. The organization has had seven *sarasanghchalaks* so far who include: K. B. Hedgewar (1925–30 and 1931–40), M. S. Golwalkar (1940–73), M. D. Deoras (1973–94), Rajendra Singh (1994–2000), K. S. Sudarshan (2000–9), and Mohan Bhagwat (2009–till date). Dr. L. V. Paranjape worked as *sarasanghchalak* during 1930–1 when Hedgewar was imprisoned on account of Forest satyagraha.

3 Golwalkar's vituperation may be seen in what he had to say in such categorical terms: "The foreign races in Hindustan…must stay in the country, wholly subordinated to the Hindu nation, claiming nothing, deserving no privileges, far less any preferential treatment—not even citizen's right." (47–48)

4 Golwalkar wrote: "To keep up the purity of the Race and its culture, Germany shocked the world by her purging the country of the Semitic races—the Jews. Race pride at its highest has been manifested here. Germany has also shown how well-nigh impossible it is for races and cultures having differences going to their roots, to be assimilated into one united whole, a good lesson for us in Hindusthan to learn and profit by." (35)

5 Shiv Sena was founded by Bal Thackeray in 1966 and he launched his party's mouthpiece *Saamna* in Marathi twenty-two years later in 1988. Its Hindi edition, intended for a larger readership beyond the Marathi, was metaphorically titled as *Dopahar ka Saamana.*

6 See his article "How to Wipe Out Islamic Terror," *DNA*, Mumbai, 16 July, 2011.

7 Quoted by Zakaria, p. 365.

8 In the last chapter of his autobiography, he made this point in quite clear and philosophical terms: "To see the universal and all-pervading Spirit of Truth face to face one must be able to love the meanest of creation as oneself. And a man who aspires after that cannot afford to keep out of any field of life. That is why my devotion to Truth has drawn me into the field of politics; and I can say without the slightest hesitation, and yet in all humility, that those who say that religion has nothing to do with politics do not know what religion means." (463)

9 In *An Autobiography*, Nehru wrote: "Muslim Communal leaders said the most amazing things and seemed to care not at all for Indian nationalism or Indian freedom. Hindu communal leaders, though always speaking apparently in the name of nationalism, had little to do with it in practice and, incapable of any real action sought to humble themselves before the Government, and did that too in vain…Muslim communal leaders said and did many things harmful to political and economic freedom, but as a group and individually they conducted themselves before the Government and the public with some dignity. That could hardly be said of the Hindu communal leaders." (138)

10 While presiding over a special session of Congress in 1923, he made a truly unique assertion: "Today, if an angel were to descend from the heaven and declare from the top of the Qutab Minar, that India will get swaraj within twenty-four hours, provided she relinquishes Hindu–Muslim unity, I will relinquish swaraj rather than give up Hindu–Muslim unity. Delay in the attainment of swaraj will be a loss to India, but if our unity is lost, it will be a loss for entire mankind." (145)

11 He made this point quite confidently in his Congress address in 1940: "Islam has now as valid claim on this land as Hinduism. If Hinduism

has been the religion of its people for several thousand years, Islam, too, has been its religion for a thousand years. Just as a Hindu can say with legitimate pride that he is an Indian and a follower of Hinduism, so can a Muslim proudly claim being an Indian and a follower of Islam." (162)

12 Writing on Muslims, he expressed his views more liberally than many others who approached this subject. A Muslim , he said, '…is an Indian and he is an Indian not as a subject, not as a ruler but as part ruler and part subject.' (38)

13 See, for example, "Minding the Minorities" and "Riots" in *India After Gandhi*. Picador, 2007, and "Hindutva Hate Mail" in *Patriots and Partisans*. New Delhi: Penguin, 2012.

14 See Rajmohan Gandhi, *Understanding the Muslim Mind*, New Delhi; Penguin, 2000. Gandhi presents a comprehensive account of Hindu–Muslim dichotomy and examines the stances of Sayyid Ahmed Khan, Muhammad Iqbal, Muhammad Ali, Muhammad Ali Jinnah, Fazlul Haq, Abul Kalam Azad, Liaqat Ali Khan, and Zakir Husain.

15 See for example works by Romila Thapar, Harbans Mukhia, and Bipan Chandra, *Communalism and the Writing of Indian History*, 1969; Asghar Ali Engineer and Moin Shakir, *Communalism in India*, 1985; Bipan Chandra and Khushwant Singh, *Many Faces of Communalism*, 1985; K. N. Panikkar (ed.) *Communalism in Indian History, Politics and Culture,* 1991; Mushirul Hasan, *Nationalism and Communal Politics in India: 1885–1930*, 1991; Sudhir Kakkar, *The Colours of Violence*, 1995; Praful Bidwai, Harbans Mukhia and Achin Vanaik, *Religion, Religiosity and Communalism,* 1996; M. J. Akbar, *Riot After Riot*, 1998; Ram Puniyani, *Communal Politics: Facts Versus Myth*, 2003; and Paul R. Brass, *The Production of Hindu Muslim Violence in Contemporary India*, 2011.

16 See "Intersection Time: 1947," *Reading Partition/Living Partition* (ed.) Jasbir Jain, 2006. Jaipur: Rawat Publications.

REFERENCES

Azad, Abul Kalam. *India's Maulana*. Centenary Volume II, Selected Speeches and Writings. New Delhi: Indian Council for Cultural Relations in collaboration with Vikas Publishing House,1990.

Gandhi, M. K. *An Autobiography or The Story of My Experiments With Truth*. Ahmedabad: Navajivan Publishing House, 1927/2010.

Golwalkar, M. S. *We or Our Nationhood Defined*. Bombay: Asia Publishing House, 1939.

Kabir, Humayun. *Minorities in a Democracy.* Calcutta: Firma K. L. Mukhopadhyay, 1968.

Khair, Tabish. *Muslim Modernities.* New Delhi: Vitasta Publishing Pvt. Ltd. 2008.

Mujeeb, M. *The Indian Muslims.* New Delhi: Munshiram Manoharlal Publishers, 2003.

Nehru, Jawaharlal. *An Autobiography.* Bombay: Allied Publishers, 1962.

Zakaria, Rafiq. *Indian Muslims: Where Have They Gone Wrong?* Mumbai: Popular Prakashan and Bharatiya Vidya Bhawan, 2004.

7

Violence that Dare Not Speak Its Name: Construing and De-construing Minority Men

Mashrur Shahid Hossain and Kazi Asraf Uddin

LEDA *VIS-À-VIS* HYLAS

Let us begin with two questions. *First,* we have heard of Leda, a woman who was raped by Zeus in the form of swan, and who later gave birth to Helen and Clytemnestra. Yeats immortalized Leda in his poem "Leda and the Swan". However, how many of us have heard of Hylas, the handsome foster son of Heracles, who was abducted and ravished by the "nymph of the spring"? *Second,* when we talk or write about violence in war, our focus is often split into two major parts: (a) killing of soldiers and (b) rape of women. Do we acknowledge that rape can happen, and does happen, to men too?

These two questions foreground a problematic that has been overlooked so far. While sexual aggression and violence committed by men are regularly represented in human discourses, sexual aggression and violence enacted against men are rarely represented, let alone highlighted, in any human discourse ranging from books of law to alternative films. It is this misrepresentation or zero-representation of "violated men" which is being addressed here. By addressing the unheard trauma of violated men, this study interrogates the definitions of "minority" and "majority" to expose how these two signs are inherently unstable and operate in certain ways sanctioned by the socio-historical scenario.

The title intertexts Oscar Wilde's notoriously famous proclamation of his "love that dare not speak its name". This reference is crucial not only because the essay has queer and transgender issues in its vicinity, but also because the phrase, "dare not speak its name" betrays the presence of a domineering hegemonic social construct that prioritizes one (in Wilde's case, it was heterosexuality) and otherizes the rest (homosexuality that Wilde was accused of), thus construing majority/minority divides. We refer to Wilde as this study addresses a kind of violence that is rarely spoken of and, when spoken of, is rarely appreciated or apprehended. For example, sexual violence against men neither sells well nor speaks clearly. Correspondingly, the second part of the title is disconcerting, as it juxtaposes two usually incompatible words: "minority" and "men". Man is the subject that is ontologically one such (Beauvoir 1984), who speaks (Lacan 1977; Irigaray 1985), who looks (Mulvey 2001), and who acts. This phallogo-centric schema goes wrong when a man is subjected to sexual violence. In spite of being men, these men are almost invariably, and inevitably, stigmatized, emasculated, and un-manned; they are "minoritized". This study contends that the word "minoritizing" embraces two opposing inflections: the popular notion of "being lesser" and the Deleuzian "being becoming". The title also has "men" in italics. Why so? It is because the definitions of "man" are at stake vis-à-vis queer theory and acts of violence.

The study is divided into three sections. The first section, entitled "Manning Majority", queers the majority/minority divides. The second section, "Minority Men" outlines four major types of violence enacted against men. Concentrating on sexual abuse, this section explores how "violated men" are pushed into the minority group and how it affects the total bringing up of the men concerned. Then follow short reading of three texts – Khaled Hosseini's novel, *The Kite Runner*, A. Revathi's autobiography, *The Truth About Me: A Hijra Life Story*, and Onir's film, *I Am* – to understand the predicaments of men who are violated. We argue that sexual and gendered violence, when enacted against and not by a man, problematizes the majority/minority divides – man/woman, masculine/feminine, active/passive, heterosexual/homosexual – and exposes a liberating but disturbing realization that the signifier, minority, slides endlessly in and through discourse. Minority may thus become, referencing Deleuze and Guattari, "minor" that not only destabilizes the notion of minority but also, rather more importantly, deterritorializes masculinity and celebrates gender nomadism.

MANNING MAJORITY

"Minority" is a hegemonic construct. It denotes not simply a relational social group; it rather refers to a group separated, or differentiated from the mainstream group(s) that has better access to power and discourse. Apart from certain cases in which the minorities are self-individuated, possess agency, and have (pseudo-)political agenda (e.g. radical subcultures, ranging from British punks and Jamaican Rastafarians to racist skinheads), a minority group is a product of the mainstream/majority culture that expels those who do not conform to its major denominators outside its vicinity.

In most cases, the terms "minority" and "majority" are related to quantity: individuals less in number in a particular community at a particular time form a minority group. Examples may include racial minorities (e.g. the visible minority or aborigines in the contemporary Australia), ethnic minorities (e.g. *santal*, an indigenous group amidst the dominating *Bangalee* ethnic group in Bangladesh), gender minorities (e.g. transvestites in a society based on male/female binary), sexual minority (e.g. gay men in a heteronormative society), religious minorities (e.g. Christians in India), people with disabilities (e.g. a visually challenged student in a class full of able-bodied boys), and so on. What is, however, important to underscore is that operation of power is not necessarily affected by the majority and the groups – "minority" and "majority" – are not water-tight compartments; they mix, merge, shuffle, and give way. Since this section of the study intends to deconstrue "minority", let us outline and question three major myths of "minority".

The first myth is that "there is a majority". For example, Muslims are a majority in Bangladesh. However, this majority group can be divided, initially, into two sanctioned gendered groups: male Muslims and female Muslims. Now, within this majority group, male beings dominate the female ones. The case is chillingly the same in one of the religious minority groups in Bangladesh: Hindus. Within this minority group, male Hindus dominate the female ones. These may lead us to further problems: which majoritarian concept – religion or sexuality? – operates when a Muslim woman encounters a Hindu man in Bangladesh? Therefore, what we contend is: there are majorities, a statement that itself destabilizes claims of any one majority group having ontological superiority.

The second myth is that "the minority is always dominated by the majority". For example, the disabled people are marginalized by the able-bodied people. There are, however, cases in which the numerically minority community dominates the people belonging to a numerical majority. Thus, there are "dominant minorities", for example, the whites in the apartheid South Africa. And there are "vocal minorities", for example, people who have access to the media are less in number but they determine how the mass see the world and their lives. Therefore, we argue that the definition and functioning of minority groups are not essentially compatible. Who dominates or controls depends not on the number of the subject; it rather depends on which subject has more access to power and discourse.

The third myth is that "a person belongs to a minority community by birth". Thus, a black girl in the USA was born as black, and a *Dalit* boy in India was born as *Dalit*. There are, however, many cases in which individuals are pushed into becoming minority groups. A bachelor is a man, and, therefore, an agent of power and domination in a patriarchal world. However, he will soon be assumed as deviant, or queer, or unmanly, or at least odd, if he does not get into a marital bond. This may lead us to further problems: a bachelor executive and a bachelor priest or *sanyasi* are viewed through different socio-cultural parameters. Thus, there are culturally-variable minority communities like bachelors which include rape victims and school-rejects. Therefore, what we argue is: creation and operation of "minority" are context-dependent.

Let us now look back at the title of this section: "Manning Majority". It connotes two practices that we address. *First*, it suggests that a "majority" is not a pre-subject ontological phenomenon. It does not occur naturally. It happens as it is, first, conceptualized (based on exclusionary politics) and, then, manned. The *second* connotation relates to hetero-patriarchal praxis: the symbolic "majority" group called "man" comprises human beings who inhabit male subject position, that is, male beings who are compatible with the definitions of man and masculinity. Thus, the group called "man" is manned by men. If so, then men who do not conform to the conceptions of "man" and "masculinity" are not eligible for or belong to the masculinized group called "man". This exclusionary strategy betrays, first, the inherent contradiction in the conceptualization of masculinity and, second, the threat to "manhood". Masculinity is plural and performative. It is plural as, for example, it has to accommodate paradoxical demands of, as outlined by Metcalf and Humphries in *The Sexuality of Men*, "aggression, competitiveness, emotional ineptitude and coldness, and … penetration", on the one hand, and chivalry, responsibility, care, and strength, on the other (Nixon: 301). It is performative, using Judith Butler's vocabulary, as a man requires citing, riterating, and performing certain rituals and praxis to become a man or, more precisely, manly. This plurality and performativity of masculinity triggers the anxiety of manhood or manning. If "aggression" and "penetration" are instrumental to become men, what happens when a man is subject to aggression and when he is penetrated? How to discern manhood in a man when he walks limp-wrist or screams in fear if a cockroach happens to lands on his shoulder? The subject position called "man" excludes these men from its vicinity both to guard its patriarchal domination and maintain its aggressive-penetrative nature.

This study concentrates on men who are sexually abused. For being juridically (not always biologically) and sociologically "men"; they are privileged in a patriarchal society. However, these men, for being sexually abused, pose threat to the concept of masculinity and are, therefore, relegated into a sub-group, oscillating between "man" and "woman", that accommodates men who are not-masculine, un-masculine, and/or emasculated. A man, an individual, can, thus, belong to both majority and minority groups. Curiously, this gender nomadism destabilizes the satisfying, apparently water-tight distinctions between majority and minority and demonstrates that movement between groups is possible. Using hardware metaphor, we can say that: "majority" and "minority" are drives that exist and operate separately but can overlap and negotiate incessantly, and may even merge.

MINORITY *MEN*

Speaking point-blank, minority men are "men" who are sexually abused and, therefore, minoritized, shuttling between, and thus destabilizing "man" and "no-man" categories. This difference is isomorphic. In terms of Algebra, isomorphism "is the system of logic which defines alterity purely through failure to be the default human" (MacCormack 114). Thus, "there is no male and its opposite female, there is only male and a failure to be such" (MacCormack 114), an essentialist subjectivization that reverberates with Freudian notion of "woman" as "less-man, the one who lacks penis". According to isomorphic categorization, "less-than-men" – queers, gay men, child men, disabled men – are not quite men" (MacCormack 114). To this list of "not quite men" that fails to accommodate guys who are force-fucked, let us add "violated men" who belonged to but later fail to fit in the category called "man".

It is important to underscore now that "violated" here does not connote "subject to violence". It rather means battered, abused, raped – words which have for long been reserved for women. In our present study, therefore, a man injured on street, or crippled in an accident, or emasculated in a battlefield is not "violated". He is violated one is he who is subjected to non-consensual, forced, sexual, or gendered abuse that often takes the form of rape. There are differing arguments regarding what rape is. To a feminist, rape is less about sex and more about violence and power. To a prison official, rape is more about sex and gendering and less about violence. To an upset gay man, rape is more about sex and less about domination. Here, we view rape as a performance that originates from and satisfies libidinal desire, desire that incorporates domination and sexual proximity. When a man sexually abuses a man, the complacent socio-sexual norms are destabilized as, in this case, both the desiree (i.e. violator) and the desired (i.e. violated) upset conceptions of masculinity. Here the "face", referring to Foucault, Deleuze and Guattari's notion of "faciality", that is, the face of a man does not guarantee heterosexual man-ness. Aren't then both the violator and violated reduced to non-man? To address this complexity, let us resort to Freud's theory of sexuality and Deleuze and Guattari's conception of signification (significance) and subjectification. For Freud, human sexuality is informed by "sexual object choice" – the biology of the person whom the sexual act is directed towards – and "sexual aim" – the act one intends to perform with the person one's sexual activity is directed towards" (Hossain "dancing": 45). Traditional hetero-patriarchal culture normalizes and privileges certain sexual "object choices" and "aims" while abnormalizes and punishes the other. Violated men are, first, signified as non-man through their failure to fit in heterosexual normativity. Along with queer and gay men, he is involved in a sex act the object of which is not woman. They are, then, subjectivized as non-masculine within the masculinist strata based on sexual role. Does indulging into sex with a man leave a man gay? When a rowdy prisoner rapes a cute fellow-prisoner only because no cunt is available, does the rapist become a gay man? These questions expose the hierarchy in the man-to-man sex scenario. To sample, Tomás Almaguer in "Chicano Men" shows that Mexican-Latin-American conception of homosexuality and corresponding "othering" is determined by sexual aim. Thus, the penetrator man is appreciated while "the anal-passive individual (the *cochón* or *pasivo*) … is stigmatized for playing the subservient, feminine role" in Latin culture (Almaguer: 539). We argue that violated man, irrespective of his sexual and gender orientation, is invariably emasculated and feminized, because he, instead of playing the role of a penetrator, is penetrated. He, thus, compromises with or fails to perform acts of domination and aggression that a man is entitled to. Doubly unmasculinized, he is now a minority, both isomorphically and numerically.

Unlike visible minority groups, minority men stay invisible. Unlike feminist sisterhood, minority men never form a group. Unlike female sex victims, they rarely make news item; they are rarely acknowledged by or included into mainstream culture; they are barely understood; they rarely speak. Thus, the case of sexual harassment of a school boy in Mumbai's Manav Mandir School in October 2011 was hushed up while representation of now-extinct tradition of sexual assault of young boys by rich zamindars in nineteenth-century Bangladesh in Humayun Ahmed's film *Ghetu Putro Kamala* (2012) scandalized a major part of its audience. The myth-network of man/woman, masculine/feminine, heterosexuality/homosexuality is so strong and pervasive that violated man is never fully comprehended, let alone represented. Moreover, heterosexual society never provides conceptual tools to conceive that a man can be sexually ravaged. In public consciousness, rape is reserved for women only.

The phrase "minority men" is further problematized if we take the transgender issue in concern. Is *hijra*, a man? Or more precisely, does a *hijra* consider "zirself" as "he"? Acknowledging that *hijras* consider themselves as women, this study accommodates *hijras* under the umbrella term "man". This is so because *hijras*, instead of being identified as a different sex, are popularly misrecognized as "men-performing-women" and till now officially categorized as men by law and jurisdiction.

We contend that minority men destabilize the majority/minority divides and expose the seditious and ridiculous politics pf minoritizing. For example, how to categorize the male rapist? As he raped a man, should he be labeled as straight? In their book *Prison Masculinities*, Sabo, Kupers, and London show how a prison rapist thinks of himself as "straight" and his victims "fags" or feminine. These, they argue, reveal "the confounding malleability of human sexuality and social definitions of gender" (109).

CAN "VIOLATED" MEN SPEAK?

Mainstream literary and film discourses pretend that sexual violence against men does not exist. Alternative literature and film trends too are not very comfortable, or careful in representing violated men. Foucault used the term "discursive regime" to designate politics of representation in a particular community at a particular time that determines what is in and what out. Hetero-patriarchal discursive regime eschews representation of violated men and, thus, renders them invisible.

There are, however, a handful of literary and film discourses that address this issue. This section concentrates on three such texts that represent and explore the predicaments of minority men. Embracing the South Asian scenario, these three texts are Khaled Hosseini's novel *The Kite Runner* (2003), A. Revathi's autobiographical text *The Truth About Me: A Hijra Life Story* (2010), and Onir's film, *I Am* (2010). The reason behind this choice is to add insight into the predicaments of violated men from different, even differing, perspectives. Regarding trend and authorship, *The Kite Runner* belongs to the mainstream high literature and the writer, Khaled Hosseini, has, arguably, no direct personal experience of sexual abuse. Revathi's *The Truth about Me* stands at the other pole; it came from the minority community of *hijra*, and the writer and the narrator are the same. In contrast stands Onir's *I Am*, an appreciable film but not of mainstream kind. Having a strong political agenda, the film exposes a number of socio-sexual predicaments that haunt contemporary Indian life, some of which are gathered from the real-life experiences of its director. *I Am* is, thus, an intervening discourse that sees violence against men both from the insider's and outsider's perspectives.

In their treatment of violence and masculinity, all these texts reflect upon how sexual abuse of a man is concomitant with power and domination and how sexual abuse minoritizes an individual. Invariably re-positioned as no-man and unmasculine, minority men are stigmatized, marginalized, and emasculated. This sense of emasculation may work to remind a male individual that the threatening castration complex has not been resolved. This castration-complex-went-reverse traumatizes victim men, leading to submission, resilience, violence, and perversion.

TOWARDS *ÉCRITURE MASCULIN*

Khaled Hosseini's *The Kite Runner* addresses different socio-sexual denominators that inform minoritization. The narrative, spread over two generations and across the globe, centres round three characters – Amir, his friend, Hassan, and his son, Sohrab. All of whom have to come to terms with racial, sexual, and gendered minoritization. Amir is uncomfortable with his effeminacy, Hassan hails from a lower Afghan caste, Hazara, and later raped by a high-caste boy, and Sohrab is a child drag queen. Quite interestingly, Amir the boy who manages to cover his effeminacy complex by letting Hassan be raped is the adult man who rescues Sohrab from a Taliban hovel.

To understand Amir's psychology in letting Hassan be gang-banged, we need to put some light on the father–son relationship between Amir and Baba. Amir is driven by a desire to win his father, which ultimately is reflected in his behaviour. He tries to please his father through writing. However, intellectual achievement does not seem to work to win Baba, rather being in Afghan patriarchal matrix, he seems to demand a macho from Amir, which Amir fails to achieve. Amir's writing excellence can be understood as a mode of representation which hints to a reversal of Hélène Cixous' *écriture féminine*, in other words, *écriture masculin*. Problem occurs only when Baba cannot take off his already-structured heterosexual values and exposes his favouritism for Lacanian "phallocentric" orientation, an attempt by the father in breaching the son's Oedipal attachment with his mother, which ultimately leads to a gender bias by the father regarding the role of the son. Hence, if we follow the series of events in the narrative of this fiction, we will perceive these two phrases – "gender bias" and "role of the son" to be the central problematic in both Amir and Hassan's life. Baba is the construct of established heterosexual gender role, hence, he resounds Judith Butler's notion of performativity.

Interestingly, both Amir's effeminacy and Hassan's sodomized status can be related to Butlerian preoccupations, namely, "performativity" and "subjection". Amir is identified not by his natural sexual identity (at least, not by his father who means the world to him), rather he faces the music of culturally formed gender identity.

His behaviour or performance as effeminate is what renders his gender fixity. In Butler's articulation, his "reiterated" acting (Butler: 1990) or role-playing which destabilizes his natural sexual identity pushes him towards the margin of a so-called heterosexual matrix. Amir must be considering Hassan's stigma as a violated man as a passage to his emancipation and a trap for Hassan's subjection (which ultimately did not work out). Here, as hinted before, Amir's subconscious jealousy and psychosexual anxiety for being girlish contribute to his allowance to Hassan's sexual harassment. Hassan, now sodomized in an Islamic culture of patriarchal Afghan society, loses his place as a representative of macho-like masculinity amidst the patriarchal hegemony.

Though Hassan does not belong to the hegemony of upper class/caste, his physical vigour (allusion to Butler's *Bodies that Matter*) was something that compensated his low social rank; he was a dear child to Babajan (Hassan's biological father) while Babajan criticizes his own son Amir for lacking masculinity. Thus, the social construct of so-called manliness disturbs any (ab)normalcy of behaviour or attributes in man. The instrumentality of stigma, attached to unmanliness creates a constant complex in Amir, which is later transformed to Hassan though he should be studied not as unmanly, rather unmanned. One's minority is the consequence of natural (later socially defined) and behavioural display of a lacking while the other's minority is a forced (power matters) one.

Hassan has been minoritized/stigmatized in two steps: first, he is raped/emasculated/sodomized; then he is accused of theft (though wrongly). Here, the question of perspective regarding stigma arises. Hassan's so-called crime of theft can be seen as a personalized/personal stigma to Babajan. Thus, stigmas are to some extent the miniature versions of cultural taboos with greater flexibility to be construed and deconstrued. Moreover, Hassan's mother's flirtatious elopement led him to face another social stigma which ultimately construes him as different from the other children, a minority.

We can interpret Assef's act of rape on two different parameters: one in relation to his so-called sense of superiority and hence the right to violate as was prevalent in Greek myth (hegemony of culture); and the other in relation to the possible interpretation of the derivation of the first in the sense that Assef's sense of superiority restrained his superego to act, or to resist, rather he indulged in his libidinal drive in a sadistic manner. Pashtun tribe, being the majority in Afghan power matrix, has rendered an unannounced racial superiority to its members. Though an Afghan man's keeping a boy lover (being a *bacha baz*) is a sanctioned Afghan custom, Sohrab's forced transvestism (i.e. drag) and service as a dancing boy is internalized by him as a shame which causes other people's "O My God". Therefore, both violence and homophobic heteronormativity are what construct stigmatized identity.

Here, we observe a revival of Freud's Victorian society hegemonic construct of an Afghan society context; but in the form of a non-straight sexual violence: a male violated by another male. We can also consider the master/slave binary as a possible catalyst for ostracizing Hassan from his so-far uninterrupted social rank, for the deconstruction of his identity from a brave manly individual to an emasculated thief.

We can assert that the homophobic or heterosexist construct of the society marginalizes the once Hassan, the Man. So his manliness can be ripped off through violence and he can be discriminated in terms of caste or race. Interestingly, it is men who apply both these unmanning techniques. Hence, men are made sexual minority and powerless by men themselves. Hassan's internalized homophobia (fear of being considered as a homosexual) might render his situation even more complex in this case. His intentional departure from Amir's place can be seen as an escape to anonymity (where less people will know him) to bury the stigma. After all, being called a 'faggot', a 'homo', or a 'sissy' is a disgrace in almost all the contemporary societies of the world. However, if Assef is deemed having a homosexual orientation, his act of rape can be understood as a male violence acted by a politico-sexual minority himself and his imposed violence will result in the creation of another stigmatized minority man with a wounded masculinity.

In Hassan's case, heterosexual praxis/norm determines his separation from Babajan's family. R.W. Connell's classification for the definition of masculinity can aptly be applied in Hassan's case; he is someone who is the formation of hegemony, subordination, complicity, and marginalization (Connell 1995). Hassan's son encountered a similar fate as his father's being raped and forced to cross-dress. Both rape and transvestism have stigmatized connotation, which can be understood as Sohrab shamefully utters, "I'm so *dirty and full of sin*. The bad man and the other two did things to me" (Hosseini: 2004). Sohrab's sense of stigma and a feeling of rejection mount in his suicidal attempt. Hence, both Hassan and Sohrab's cases might be read as the incidence of forced stigmatization. The above discussions on some of the considerations of *The Kite Runner* should open up further discourses on the issue of minoritizing the male. In the age of third wave feminism, quest for subjective identity has become a popular psychoanalytic practice in the academia, diversifying the minority issues and complexes still further.

In *The Kite Runner,* Hosseini's treatment of rape and sodomite violence generates rage and fear, compassion and tragic sense. In the first case, rape is less about sex: it is more about dominating or ravishing an individual belonging to a lower caste. In the second case, child assault is more about sex: it is a legitimized but clandestine sexual practice aimed to satisfy libidinal desire within the vicinity of religion. In both cases, Hassan and Sohrab are robbed of their agency as man and masculine because of being violated. In between stands Amir. If Amir is the boy who manages to overcome and cover his effeminacy complex by letting Hassan be raped, he is also that adult man who rescues Sohrab from a Taliban hovel. Rescuing Sohrab is more than showing respect to Hassan. It is also rescuing the subject's arrested masculinity. *The Kite Runner*, a kind of *l'écriture masculin*, exposes inherent instability and migrancy of what we call "man" and the irony of minority and majority.

BECOMING A WOMAN

Unflinchingly unabashed, A. Revathi's *The Truth About Me: A Hijra Life Story* attests to a dissent against the hetero-normative contemporary Indian society that appreciates deviation neither from heterosexuality nor from male/female binary. In zir (gender-neutral pronoun) life story, Revathi, the *hijra*, encountered a plethora of abuses – domestic, social, cultural, and sexual – chiefly because zie denies neatly fitting into established gender categories: man and woman. When a young Tamil village boy called Doriasamy became Revati through *nirvanam*, a gender-transformation surgery, zie becomes and accommodates many identities in one: zie is a man, a woman, a *hijra*, a *pottai*, a dancer, a bread-earner, a son, a sex-worker, a lover, a wife, a *chela*, a guru, and a social activist. Revathi's glib movement through and across diverse identity modalities problematizes heteronormativity and binarized gendering, demonstrating heterogeneity of sexuality that Foucault argues in his discussion of Herculine Barbin, a nineteenth-century hermaphrodite, and destabilizing "the metaphysics of sex" and "identitarian categories of sex" (23–4) that Butler critiques in *Gender Trouble*.

Deconstructing Beauvoir's suggestion that "one is not born a woman, but, rather, becomes one". Butler questions if such becoming is a matter of "compulsion" or "choice," and if the "one' who becomes a woman is necessarily female" (12). The answers that she offers are imbricated upon her notion of "performativity". If gender is performative, that is, assumed by "repeated stylization of the body" regulated and monitored by heteronormative social frames (33), gender is a matter of compulsion and choice as well, and the "one" in Beauvoir's formulation is not always a female: *a man who is not born a woman can become a woman*. Revathi testifies to this statement. Zie made a curious gender travel, out of compulsion and choice, from majoritarian man to minoritarian woman that left zie oscillating in liminality: zie becomes a hijra who is neither a man nor a woman, or who was born as a man but wants to be a woman, and, after, *nirvanam*, belongs to none. Revathi is doubly minoritized.

Doriasamy discovered his difference from other boys in school at an early age. He like female demeanour, "behaved like a girl" (7), and preferred dancing to playing football. Being handsome, he was invited to a number of dance and theatre performances where he played the role of woman and was highly applauded. He was attracted towards his male school mates and stealthily fell in "love" (9) with some. All these strengthened his conviction that he was a woman trapped in a man's body. Now traumatized for being "a flawed being" (15), now disgusted for being in "man's garb" which he considered, paradoxically, his "disguise" (16), Doriasamy got desperate to live the life of a woman. He left home, became a *chela* of a *hijra* guru, and made arrangement for *nirvanam*: "To undergo *nirvanam* is to submit to castration and turn into a full woman" (22). Full woman? Doriasamy understood that "it's not easy to become a woman" (82). The operation was excruciatingly painful and potentially fatal, but because of strong determination and obsessive desire to be a woman, zie survived castration and was turned into a *hijra*. Revathi initiated and celebrated zir deviation that not only deconstructs notions of normalcy but more importantly, destabilizes the minoritarian position called man.

If it is difficult to become a woman, it is far more difficult to live as a woman. Sex-shift left Revathi vulnerable to a series of humiliation and violence: ideological (for being a castrated male), legal (for being deprived of ownership), familial (for defaming the family), social (for being a *hijra*), physical (for being a sex worker), gendered (for being feminine), and sexual (by being sodomized). Let us concentrate on two events that violated zir body and mind as well. The first incident relates to her sex work. Traditionally, sex work is not welcome among the hijra community. Correspondingly, sexual craving for man is not encouraged. Revathi's first *nani* told zir, "We must not desire men, and seek not to misbehave with them" (45). Rebellious and self-indulgent, Revathi started doing *danda* (i.e. sex work) only to satisfy zir libidinal urge. Soon, however, zie found out that sex work does not resource a *hijra* pleasure: "I did not like doing sex work, but now found myself doing it. I wanted to experience sexual happiness, but I found myself having to treat sexual experiences as work" (106). Instead, sex worker *hijras* are routinely violated, assaulted, and murdered both by customers and police officers, and neither public nor the law of the country are there to protect a *hijra* (Hossain "enforced" 126–7). More often than not, a hijra has to submit before the whims of men: "If you are a girl-boy you have no choice" (19), once a hijra told Ravathi when zie was a young boy. Revathi likes men but zie did not like doing anal and zir customers somehow respected her choice until one day when a "large, dark rowdy" guy force-fucked her in zir *jopdi*: "When I screamed in pain and yelled for my guru, he shut my mouth with one of his hands ... The skin down there felt abraded and I was bleeding" (108). The matter-of-fact description of this heinous act betrays Revathi's trauma and zir attempt to escape it by backgrounding it in the memory.

Curiously enough, this incident stalled Revathi's sex work for a considerable period of time. Soon did zie resume doing *danda* chiefly because zie had no other option. However, a new kind of trauma was awaiting her. This time, it came through local *gundas* and police who often demanded bribe from the street sex workers and behaved like a rowdy if a *hijra* protested: "How many times they've caught men thus, beaten me in full view of the road, snatched money from me as a bribe and sent me off" (202). Once it went too far. Ravathi was taken to custody, accused of blackmailing clients, and forcibly stripped before a policeman and a prisoner. When she stood naked, he "stuck his *lathi* where [zie had zir] operation" and demanded that [zie] stand with zir legs apart, "like a woman would". Repeatedly striking that part with his *lathi*, he said, "So, can it go in there? Or is it a field one can't enter? How do you have sex then?" (206) As if to find answer to this question, he asked Revathi to bent and hold zir "buttocks apart so that he could see [zir] anal passage," and forcefully thrust his *lathi* up there: "So you get it there?" (207) Endurance of this and many such "physical violence and torture of the mind" (210) left Revathi more matured and tolerant but it also made him more aware of zir being a *hijra* and more critical of the society that considers it wrong: "The world looks askance at me. It holds me wrong for having turned into a woman after being born a man" (219).

Revathi is doubly minoritized. *First*, zie transforms "him"self into "her"self, thus attempting a shift from a majoritarian group to a minoritarian one that stops in between. *Second*, zie assumes sex work for livelihood and is sodomized by force. What is important to underscore is the tone. Zie is often frustrated, upset, and complaining, pleading for sympathy and respect from the non-hijra communities. But, zie is equally strongly resourceful, energetic, and assertive. Written from within a minor community, Revathi's narrative makes a shift and questions dominant modes of representation. Gamble argues that autobiography and Obligatory Transsexual File (OTF) became a dominant generic mode for transgender authors and theorists since the 1990s as a counter-discursive regime to resist non-transgender representational politics and open up new spaces for the transgendered to speak (45). Revathi's *The Truth about Me*, being a minority discourse and a powerful exposé of India's closeted queer praxis, has challenged complacent heteronormativity and queered discursive space: to become a woman is a matter of choice and volition.

TRANSGRESSING COMPULSORY MASCULINITY

The title of Onir's *I Am* alludes to the establishment of the Cartesian subjectivity. However, the protagonists of at least three episodes (out of four) tag themselves with stigma while representing their own subjective desire and psycho-sexual orientation. They willingly opt for non-representation. Such voluntary silence arises out of the cultural construct of the society; in this case Indian society. Film director, Onir, has earned a reputation in dealing with the problematic of social acceptance of males among the hegemony of patriarchy. Issues like AIDS (in *My Brother Nikhil*), sperm donation, homosexuality, childhood abuse, trauma, etc., have been aptly addressed in his films. Onir's portrayal of marginalization of the male characters with the afore-mentioned so-called anomalies questions the established normativity of the society. In doing so, Onir, being a male (we are going into the structuralist debate over sex and gender), also asks an original question alluding to Gayatri Spivak: "Can the violated men speak?" Onir's answer is: yes.

In *I Am*, Onir investigates into three different categories of socio-sexual reality that drive the males to the margin of normalcy. Such realities also collectively contribute to the silencing process of the social minorities, such as the sperm donors. In the first episode, Afia's (single mother collecting sperm to conceive) response to stigma, politicized by the fertility clinic's vow to anonymity of the sperm donor, reinforces the normativity of a pregnant woman having a legal partner to be a mother. However, Afia's insistence on the disclosure of the donor's identity and Suraj's intended resort to anonymity portray the tension between the social taboos in a subtle manner. None of the situations can be voiced. Conventionally Suraj's reliance on anonymity can be imagined as Judith Butler's concept of "subjection" as the last resort of survival in a society which brands shame with sperm donation, a male's vocation. Considering the fact that the sperm donor (Suraj) does not have the right to be the legal or *de jure* father of the child despite being the normal/biological father, the sperm donor challenges the socially structured notion of father. Is it like a minority group of father denouncing the established concept of fatherhood?

In the "Abhimanyu" episode, the childhood sexual harassment of Abhimanyu by his stepfather interferes in the formation of his sexual identity/subjectivity. Here (male) violence together with homosexual stigma haunts Abhimanyu's memory, and acts as the Freudian "return of the repressed". Though, his apparent escape from such non-straight abuse was predicted through his admission into the film institute and engagement with creative affiliation, the return of his childhood memory and his hallucinating young abused self (a teen alter-ego) disturbs his growth, both sexual and emotional. Every time Abhi(manyu) looks forward to a straight interaction with Natasha, the ghost of his (non-straight) abused child self returns. He, in a way, encounters a reverse "eternal child" complex. He wants to grow up to forget the past, but melancholic past reappears in his hallucinating child self as a stigmatized trauma. Such non-straight violence "dare not speak its name", rather complicates the individual psyche. Stigmatized and forced silence of such non-straight sexual experience amidst the "heterosexual praxis" imposes psychosexual complex on Abhimanyu which ultimately makes him look at himself as different (a self-othering attitude) from others, a transgresser of the so-called normativity. Even his negotiation with his mother and fiancée cannot really re-settle him without a psychosexual trauma. The moment Abhimanyu utters his step-father's violence towards him, his mother's already constructed image of an ideal homophobic husband deduces Abhimanyu's account as lie straightaway. Hence, Abhimanyu's crisis is not only limited to the abuse, but his also being a source of incredible information concerning the sexual orientation of his step-father. Furthermore, Abhimanyu displays number of symptoms of body dysmorphic disorder, such as social isolation, depressive disorder and anxiety. Though his body is not a deformed one, it contributes to his melancholia. He can never accept his mirror image/self-image in his younger self thus making himself different than the others in his vicinity. The forbearance of a silent stigma is what perplexes him. Therefore, Abhimanyu's marginalized status can be reckoned as the joint consequence of patriarchal (by a strong authoritative father figure) violence and social stigma attached to it.

Unlike Abhimanyu, Omar (in the "Omar" episode) has a categorical homosexual orientation. However, such categorical detection of one's own sexual drive problematizes itself when it has to be silenced. In "Omar", however, the stigma tagged on non-straight sexual orientation is promoted by the state itself through Article 377 of Indian Penal Code, which criminalizes sexual act "against the order of nature". Both the terms "order" and "nature" establish a certain normativity violation which is subject to either social ostracism or judicial punishment. As we can observe, such anti-homosexual praxis never hesitates to physically assault the gay man (Jai) and male prostitute (Omar), and lock them up in the prison, a reminder of Foucauldian "birth of a clinic". Here, we can read Foucault's notion of power/authority in defining the sanity (normativity in this case). And of course, the same authority unhesitatingly harasses the (ab) normals. It seems that there is no space for gay men (a real crisis for sexual minority) in India as the policeman asks them if they can find no place for lovemaking other than in a taxi. For the policeman, homophobia seems to be the central tenet for the cultural definition of manhood. Interestingly, even the policeman cherishes his homo/bi-sexual interest discreetly when Omar was away. Both Jai and the police apparently bear the same sense of stigma of being disclosed as gay in front of the society. Added to that, the film's dark setting in the time of their (homo) sexual attachment supports the secrecy of homosexual praxis. Moreover, the lack of space for homosexuality might potentially refer to a lack of tolerance among the people in accepting such non-straight practices; in other words, people's normative expectations are asserted here either honestly or hypocritically. These men are reduced as the subcultural minorities with a surface-level representation. They can never speak of their psycho-sexual orientation; their only abode is discretion and repression, a form of Freudian defense.

In all these three episodes of *I Am*, men are victims of cultural norms created by the male-dominated society. Specific heterosexual responses and rituals that the male body is expected to perform is what problematizes the subjectivity of Abhi and Omar. Violence, taboo, and stigma are three instrumental aspects that drive these men into a sub-category of "man".

BECOMING MINOR

Addressing the still-taboo issue of sexual abuse of men, these three texts, we argue, destabilize our received notions of gender and sexuality, as they also reveal how subtle is the movement of signifiers between masculinity and femininity, heterosexuality and homosexuality, majority and minority. We contend that sexual and gendered violence when enacted against, and not by a man, problematizes the majority/minority divides. It thus exposes a liberating but disturbing realization that the signifier – "minority" slides endlessly in and through discourses.

Let us now attend to a potent question: are these texts transgressive or assimilative? Does Revathi's narrative, for example, really affect transgression of gendering and gender hierarchies? One might argue that Revathi never seeks for transcending gendering. Zie is rather obsessive in zir desire to become a woman. Zie suffered a lot and was often dehumanized for being a woman, but we never see zir critique her desire of being a woman, or reject femininity. Zie allows herself to be trapped within gender binaries. We, however, contend that Revathi, and also Amir, Hassan, Abhi, and Omar's oscillation between masculinity and femininity, aggression and submission, action and silence, betrays the predicaments of minoritization that invokes what Deleuze and Guattari called "becoming". In *A Thousand Plateaus,* they use the word "majoritarian" to designate a mode that is expressive and views binary opposition as fixed and given. Thus, "man" is a majoritarian term; we think of "woman" as other-than-man and queer as not-quite-man. On the other hand, "woman" is a minoritarian term as it, according to Deleuze and Guattari, does not pre-suppose ontological norms. "Woman" is minoritarian in the sense that it is always in-process, always creative, always becoming, thus subverting the normative and exclusive existence of "man". If "woman" is always "becoming-woman", we argue that "minority" is always "becoming-minor". Minority is "minor" because it does not claim to have any unified image, rather it questions, because of its very existence, the normativity and normalcy of "majority". We propose to view "minority men" as minor; instead of a being, it is always becoming, always shuttling between this and that, and thus not only debilitating hetero-patriarchal masculinity, but also opening up dialogic spaces to acknowledge deviations, accommodate possibilities, and celebrate diversities in identity and experience that human can overreach.

One is not born a man, but, rather, becomes one. The transition/movement from the first one to the second one is becoming minor.

REFERENCES

Almaguer, Tomás. "Chicano Men: A Cartography of Homosexual Identity and Behavior", *Social Perspectives in Gay and Lesbian Studies: A Reader*. Eds. Peter M. Nardi and Beth E. Schneider. New York and London: Routledge, 1998 537–52.

Beauvoir, Simone De. *The Second Sex*. Trans. H. M. Parshley. 1949. Harmondsworth: Penguin, 1984.

Butler, Judith. *Gender Trouble: Feminism and the Subversion of Identity.* New York: Routledge, 1990.

Connell, R. W. *Masculinities*. California: University of California Press, 1995.

Gamble, Sarah. "Gender and Transgender Criticism." *Introducing Criticism at the 21st Century* Ed. Julian Wolfreys. Edinburgh: Edinburgh UP, 2002, 37–56.

Hossain, Mashrur Shahid. "enforced ab/normalcy: the sex worker *hijras* and the (re)appropriation of s/he identity." *Sex Work Matters*. Eds. Melissa Hope Ditmore, Antonia Levy and Alys Willman. London: Zed Books, 2010, 117–39.

——— "dancing like a man, fighting like a queen: queering querying gendering (read: how 'queerity' destabilizes gendering)." *Harvest, Jahangirnagar Studies in Language and Literature*, Vol. 25., Department of English, Dhaka, Bangladesh Jahangirnagar University, 2010.

Hosseini, Khaled. *The Kite Runner*. London: Bloomsbury Publishers, 2004.

I Am. Dir: Onir. Anticlock Films, DVD, 2010.

Irigaray, Luce. *This Sex which is not One*. Trans. Catherine Porter and Carolyn Burke. 1977. Ithaca: Cornell UP, 1985.

Lacan, Jacques. *Écrits: A Selection*. Trans. Alan Sheridan. 1960. New York: W.W. Norton & Co, 1977.

MacCormack, Patricia. "Queer Posthumanism: Cyborgs, Animals, Monsters, Perverts." 111–26, *The Ashgate Research Companion to Queer Theory*. Ed. Noreen Giffney and Michael O'Rourke. Surrey: Ashgate, 2009.

Mulvey, Laura. "Visual Pleasure and Narrative Cinema." *Media and Cultural Studies: KeyWorks*. Eds. Meenakshi Gigi Durham and Douglas M. Kellner. Malden: Blackwell, 2001.

Nixon, Sean. "Exhibiting Masculinity." *Representation: Cultural Representations and Signifying Practices*. Ed. Stuart Hall. London: Sage Publications, 1997. 159–210.

Revathi, A. *The Truth About Me: A Hijra Life Story*. Trans. V. Geetha. New Delhi: Penguin, 2010.

8

Negotiating Difference: Minority Discourse and Translation

Assumpta Camps

This essay makes an attempt to show how difference is currently negotiated from the perspective of minority discourses, and how such negotiation concerns the task of translation, when the dynamics of intersections and mediations that largely shape today's developments in contemporary literature, fall under the rubric of cultural translation. Let it be posited first that linguistic conflict is crucial to the creative trajectory of transcultural authors. As bilinguals, these authors are torn between their mother tongue and the majority language that many of them choose to write in. Caught between languages and cultures that are sometimes very distant from one another, their experience in these interstices gives rise to a need for finding a literary voice that can express their cultural, linguistic, and social reality. The challenge for them is to find a form that pays respect to their own minority cultural universe (often oral in nature), a universe to which they wish to give visibility and literary substance. This search takes transcultural authors on a journey of exploration that not only arrives at no easy solutions, but also aims at giving shape to a genuinely intercultural communication from which minority discourse can emerge. In this effort, translation plays an absolutely critical role. Quite often, these authors negotiate with the dominant culture through translation: they perceive themselves through translation; they write and are written about through translation; and through translation they aspire to make space for their own voice within the dominant discourse.

From this perspective, it is necessary to bear in mind that transcultural literatures involve a process of translation in and of themselves. As the Indian critic G. N. Devy (1998) reminds us, many literary traditions in post-colonial spaces have been born precisely in the acts of translation. In Devy's view, communities possess translating consciousness, a consciousness which emerges in multilingual communities where the language of colonial domination has attained a privileged status in terms of its communicative and creative possibilities without overriding the various autochthonous languages within such communities. Similarly, Pérez Firmat speaks of translation sensibility in his study on the importance of translation in the development of Cuban literature, and Bergvall refers to translative awareness (Bergvall 2000: 252) to describe the narrative of multilingual authors who continually develop their fictions around the complex concept of (un)translatability between two or more languages and cultures. As we have seen, these are similar approaches to the same transcultural experience that, in its negotiation of difference in order to make room for minority discourse, draw on the idea of writing from the standpoint of translation.

TRANSCULTURAL LITERATURES

Located between frontiers, in the problematic cultural and linguistic interstices created by the clash and interaction of various cultures in tension, the narratives of transcultural authors, who are largely immersed in the post-colonial sphere, encompass an emerging area where the forms of these encounters have taken on their own voice. Their literary efforts have a dimension that is also critical in that their aim is to rewrite and move away from the representation that others, within the dominant discourse, have made of them, marginalizing, censoring, hiding, or stereotyping their cultural identities then in a colonial, and now in a post-colonial setting.

This essay makes use of the concept of "transculturation", borrowed from Latin American cultural criticism. In broad strokes, transculturation refers to the process by which cultures meet. This meeting produces changes in the societies in contact with each other, and causes creative response that arises in the transitivity between cultures, particularly when these cultures come from dissimilar positions of power. Transculturation is an avenue by which minority discourses make their way in this intercultural relationship; it is not predicated on the idea that individual cultural traditions disappear, rather they undergo continuous development through dialogic interaction. In this process, some features of both the cultures are lost, while others are gained, giving rise to new communicative forms and possibilities (Sales 2001).

We start from the premise that the minority discourse makes room for itself through the narratives of transculturation produced by bilingual and bicultural authors, who fictionalize a communicative issue that is resolved by an operation of translation. Bicultural (not merely bilingual) authors are also, and above all else, translators; they are mediators between the languages and cultures that make up who they are, and yet do not exist on the same plane. Their work leads to a dissimilar intercultural dialogue that involves taking a stance with respect to the dominant, hegemonic discourse. Writing in this context is, without doubt, translating. At the same time, however, it involves negotiating difference between the autochthonous culture and the hegemonic culture, which is typically Western, and projects itself up as central and canonical.

As we know, translation and power are inextricably linked. From the post-colonial sphere, retranslation, or the use of translation is postulated as a means of resisting hegemonic structures. Indeed, translation studies in recent decades, particularly from the nineteen nineties onwards, have assumed that translation goes beyond the strictly linguistic area, functioning as an activity of intercultural, creative, and social mediation, a communicative process that always unfolds within a social, cultural, and political context. It is not necessary to insist here that one of the main avenues of imperial oppression is precisely the exercise of control over language, which is not only a social phenomenon, but can also become an instrument of institutional power. Seen from this perspective, the post-colonial use of non-dominant and minoritized languages poses a real challenge in the social and political sphere, because many transcultural authors adopt what has come to be called the Caliban strategy, formulating their response in the "language of empire" in which they have been educated.[1]

For better or worse, the global expansion of languages, such as Spanish or English, cannot be denied in today's world. As we know, such languages do not belong to a single nation in particular. A multitude of communicative varieties have sprung up in places where they have been introduced as official and they have, over time, taken on a life of their own. In the confrontation between the so-called global languages and minoritized languages, transcultural narrators see a possibility of transforming and promoting the hybridization of hegemonic languages, the languages of power, from within and through the lens of minority cultures.

Today, choosing the dominant language, that is, a global language for literary creation is an increasing and common phenomenon. In some sense, the choice can be viewed as an act of submission to the dominant discourse and the suppression of minoritized languages and cultures. However, it also marks a privileged space *from which* to undertake resistance and promote transcultural interaction: a space where the discourse of power can be made plural from within the system. This involves using the language to communicate what would otherwise remain unvoiced, concealed, and marginalized. Preserving a minority language and culture from annihilation is also possible through an artist's choice of creating in a global language, as a valid communicative intermediary, and inserting into that language the cultural features of an artist's minority tradition, language and culture, turning the global language into a hybrid vehicle of this other language and culture. With this translinguistic option, the transcultural writer has established that a translingual writer is one "who resides between languages into the transnational repertoire and market". Steven Kellman (2000: 9) has posited, that "inhabiting" this interstitial space in order to establish authority, and to find a voice in a foreign language may, at the same time, cause major reluctance in the writer because of earlier social or colonial imposition. For the narrators of bilingual capability, writing in a language other than their mother tongue, is sometimes a choice and sometimes a necessity, arising from the reality of social imbalance between languages. Whatever the case may be, the choice is never innocent. It has a political dimension. Such authors aspire to convey their culture and their vision to the world. The challenge lies in finding expression in a language that they must learn to make their own. Literary creation that brings out the minority discourse of languages and minoritized cultures, originates in an operation of cultural translation which is taken as an activity that is not only creative, but also fundamentally critical. Indeed, such authors create narratives in which the language of writing, just as a palimpsest, does not succeed in fully covering the linguistic and cultural diversity that nurtures their works.

Contemporary transcultural literature features a wide panorama of bilingual subjects writing in a global language. Examples abound: Indians writing in English (e.g. Salman Rushdie, Vikram Chandra, and even V. S. Naipaul born in Trinidad and Tobago), Maghrebi authors writing in French (e.g. Tahar Ben Jelloun and Assia Djebar), Egyptians writing in English (e.g. Ahdaf Soueif), Turks writing in German (e.g. Emine Sevgi Özdamar and Jakob Arjouni), Iranians writing in Dutch (e.g. Kader Abdolah), Africans writing in Spanish (e.g. Donato Ndongo and Mohamed El Gheryb), Tunisians writing in Italian (e.g. Salah Methnani), Quechua-speakers writing in Spanish (e.g. José María Arguedas), and many more. In the same vein, some multicultural literary experiences in the US are of great interest. For example, Rosario Ferré and Esmeralda Santiago are Puerto Rican authors who are bilingual writers in Spanish and English, and self-translate their novels from Spanish to English (Ferré) or vice versa (Santiago), noting the painful recreation of the narrative subject in the process of cultural translation in which they are consciously inscribed. By contrast, the Dominican-American Julia Álvarez and the Cuban Cristina García have Spanish as their mother tongue, but they write in English, the language that they have learned and mastered, and in which they have (re)created themselves.

THE CHICANO LITERATURE: A CASE STUDY

A particularly interesting case is that of Chicano writers, such as Sandra Cisneros, Carmen Tafolla, Lorna Dee Cervantes, Ana Castillo, and Gloria Anzaldúa, who negotiate difference with the hegemonic discourse based on their bilingual and bicultural stance in a unique space, that is, the borderlands of the US and Mexico where they live. Their works shift back and forth between Spanish and English, adopting extremely interesting code-switching in their narratives, and this allows for a bilingual reading of their texts.

The border is a territory full of contradictions and conflicts, of contacts and transgressions, where the frontier is an "open wound" that delimits a space in which safety and risk co-exist, and which defines what we are, and what we are not, in terms of belonging and exclusion. The borderland is a space of uncertainty, a contradictory place of double inscription – neither the one nor the other, but both at the same time. Following Bhabha, we may argue that it is the uncanny space of imposture.[2]

Living on the border means living on the margins and, at the same time, preserving intact the ability to move from one space to another, from one identity to the next, from one language to another, not only from English to Spanish (or vice versa) but also from standard English to slang, to standard Spanish to Mexican Spanish, to the dialect of northern Mexico to Chicano language and its varieties, to Tex-Mex Spanglish to Pachuco, etc. At the point where cultures meet, languages contaminate one another and take on new life in the form of Chicano Spanish, a language born out of the reality of the new borderland identity, almost like a secret language, like one's own homeland.

Those who live on the border tend to be alienated from both their own mother culture and the dominant English culture: they live on a cultural border, at the limits, in a reality where translation and cultural transfer are common, and where hybridization is not only a natural feature but a defining one, observable at both the levels of ethnicity and language. As Samuel Weber has pointed out, subjects under those conditions experiment the anxiety of that double inscription, since anxiety is the affective address of a "world [that] reveals itself as caught up in the space between frames: a double frame or one that is split".[3]

The borderland exists beyond the purely geographical, for it is a metaphor not only for the clash or contamination between cultures but also of a certain state of mind. As H. Bhabha has aptly stated:

> [the] borderland culture of hybridity [...] articulates its problems of identification and its diasporic aesthetic in an uncanny, disjunctive temporality that is, at once, the *time* of cultural displacement, and the *space* of the 'untranslatable" (Bhabha 1994: 322).

The borderland as a metaphor of this "in-between space" that celebrates cultural mixing and hybridism can be projected towards other realities not necessarily identified with a political frontier. In fact, it appears in any context of cultural hybridization, be it a post-colonial context, or the settling of minority cultures in first world countries. What is interesting here is to analyse this cultural hyphenation and the effect of this mixing on the textual experience of these authors from the point of view of the negotiation of difference in the minority discourse, and beyond this liminal space for erratic cultural identities, to study its implications for translation. This is particularly so because, as in the work of Sandra Cisneros, we are facing not just one frontier – the Mexican-American frontier – but several: as a woman, as Chicana, and as a writer.

The border, therefore, is a privileged place in which to consider issues of cultural transmission and the relationship with the Other, as well as to redefine ourselves in the light of how the Other sees us. In other words, it is an ideal viewpoint for observing the cultural centre from the periphery and the cultural periphery from the centre allowing the emergence of silenced minority discourses.

Cisneros' work, arising out of this plural reality, is almost inevitably bilingual, and we often find words in Spanish in its different varieties. Her writing, however, is a case of more than straightforward bilingualism: Cisneros writes in English, but she often uses Mexican syntax, introduces numerous set phrases, Mexican idioms and proverbs, which are sometimes translated literally into English and in Texan Spanish. Her writing is thus not only bilingual, but bicultural; it supports itself through translation, where language, identity, and culture become concepts that are subject to continuous negotiation. Through this peculiar form of writing, the author is constantly seeking to create an effect of strangeness that surprises the reader.

A brief extract from the novel *The House on Mango Street* by Sandra Cisneros offers a suitable example:

> My Name
>
> In English my name means hope. In Spanish it means too many letters. It means sadness, it means waiting. It is like the number nine. A muddy colour. It is the Mexican records my father plays on Sunday mornings when he is shaving, songs like sobbing. [...] At school they say my name funny as if the syllables were made out of tin and hurt the roof of your mouth. But in Spanish my name is made out of a softer something, like silver, not quite as thick as sister's name – Magdalena – which is uglier than mine. Magdalena who at least can come home and become Nenny. But I am always Esperanza. (Cisneros 1989: 10–11)

Demonstrating an astonishing degree of metalinguistic reflection, the girl narrator, who is a Chicana and a bilingual, centres the enormous experiential weight of her bicultural dichotomy on the meaning of her name, which she is able to translate into English, acting as real bridge to mediate between the languages and cultures that make up who she is. In this way, the author reflects in her work how such an experience can also be difficult and even harrowing, particularly in childhood.

In the field of translation studies, this proximity between the translation process and creative writing has been described differently by Maria Tymoczko (1999: 2000), whose view is that translation and post-colonial literature are both instances of intercultural writing that emerge from the intersection between different literary systems. In Tymoczko's view, the translator and the post-colonial writer are mediators who can only be differentiated by the greater degree of the writer's endeavour. The writer transposes and translates not only a text, but also an entire cultural universe:

> The primary difference is that, unlike translators, post-colonial writers are not transposing a text. As background to their literary works, they are transposing a culture — to be understood as a language, a cognitive

> system, a literature (comprised of a system of texts, genres, tale types, and so on), a material culture, a social system and legal framework, a history, and so forth. (Tymoczko 1999: 20)

However, Tymoczko continues to note that a more significant disparity between these two literary activities concerns the demands that they make. While the translator faces the dilemma of fidelity to the text that must be translated, the writer has greater freedom to select cultural elements that will be translated into an original text. In her conclusions, Tymoczko does not go so far as to claim that post-colonial fictions are translations, but rather offers the statement as metaphorical and suggestive. Certainly, they share formal and functional elements in common. Without lapsing into generalizations, I would say that transcultural cases exist in which a fiction is and functions as a translation: of itself and of an entire cultural world. Transcultural narratives are peculiar examples of self-translation arising from the bilingualism of their authors.

However, the situation grows in complexity when we confront the translation of transcultural narrative, which involves an operation of translation on its own. Translating Chicano literature, as with any borderland reality, is undoubtedly a complex procedure because the original texts are already loaded with a textual and contextual plurality that is difficult to transfer. This multiplicity involves, on the one hand, a special relationship between the original text (hybrid) and the translation (which, it could be argued, is of necessity also hybrid). On the other hand, it obliges us to adopt a different positioning with respect to the subject/object of the translation, such that in approaching the original (and its meaning) the reader is ultimately involved in a shifting experience (Joysmith 1996). For many people, the translation of borderland textualities is a *talking back*, that is a procedure of reversed (re) writing which would only be strictly true in the case of a translation into Spanish). What emerges is thus a hybrid translation, neither Mexican nor American, of a hybrid original text that likewise is neither American nor Mexican.

The translation of this type of transcultural writing calls for special translation strategies, as well as the commitment of the translator.

Gayatri Spivak, poses an interesting case of a visible translator committed to cultural subalternity. She says, "You cannot translate from a position of monolinguist superiority" (1993: 195). In addition to other aspects of this indisputable truth, Spivak offers interesting reflections on the ethics and politics of translation, particularly in her well-known text *The Politics of Translation* which takes a feminist and post-structuralist approach to post-colonial translation and critiques Western strategies of translation as "Westernizing". She points to their tendency to homogenize, approaching the so-called "Third-World literatures" without mediation of any sort, as though they were immediately accessible. In common with Berman (1984: 1985), Spivak takes a stance in favour of a specific degree of literalness. That is, she supports an intermediate discourse that breaks the effect of immediacy that the reader can have of the text, offering a sense of the differential specificity of the original. Spivak also holds the view that the most appropriate approach to take when introducing texts of minority cultures, particularly from the so-called Third World, to Western culture is that the translator needs to have a sound familiarity with the literary production of the language being translated in order to know how to discriminate some texts from others. Beyond these reflections, Spivak's contributions in this area are also of great interest when she puts her principle into practice, for example, when translating into English from Bengali – a language that is already a hybrid – the works of a post-colonial author like the Bengali activist Mahasweta Devi, who has a strong commitment to the tribal communities of India.[4]

In conclusion, in the context of transcultural literatures, when narrating constitutes translating in and of itself, the act of translation challenges us to assume an ethical commitment born out of respect not only for cultural and linguistic diversity, which nourishes the text from the start, but also for the minority discourse that sustains it. Today, more than ever, translation as a constant negotiation leads us into dialogue with difference and it may even open the way for the emergence of a minority discourse kept silent until now.

NOTES

1 Weber, S. (1991). *Return to Freud: Jacques Lacan's Dislocation of Psychoanalysis*. Cambridge: Cambridge University Press, p. 161.
2 See Bhabha, Homi K. (1994). *The Location of Culture*. London-N.Y.: Routledge (especially Chapter 8).
3 In the famous words of Caliban to Prospero: "You taught me language; and my profit on't is, I know how to curse. The red plague rid you for learning me your language!" (Shakespeare 1610: 976).
4 As we know, Mahasweta Devi writes in English (the language in which she studied) as well as in Bengali, but she has written most of her literary works in Bengali, employing it as a dominant code that hybridizes English and other languages used in India.

REFERENCES

Albertazzi, Silvia. *Lo Sguardo dell'Altro. Le letterature postcoloniali*. Roma: Carocci, 2000.

Bhabha, Homi K. *The Location of Culture*. London-New York: Routledge, 1994.

Berman, Antoine. *The Experience of the Foreign*. S. Heyvaert (trad.) (1992). New York: State University of New York Press, 1984.

——— "Translation and the trials of the foreign" (Lawrence Venuti translator). In: Venuti, Lawrence (ed.). (2000). *The Translation Studies Reader*. London/New York: Routledge, pp. 284–97, 1985.

Cisneros, Sandra. *The House on Mango Street*. London: Bloomsbury, 1989.

——— *Caramelo o Puro cuento*. Liliana Valenzuela (tr). (2003). Barcelona: Seix Barral, 2002.

De Courtivron, Isabelle. (ed.). *Lives in Translation: Bilingual Writers on Identity and Creativity*. New York: Palgrave MacMillan, 2003.

Devi, Mahasweta. *Chotti Munda and His Arrow*. 1980, Gayatri Chakravorty Spivak (tra). (2003). Oxford: Blackwell.

——— *Imaginary Maps*. Gayatri Chakravorty Spivak (translation and introduction). London/New York: Routledge, 1995.

Devy, G. N. *Of Many Heroes: An Indian Essay in Literary Historiography*. New Delhi: Sangam Books/Prestige, 1998.

Kellman, Steven. *The Translingual Imagination*. Lincoln/London: University of Nebraska Press, 2000.

Pérez Firmat, Gustavo. *The Cuban Condition: Translation and Identity in Modern Cuban Literature*. Cambridge: Cambridge University Press, 1989.

Sales, Dora. "Transculturación narrativa: Posibilidades de un concepto latinoamericano para la teoría y la literatura comparada intercultural." *Exemplaria. Revista de Literatura Comparada/Journal of Comparative Literature* 5: 21–37, 2001.

Shakespeare, William. "The Tempest". *The Complete Works of William Shakespeare.* W. G. Clark and W. Aldis Wright (eds.) (s.f.) 2 vols. New York: Nelson Doubleday, vol. II, 971–92, 1610.

Spivak, Gayatri Chakravorty. "The Politics of Translation". In: Spivak, Gayatri Chakravorty. *Outside in the Teaching Machine.* London/New York: Routledge, , 2003, 179–200.

——— *Death of a Discipline.* New York: Columbia University Press, 2003.

St-Pierre, Paul. "Translating Cultural Difference: Fakir Mohan Senapati's *Chha Mana Atha Guntha*". St-Pierre, Paul (ed.). *Translation and Postcolonialism: India.* Numéro spécial, *Meta. Translator's journal,* 42 (2): 423-38, 1997.

Tymoczko, Maria. "Post-colonial writing and literary translation." Susan Bassnett and Harish Trivedi (eds.). *Post-colonial Translation: Theory and Practice.* London/New York: Routledge, 1999, pp. 19–40.

——— "Translations of themselves: The contours of postcolonial fiction." Sherry Simon and Paul St-Pierre (eds.). *Changing the Terms: Translating in the Postcolonial Era.* Ottawa: University of Ottawa Press, 2000, 147–63.

Weber, S. *Return to Freud: Jacques Lacan's Dislocation of Psychoanalysis.* Cambridge: Cambridge University Press, 1991.

Section 2

In-Text

9

Redefining the Secular and the Modern: The Politics of Identity and the Minority Discourse in Contemporary India

E. V. Ramakrishna

I

With the advance of modernity, religion has not disappeared from the contemporary world. The emergence of modern institutions has redefined the social significance of religion. We tend to associate religious practices with pre-modern world-views, but secularization has not rendered the religious practices and ideas redundant. Carl Schmitt has observed that "all significant concepts of the modern theory of the state are secularized theological concepts" (36). As an ideology, secularism reconstitutes the self in relation to a new set of paradigms derived from Enlightenment rationality. Secularization is a process that has taken different trajectories in different countries. The formation of the secular is not always accompanied by the shifting of the religious from the public to the private domain. In England, one can see close links between the state and the church, but the people tend to be secular in their views, while in the United States the federal state is strictly secular even as the population professes their religious faith openly. In India, despite a strong narrative of the secular articulated by the constitution that sanctifies the state, the nation as represented through symbols and images is mediated through a refined Hinduism that has clear elitist associations. Talal Asad argues that "the secular" should not be thought as "the space in which *real* human life gradually emancipates itself from the controlling power of *religion* and thus achieves the latter's relocation". This also explains the deep sense of ambivalence that surrounds terms such as "minority" and "minority experience" in contemporary discussions of the secular nature of the Indian society (190–91).

The ambivalence built into the minority discourse in India has become more intractable in the last two decades. Even among those who subscribe to the secular-modern, there is a great deal of ambiguity when it comes to recognizing the minority as a historical category. The process of minoritization of communities did not take place in the same way, and even among the religious minorities their relation with their majoritarian community is not the same in every part of India. The minoritization of the Muslim community and the Dalit community has followed different trajectories. Following D. R. Nagaraj, I would like to argue that Dalit movement articulated Dalit identity through the mode of "self-minoritization and self-closure" (115). Ambedkar had stated before Simon Commission: "We claim that we must be treated as a distinct community, separate from the Hindu community, our minority character has been hitherto concealed by our inclusion in the Hindu community, but as a matter of fact, there is really no link between the Depressed classes and the Hindu Community" (117). D. R. Nagaraj argues that Ambedkar created a new identity for Dalits "by treating them as an embodied mass of humiliation" (118). He comments: "Self-minoritalization in this case meant the removal of spiritual, or ideational, link with other forms of protest, ignoring the idea of a common historical fate that binds Dalits with other subaltern producers" (118). Ambedkar's strategy of limiting the Dalit identity to those communities and castes that had a common history and shared memory created a self-definition that cleared social space of resistance, but did not open up a larger unity among the similarly oppressed minorities.

Unlike the Dalit movement's conscious strategy of minoritization to negotiate with colonial modernity, the Muslims did not have a vantage point to engage with the same historical situation. Partha Chatterjee observes that "the tendencies of religious reform with the minority communities were blocked by the fears that reform would mean capitulation to majoritarian homogenisation and the loss of identity" (3). Reform of personal law has remained a particularly intractable problem because the way the secular-modern has been defined by the imagined community of the late nineteenth-century India, it left no space to accommodate the self-definition of the dominant religious minority of Muslims. Talal Asad has observed that secularization (which according to Max Weber is the dominant feature of modernity) is a coercive process even in the West. The religious minority's ability to represent itself becomes seriously compromised when the experience of religion is confined to the private, domestic sphere. The subjectivities born of the "private/domestic" religious experience could not find articulation in the public sphere without seriously disputing the dominant feature of the secular modern as inscribed in the narratives of the nation and the nation-state. This means that the secular-modern needs to be redefined to address the anxieties and compulsions of the minoritarian discourse.

II

I intend to focus on Kerala and Malayalam fiction in the rest of the paper, since the only way to historicize the minoritarian discourse is to regionalize it. It is not possible to posit a monolithic Muslim identity for India. Even within Kerala, the north Kerala or Malabar presents a distinctively different experiential site from the rest of Kerala in historical terms. The Muslims in the interiors of Malabar (North Kerala) are largely converts from the lower castes, unlike the rich Muslims in the coastal area. Malabar witnessed a series of conflicts in the nineteenth century and early twentieth century between the Muslim peasants and the Hindu landlords that culminated in the Mappila rebellion of 1921 during which large parts of South Malabar were "liberated" by Muslim rebels who ran a parallel government till the British army brutally suppressed the armed rebellion and banished or hanged all its leaders. As Shahid Amin points out in his study of Chouri Choura incident, the nationalist and the regional narratives contradict each other as the same facts are deployed differently in their formulation (35–41). The root cause of Mapilla rebellion was the intervention of the colonial government in the revenue system, empowering the landlords to evict tenants from their land for failing to pay taxes. The protest by tenants who were mostly Muslims often resulted in violence against the landlords. Between 1836 and 1919, there were 29 episodes of rebellion. As this, protest found patronage from the religious leaders of this sub-region it assumed communal overtones. As M. T. Ansari shows in his essay in *Subaltern Studies* XII, the figure of the fanatic Muslim gets articulated in the colonial discourse during this phase. This figure gains currency in the popular imagination and circulates in the literary discourse throughout the twentieth century, erasing the Muslim's material life and excluding him from the nationalist discourse of the secular-modern. The framing of the Muslim into a fanatic dehistoricizes him, metamorphoses him into an illiterate, irrational savage who has to be feared and tamed. Some of the major Malayalam literary texts, *Duravasta* by Kumaran Asan, a long poem on inter-caste marriage between a Dalit youth and a Brahmin woman set against the background of Mappila rebellion and a novel by Uroob called *Sundarikalum Sundaranmarum* (The Women and Men of Beauty) refer to the "cruel Muhammadan" who is marked as the other.

This "othering" of Muslim in the mainstream culture/popular imagination has rendered his material reality unrepresentable. As opposed to the savage Muslim in the writings of the mainstream, we also come across in the popular narratives (in fiction, films, and plays) the figure of the "good Muslim" who is always shown with a cap, a beard, and a belt, eager to help the Hindu neighbours. This crisis of representation has found articulation in the fictional works of a major writer of Malayalam, Vaikom Muhammad Basheer (94). Basheer, who was inspired by the Progressive movement, and was a nationalist, valorized the secular-modern as a desirable ideal but finds the assimilation of the Muslim community into its logic, leading to the loss of its difference without which the community cannot sustain a viable mode of belonging in society. We will briefly discuss the novel, *Me Grandad 'ad an Elephant* (hereafter mentioned as *Me Grand 'ad*) which brings out the implications of the project of modernity for the minority Muslim community in Kerala.

Written in 1951, *Me Grand 'ad* addresses the question of reforms in Muslim community with a sense of urgency. In the course of negotiating the question of modernity, Basheer has to face some of the basic paradoxes implied by modernity. *Me Grand 'ad* may be read as a critique of the project of modernity embodied in the nationalistic discourse. The central character in the novel is Kunjupathumma who moves out of her minority "subculture" to "national" culture through a series of encounters and decisions. Brought up in the closed world of the Muslim culture, Kunjupathumma shares the "common sense" of the typical Muslims who are illiterate and pious to a fault. With characteristic irony Basheer writes:

> In the world there are only two classes, Muslim and Kafir. Whether they are men or women, after death all kafirs will go to hell. They are all fallen ones. If Muslims imitate them they will become lost souls worthy of hell. The kafirs Kunjupathumma saw were schoolmistresses.
>
> Although they are kafirs, they smell nice. They all wear saris. They all have those small kuppayams known as blouses. Underneath the blouse they have a thin, tight bodice. What is more, they wear flowers on their head. (54–5)

Muslim and Christian communities in Kerala, in the first part of the twentieth century, had their own distinctive way of dressing. Joining the mainstream meant moving out of these culture-specific markers of identity. The novel portrays the reforms that were sweeping the Muslim community, which stressed education, standardization, and integration into the mainstream community. The formation of the linguistic state of Kerala in 1956, unifying the regions of Malabar, Kochi, and Travancore, also set in motion a process of standardization in educational curriculum and linguistic usage. Caste markers had come to be associated with regressive worldviews. The Communist government came into power in 1957 and this also accelerated several progressive legislations that dismantled the feudal power structure. That Kunjupathumma's mother always invokes the family's feudal past as the paradise long after they have been reduced to penury, indicates the underlying conflict in the novel.

Nisar Ahmad and his sister Ayesha represent the progressive Muslims in the novel. They take it upon themselves to "reform" Kunjupathumma, the illiterate, orthodox girl who speaks the Muslim dialect to their utter shock. But Basheer portrays the fables and myths that inform the world of Kunjupathumma bestowing on her a unique power of imagination which one does not associate with the world of modern rationality. Nisar Ahmad and Ayesha "teach" Kunjupathumma to speak "proper" Malayalam which is closer to the written standard Malayalam. Kunjupathumma can traverse this distance between the dialect and the standard speech only through cultural assimilation. She has to transform herself into a national subject partaking of the larger process of modernity that has no space for her "differences". At one point, Kunjupathumma asks Ayesha: "If you learn to read and write....... And if you are well informed, it is not possible to live like a Muslim? Is it true?" This question has greater significance than the context seems to imply. Can the Muslim retain his/her unique community-specific markers of identity and still enter into the domain of modernity? Does membership in the world of modernity imply a loss of all that specifically contribute towards their collective identity? Kunjupathumma's assimilation into a standard "national" identity alienates her from the larger bonds of community. One needs the specific culture of a local, living community to relate oneself to a larger "national" identity. The local and communal are not negative sources of identity but affirmative modes of belonging to a larger collectivity. Basheer demonstrates how the local is constituted in terms of specific modes of knowing and experiencing the world. Subcultures have their collective wisdom and their native ways of perceiving the world. Such cosmologies inform the larger narrative of the nation. Though Basheer is on the side of the progressive Muslim and endorses Kunjupathumma's assimilation into secular modernity, he is aware of an uneasy resolution here since this assimilation does violence to the process of belonging to a culture-specific identity.

The minority discourse becomes a possibility only if the members of the group can operate as meaningful collectivities with their specific experiences rooted in separate social contexts. Minority discourse in this sense is an "ethical-political" discourse which in the view of Habermas, would pertain to group or collective identity and enable members of a community to see themselves as inhabitants of a specific region, as heirs to a specific culture, allowing them to decide how they want to deal with their historical destiny, with one another or with nature. Plamen Makariev commenting on Habermas's views on minority discourse writes:

> Habermas regards ethical political discourse as being twofold in character. On the one hand, they can be self-reflexive to a certain extent insofar as they are not based upon a fundamentalist mentality. As such they enable groups to critically appropriate their own traditions. On the other hand, however, they cannot be completely dissociated from the respective domain of the lifeworld (24).

Minority discourse as an ethical-political discourse provides a means of explicating and articulating a shared value orientation. The secular-modern as a normative hegemonic source of validation of collective needs and self-understandings will impact upon the manner in which minority discourse projects the self-understanding of the community. The larger framework of citizenship will form the foundation for this negotiation between the particular demands of the community and collective will of the society. As Habermas says: "Reason and will reciprocally determine each other in ethical discourses, for these discourses remain embedded in the context they thematize" (167).

In the context of Kerala, the Marxian discourse of emancipation has subscribed to the rationalist ideal of the secular modern complicating the legitimacy of the marginalized minorities as a separate group. The Marxists have strongly disputed the claims made on behalf of the politics of identity. The appeal to the authenticity of the self, derived from the daily experiences of exclusion, or violence calls into question the claims made on behalf of the class struggle. What is disputed is the claim that class transcends all such divisions such as gender, caste, religion, region, and race. In the last three years, the organs of the Marxist Party in Kerala have found it necessary to refute claims of the politics of identity as conspiracies of capitalism. Prakash Karat, in an essay on the politics of identity observes that "the impetus to globalization provided by capitalism and the setbacks suffered by the socialism were primarily responsible for the legitimacy gained by the politics of identity" (Govindan Master 12). However, the arguments put forward by the party ideologues betray the inability to engage with anxieties and insecurities of Muslims in the post-Ayodhya Kerala. K. N. Panikker in his essay in the same volume argues that traditionally the organizations based on caste and religion, have played a dual role, both constructive and regressive, in the social formation of India (33). Since all societies have multiple identities, it is natural that identities based on region, caste, religion, ethnicity tends to assume significance in a society that is yet to develop class-consciousness. Citing Gramsci, he argues that man-in-mass is bound to have a "contradictory state of consciousness" that will result in an ambivalent attitude towards questions of social change (34). Citing the example of Muslims in Kerala, he says that large sections of them are extremely poor. The assertive attitude of the majoritarian forces, particularly in the wake of the communal incidents after Ayodhya, makes them vulnerable. Hence, Muslims in Kerala find themselves in a double bind. Without the larger support of the community, they cannot shape an ethical-political discourse on their culture-specific identity. However, the community is economically and socially divided, creating a conflict of interests regarding the larger commitment to the well-being of the community, particularly its most vulnerable sections.

III

In the post-Ayodhya situation, the Muslims in Kerala are increasingly seen as part of a pan-Indian or international religion of Islam, though such a perspective falsifies their lifeworld constituted by Malayalam language and immersion in local reality. The culture-specific nature of their identity gets erased when they confront the challenges of fundamentalism. Here, I would discuss some short stories from a volume called, *Ariku* edited by Samad Kunnakkavu with an introduction by me in Malayalam, which showcased issues of communal and cultural identity in the context of the minorities in Kerala. The stories in the volume show how the secular-modern legitimates only certain kinds of identities as "modern". This "othering" process is a major theme in these stories.

In the story, "A Cow in Aligarh" (Samad 110–23) by Anwar Abdullah, the narrator speaks of a harrowing time he had in Thiruchirappalli when preventive arrests were made in connection with the visit of the Central Home Minister to Coimbatore. They found that almost all male members of the family had disappeared from the Muslim-dominated areas fearing arrest. Anis, one of the members of the group, narrates an episode from his life in Aligarh while he was studying there. It was in 1993. After the widespread communal riots in Bombay and other parts of the country, the students on the campus were filled with anxiety and fear, though they found the place fairly secure. Then, suddenly the dead body of a cow was discovered on the campus and the needle of suspicion was on the students of Zoology on the campus. Anis, one of the Zoology students, was among the students who were threatened with dire consequences. This was the first time he had felt as a proclaimed victim. There were rallies and processions demanding action against the culprits. The district magistrate ordered for the post-mortem of the cow. The night before the post-mortem, the district authorities shifted all students under suspicion to the railway station where they were kept under guard. Anis described the trauma he went through, fearing that he could be attacked any time. The plight of his classmates was equally harrowing. Though they were asked to leave for their native places, nobody had the courage to step out of the room alone, as they knew they could be attacked. Then the station master brought the newspaper which reported that the cow had died of natural reasons, and it was not an unnatural death. The story clearly shows that Anis was a changed person after that. He has become a drifter, feels vulnerable and is clearly confused about his own identity in a free India.

In another story, titled "The Pedestrian Called Badusha" (*ibid*: 95–101), R. Unny shows the plight of an elderly Muslim who is fond of walking around, enjoying the landscape and the sights and sounds of nature. His wife cautions him when he goes out to the beach in the dead of night asking him, "Are you mad to go for a walk at this time of night?" He is picked up by the police and brutally beaten up. The very fact of his appearance with a beard is enough to confirm his identity as a criminal. Something similar happens in the case of a lunatic in the story titled "The Fanatic" (27–38) by Shihabuddin Poythumkadavu. Here, a mentally unstable person is taken into custody by the police after a bomb goes off in the city. He was searching for food in the garbage heap and his bearded visage caught in CCTV camera becomes an evidence against him. He was retrieving some leftovers; but in the dimly lit photo, he is seen planting a packet. Since the bomb went off in the vicinity, his arrest is the breakthrough the police celebrate. He is seen as a hardened criminal, his incoherent answers confirming him as a trained terrorist who has been taught to mislead the police.

In all these stories, the Muslim identity is seen as potentially disruptive to the nation-state by the law-enforcing agencies. The majoritarian worldview has come to be internalized by the nation-state which as a republic has to guarantee equality before law for all citizens. These stories are about the moral failure of the nation-state. K. P. Ramanunni's story, "A few secular conversations" (17–27) lampoons hypocrisy of the elites who pose as secular but profess deep-rooted hostility towards the minority. One of the speakers in this story who happens to be a university professor is unable to stand the appearance of a Muslim, Bavootty who always wears traditional "Mappila" (North Kerala Muslim) dress and has a beard and a cap. This Muslim happens to be a philanthropist who generously donates to the cause of education. But his manners and appearance mark him as an obscurantist. It does not take long for his son to be arrested for his alleged links with an organization that is supposed to be extremist in nature. Bavootty is taken into custody for questioning, is beaten up for speaking in Arabic, and finally dies on the way to hospital. The university professor invites all his friends including the moderate Muslim, Aryankav who edits a progressive journal, *Navakeralam*, for a get-together for "celebrating" the event. The case of Aryanakav also sums up the dilemma of the moderate, "modern" Muslim. To become a member of the secular society, he has to disown his own community. The title of his periodical, *Navakeralam*, clearly points to the democratic ideals once held up by the progressive reformist sections of Kerala society. As shown above in the discussion of Basheer's novel, Muslims in Kerala had clearly endorsed modernity through education and social reforms. But the events after the 1990s, globally and nationally, have brought into focus a certain crisis of identity among the Muslims, in general, and the Kerala Muslims are caught in the nightmare of history, with the secular-modern discourse offering no safe passage. We need to bring into the minority discourse the larger framework of citizenship which is an indivisible and irrefutable right guaranteed by the constitution and that alone can bring back legitimacy to the representation of minority subjectivity in our troubled times.

REFERENCES

Amin, Shahid. *Event, Metaphor, Memory: Chauri Chaura 1922–92.* Delhi: OUP, 1995.

Ansari, M. T. and Deeptha Achar. Ed. *Discourse, Democracy and Difference: Perspectives on Community, Politics and Culture.* New Delhi: Sahitya Akademi, 2010.

Asad, Talal. *Formation of the Secular: Christianity, Islam, Modernity.* USA: Stanford University Press, 2003.

Basheer, Vaikom Muhammad. *Me Grandad 'ad an Elephant!* Trans. R. E. Asher and A. C. Chandrasekharan. New Delhi: Viking, 1980.

Chatterjee, Partha. "Fasting for Laden: The Politics of Secularization in Contemporary India" in *Discourse, Democracy and Difference* edited by Ansari M. T. and Deepatha Achar, *op.cit.*

Habermas, J. "Faith and Knowledge" in Habermas, *The Future of Human Nature.* Malden: Polity Press, 2003, 101–15.

Habermas, J. "Religious Tolerance: The Pacemaker for Cultural Rights," *Philosophy,* 79, 2004, 5–18.

Habermas, J. *Between Facts and Norms.* Cambridge: MIT Press, 1996.

Makariev, Plamen. "Cultural Rights and Deliberative Policy: Beyond Habermas" in *Journal of Public Deliberations,* Vol. 9 (2013; Issue 1), 2013.

Master, M. V. Govindan. *Swathwarashtreeyathepatti* (Regarding Identity Politics). Chinta Publications, Thiruvananthapuram. 2010.

Nagaraj, D. R. *The Flaming Feet and Other Essays.* New Delhi: Permanent Black, 2010.

Samad, Kunnakkavu. *Ariku: Orangalil Aakkappettavarekurichulla Kathakal* (Margin: Stories about the Marginalized). Kozhikode: Prateeksha Books, 2012.

Schmitt, Carl. *Political Theology.* Cambridge: MIT Press, 1985.

10

The Artiste as Woman: The Seeking Spirit of Vidya Rao and Tulsi Badrinath

Laxmi Kannan

My role in society, or any artist's or poet's role, is to try and express what we all feel. Not to tell people how to feel. Not as a preacher, not as a leader, but as a reflection of us all.

—John Lennon, Musician (2012)

I

This is an attempt to make a comparative study of two books – *Heart to Heart: Remembering Nainaji* by the thumri-dadra[1] singer Vidya Rao and *Meeting Lives* by the Bharat Natyam dancer and writer, Tulsi Badrinath. The very fact that I present this study on two well-known artists in a conference on *Minority Discourses* should speak volumes about the paradox in a woman's life. This is a unique opportunity to re-think about what really constitutes the status of a "minority". Let me cite a few definitions of minority that many of us already have at the back of our minds. It refers to "persons belonging to a smaller group" according to the *Cambridge Advanced Learner's Dictionary*; while it is "a sense of separate identity and awareness of status apart from a large group" according to the *Webster's Third New International Dictionary.* A rather simpler definition comes from the *Oxford Advanced Learner's Dictionary* which says that it could mean "a small group in a community or a nation". The hard fact, however, remains that one does not really need dictionaries to define the sense of someone being in a minority. Having said that for the sake of a broad reference, let me now get back to the texts I wish to study.

Heart to Heart: Remembering Nainaji by Vidya Rao is a memoir of her former guru, the legendary singer Naina Devi. In tracing her life, Rao finds many similar paradigms and patterns that she comes across in her journey as a singer. *Meeting Lives*, by Tulsi Badrinath, a dedicated Bharat Natyam dancer trained under the renowned gurus, Dhananjayans, in Chennai, was long listed for the Man Asian Literary Prize 2007. A novelist, critic, reviewer, she raises gender-related questions regarding wifehood, motherhood, and all the usual roles that a woman is expected to conform to. For both Rao and Badrinath, music and dance are the sources of spiritual quest respectively, which offer them a medium through which they can transcend their bodies and the constraints of domesticity, or patriarchy that would otherwise circumscribe their growth. They know very well that they can reach for excellence in their field only through the rigours of an intensive training and hours of dedicated *riyaz* (practice). Having laid out the basic parameters for the sake of a broader reference, let me now engage with the two texts I wish to study.

II

In her book, Vidya Rao addresses many gender issues head on. First, there is the societal pressure to conform to the norms for respectability, or to what is appropriate for women, most of which are brought about by their familial roles of being a wife, mother, daughter, sister, daughter-in-law, and so on. Next, there are parameters within the conventions of classical music and dance, given the public role of a "performer", and the convoluted path an artiste has to traverse before she reaches a level playing field. It entails waiting with patience for the right time and enduring many a bumpy ride with fortitude. Rao admires Naina Devi not just for her fortitude, but more for the creative way she handles the rough with the smooth in life. She puts it succinctly: "It seems to me that she (Naina Devi) learnt how to make bandhan into bandish" (141).

Born Nilina Sen into a Brahmo Samaj family in Calcutta, she had to take another name, as Naina Devi, in order to transform herself for her role as a staff artiste with All India Radio, and eventually evolve as one of the foremost singers. While she was encouraged to dance, sing, act and write in her parents' house, marriage at the age of seventeen to the prince Ripjit Singh of the Kapurthala *rajwada*, put an end to her singing when she became a young Rani. It was not considered proper for her to sing any more. From then on, she could only listen to music concerts, or see performances of dance in her palace through a *chilman*.[2]

The idyllic marriage comes to an end when a very young Nilina loses her husband following a brief illness after which litigations, family jealousies, and rivalries surfaced, and her in-laws turned hostile. Perhaps, that made Nilina realize, in Rao's words: "we belong nowhere, are related to no one" (63). This in itself, according to her, helped Nilina achieve "the centeredness that is the mark of an artiste," hastening to distinguish it from a mere selfishly inward self-centeredness. "As a singer she found herself again" (76) says Rao, introspecting about the wave of feminism during the 1980s when it urged women to claim and defend their space. That seemed to be adversarial in comparison to Nilina's centeredness which was all inclusive and non-oppositional.

A few recent critical studies of feminism take cognizance of this new perspective of women who have a different take on what life, or marriage, holds out for them. Radha Chakravarty's sensitive analysis of "alternative forms of liberty," as she phrases it, is one such study that declares in its subtitle the need for a review. In *Feminism and Contemporary Women Writers: Rethinking Subjectivity*, she says:

> The idea of freedom is thus paradoxically combined with a strong emphasis on responsibility towards oneself and others, which suggest alternative forms of liberty, beyond current notions of individualism so popular

> in the "West"...The idea of freedom in these texts is based less on separateness and unique destinies than on fluid subjectivities with porous borders...The suggestion rather, is of an alternative model of emancipation, one based on a productive tension between personal rights and duties towards a larger collective. (18)

In this book, Chakravarty engages with the feminist philosophy of six contemporary writers who declared publicly that they do not fall in line with the conventional canons of feminism found in academic discourses.

It is only after the death of her husband that Nilina Sen resumes music earnestly, and this time, she does not look back. In deference to the royal background of her marital family, she decides to camouflage her lineage with the anonymity of her new name Naina Devi, a name that was inspired by her indelible memory of a woman she saw as a child, sitting on a *ghat* along the river Ganga in Benaras, as she sang with a rich tonality. Not knowing who she was, what stayed on the mind of the child Nilina was the beauty of her eyes, and she chose the name Naina Devi as a tribute to her. It was much later that she got to know a few details about the woman that she was once a famous *tawaif*, a courtesan, but had given up everything—fame, possessions, jewellery—and donned the white saree of a widow and sat by the Ganga, singing a prayer for deliverance.

Nilina Sen continued singing *incognito* as Naina Devi for a long time, not wanting to offend her in-laws' family. There is a humorous incident involving Ghulam Sabir Khan, a man with a huge physique who played delicately on the sarangi.[3] When her father-in-law paid her a surprise visit, Ghulam Sabir Khan understood the sensitivity of the situation and suddenly jumped out of the window, so that there was not a trace of music or *riyaz* in the room.

What touches a chord in the reader here is the way Naina Devi's life reaches Rao as an archetypal story that she recognizes in her own racial memory, something that we know as the Jungian collective memory. "I have heard this story before," she writes. "It is the story of so many women, the story of Ambapali, of Sufan Moti, Madhavi and Manimekhalai". These are stories of women who gave up their wealth and comfortable lives "to become wanderers on the spiritual path". In what is perhaps one of the most disturbingly profound observations in the book, she says of the tawaif: "her other face is that of the bhikkuni, the jogan, the sufan" (123). Rao then asks herself a series of questions that lead her – and us – to the realization that it is also the story of every woman who is an artist:

> In these stories then I hear these women to be saying that for them, as for me, as for all of us, the path is but a metaphor for our choosing, our determination to journey, to search. I see this story as my story too, as it is the story of every woman who is an artiste. Because while all artists confront the paradox of the ascetic and the erotic, perhaps for women this is experienced in a particularly poignant way. (124)

Women writers too can find many a paradigm in the life of Naina Devi. Notions of a prescriptive respectability, an imposed domesticity, and a subtle if invisible control exercised over their creativity are some of the patterns of patriarchy *within* the fraternity of writers. They can constrain her fecundity if she is not alert enough to salvage her writerly self from these forces that lurk around her.

Does one barter the security of marriage for art in the end, is a rhetorical question Rao asks when Nainaji recounts the life of Zohra Begum, a *tawaif* who completely gave up singing after she got married. There are many questions that go unanswered, and many things that remain unsaid, because Nainaji chooses to be reticent about her life. But the medium of written discourse helps Rao – and us – to explicate the gaps to an extent and piece together the various phases of her life. "I have asked her about her own marriage many, many times...How could she have borne without sorrow, anger, despair, or a sense of injustice, the long years of silence imposed on her by her role as a wife?" (31).

Later, Rao remarks about Nainaji's marriage to the prince Ripjit Singh: "The years of her marriage were happy years. Of that I have no doubt. But in the story of her life as I think she wanted me to hear it, were they years to be glossed over quickly, compressed into brief statement?" (58) A page later, she says in a definite tone: "Those were happy years. And yet, there was an emptiness. There was no music" (59). Nainaji seems to accept with equanimity the phase in her life when music as an option "was not available to her." (60)

For a woman singer, as for any artist, sensing a self that is separate from all her given roles is perhaps the first step towards realizing that she has a calling from within. Says Rao:

> But learning, teaching and performing music provide her a space where she can experience and express a self separate from the given familial roles. A woman singer, especially one not born into a family of traditional performers, must however, renounce the home of her birth, her religion, her relationships and all the excess baggage of appropriate feminine behaviour before she can claim this space as her own. (77)

In her recent book *Indigenous Roots of Feminism: Culture, Subjectivity and Agency*, Jasbir Jain rightly emphasises the importance of this self-image for an individual and her inner consciousness: "Feminism has deeper roots in the individual consciousness than the basic fact of being a woman. Both self-image and social image come together in this. The perception of the outer reality is guided by this. The two terms – 'woman' and 'feminine'– feed on each other" (2). What Jain says two pages later, can have a bearing on both Rao and Badrinath: "Feminism is recognition of this 'wholeness' of existence that encompasses all three – body, mind and soul. And for this recognition, it also forces a rethinking on the idea of masculinity" (5).

About women Rao observes: "A temporary guest in the homes of our birth, never quite assimilated in the houses of our in-laws, there is no place we can truly call home.' (78) Nainaji moved on to other families – "the family of music, the gharana,[4] and the spiritual family of the pir" (79). In the *gharana* of Rampur, she finds her fathers and mothers in her many gurus of thumri. A woman is the eternal outsider, and Rao quotes Amir Khusrau's *bidai* song: "To my brother you give your beautiful palace, to me, an alien land." The dualities in a woman's life are assimilated through the motif of music. A song in praise of Kali that Rao learns from Nainaji leaves a lasting impression on her because it carries, in turn, the impact of her guru's own memory. Writes Rao: 'And I will wake to remember again, this strange, precious gift from my guru that brings together the beginning and end of her life, and that blurs and softens the dualities of my own' (127). Nainaji learnt the song from a hideous looking beggar named Khendi. She was "ragged, sickly...Her skin was rough and scaly, covered with sores". But stark images of surprising beauty overlap the physical ugliness in a powerful description that shows all three women – Khendi, Nainaji, and Rao – in a strange, wild bond in which music floats up as something pure and unsullied: "Nainaji says of Khendi that one forgot she was a beggar, for there was only 'her sweet, powerful voice'" (128) And Rao says of Khendi: "She travels Khamaj's landscape without map or compass, without accompanists or instruments, without fine clothes, or jewellery, or listeners," till she, that is Rao, can see the great goddess "in all her terrible beauty" (128).

In thc memoir, we see Nainaji as a gifted woman who negotiates her space with a quiet dignity. If, within the tradition of music, only *ustads* tie a *ganda*,[5] Nainaji followed that without demur, even as Rao remarks in her narrative: "I mourn that. I would like my wrist to carry the mark of her teaching. I would like to carry and show to the world an unbroken thread that links me to her, and through her to Rasoolan Bai, Girija Shankar Charkravarty, Moujuddin Khan," listing all their seniors and gurus. Earlier on, she writes about how the dadra she has received comes to her "not in a clear, unbroken line, but in swirls and eddies". There is a direct line of musical descent through the male performer. "Both blood and art are handed down from father to son" in what she terms as "musical patrimony" and for female performers, "blood and art are not necessarily congruent" (87).

Yet, training in thumri is in itself, a way of learning to question accepted notions of gender, musical form, and growing in maturity, says Rao (84). Recalling the lines of Rabindranath Tagore – "Deliverance is not for me in renunciation/I feel the embrace of freedom in a thousand bonds of delight," Rao says thumri also delights in the drama of life and leads both singer and listener to deliverance through this very steeping in the ties of the world. These are some of the transitions that need to be factored in when we trace the moving curve in contemporary feminist philosophy. A recent feminist study takes cognizance of the changes in the attitude of women. In the Introduction to *Transformations: Thinking through Feminism*, the Editors write:

> The desire for transformation animates feminist praxis. As a politics seeking radical redress, feminism is driven by an imperative for change. In this sense, the hope for transformation calls feminism into multiple and diverse existence. Contemporary feminism is imbricated in ideas of and expectations of transformation.' (Ahmed 1)

The editors further point out the highly individualized take of women about areas that have so far been issues:

> In this respect, feminism is not one set of struggles: it has mobilized different women in different times and places, who are all seeking transformations, but who are not necessarily seeking the same thing, nor even necessarily responding to the same situation. (11)

III

Women are indeed looking for different things now, and where they have a seeking spirit, they wish to traverse a different path. Tulsi Badrinath, the well-known Bharat Natyam dancer and writer has recorded this spirit in *Meeting Lives*. The entire narrative is soaked not just in the philosophy of art, but in the philosophy of life as well. There are questions of being, of becoming, of breathing life into dance, of forgetting the body and merging with the soul of the song. The novel is structured around the cyclic recitation of the verses from the Devi Mahatmaya, with the verses beginning and ending each chapter. To give a sample, chapter 1 starts with a verse:

> *That divinity abiding in every human being in the form of illusion,*
>
> *I bow my head before Her, again and again and again and yet again* (9).

The chapter closes with another verse in the same rhythm:

> *That divinity abiding in every being in the form of consciousness,*
>
> *I bow my head before Her, again and again and again and yet again (33).*

Likewise, the rest of the chapters begin with one verse, and close with another. This continues as a refrain that holds within its expanse the slow unfolding of the theme of Aditi, a young mother trained in Bharat Natyam, who struggles alone with her small, somewhat accident-prone child who also needs to be constantly coaxed into eating. She yearns to return to the rigours of her *riyaz*, to the artistic demands of her exacting guru, and to the arc lights on the stage on which she is not just a dancer, but a spirit embodying the very soul of the song that is fleshed out in her dance. In addition to being a dancer, the young woman is also a writer who is itching to polish her unpublished manuscript and send it on to a publisher. The author Badrinath, who has a Masters degree n Business Administration from Ohio, University at Athens, and who once had a lucrative job in a multinational bank, decided to chuck it all for pursuing her twin passions – dance and writing. She has since performed widely in India and abroad and participated in the Festival of India at the USSR in 1987.

In the novel, Aditi, a disciple of the famous guru Tanjavur Santhanam, is clearly exhausted by the need to constantly keep an eye on her child so that he does not hurt himself. Her US-based friend Aasha, who is not into dance, is also seen struggling to bring up her two small kids. Aasha, however, slips into clinical depression, as an alarmed Aditi notes the state of her friend:

> She can no longer summon the will to care for herself. When the children nap, she curls up in a chair, unwashed, her hair in a mess, teeth furry, her mind incapable of cheer. She finds herself sliding, sliding endlessly down a deep well, into nothingness.' (198) Aditi reflects on herself: 'I catch sight of myself in the mirror. I stare at the reflection of the girl. *Girl? Woman?* I am not quite able to find myself there. My face is puffy with tiredness...My thigh muscles resemble those of a weightlifter, developed over years of practice. (35)

> The tears start, but the sobs are muted for close by sleeps my child, his hands bunched under his chin. I have come upon a great secret hidden in the open, it seems. All those mothers with babies, idealized up until the time I became one myself, were all bravely fighting tiredness and anxiety and low spirits. (75)

This is an extremely honest admission. When depression threatens to engulf Aditi, she combats it with the help of Vedanta for which she has a propensity, as well as aptitude. It helps her understand the many contradictions in her life, and in the life around her. In a move that is rarely to be found in someone so young, Aditi comes to realize the implicit potency and power of prayers. Perhaps, she owes it in part to the comprehensive cultural education that classical music and dance can give a devoted practitioner. She sums up the contrast between her therapist-treated friend Aasha and herself succinctly: "This is how we cope: she, buffered by Prozac, I, on the seat of prayer" (202).

After a long lapse of time, Aditi sets out to watch her guru perform a piece from *Krishna-karnamritam* in which we have a scene when he masterfully silences the bells on his ankles to become the stealthy young Krishna who quietly steals butter: "Hundreds of bells on Sir's ankle lie still at his command as he places foot after tentative foot in search of butter. The cymbals that accompany each movement of the dancer, helping to create effect, fall silent as well." (180). After the mesmerizing performance, she returns home to hear the complaints about the pranks of her little son in her absence: "The joy I have carried all the way home, drains from my heart, ebbs away. Dancing *vatsalya* – love for a child – is perhaps far easier than bringing up a child in real life,' remarks Aditi on the irony of art mimicking life! (183)

These portions, like many others, reach us with immense credibility because Aditi is candid in the narrative and does not resort to dissemblance. She loves her baby to distraction and says: "I enfold him, contain all his limbs within me, inhale the essence of his being," and adding a line that is disarmingly tender: "may it be that my years are added to his" (51) in what seems to be a translation of a popular saying in Hindi. And when she asks her mother what is wrong in saying that she is tired, looking after him, we find ourselves echoing: yes indeed, what is wrong? In her inclusive assessment of some of the recent trends in women's consciousness, Radha Chakravarty remarks: "The normative value of stereotyped gender roles such as marriage and motherhood is interrogated. At the same time, traditional values such as love, nurture and mutual caring are not abandoned and are off-set against prevailing notions of 'power' as alternatiye modes of agency" (18). Let us take a look at a brilliant exposition of the paradox in Aditi's situation:

> It is a paradox. As a dancer in the classical idiom, I was taught to transcend the body. In forgetting the body, the awareness of self, through *bhava*, one comes closer to finding the truth, that one Reality. After years of thinking that the world was mine to conquer, this role that emphasizes my female body comes as a shock. (76)

New insights in feminist philosophy accommodate the very real and un-doctored response of women to the changes in their lives. One such study is Melissa Moschella in "Personal Identity and Gender: A Revised Aristotelian Approach". She writes:

> In recent years it has become increasingly clear that what most women want above all – especially if we include the preferences of non-Western women – is not liberation from maternity and its responsibilities but rather recognition of its social importance and politics that make it possible for them to carry out these responsibilities, without necessarily having to forfeit professional goals as a consequence. Even such landmark feminist thinkers such as Betty Friedman, Germaine Greer and Noami Woolf have modified their initial views after coming to recognize the importance of motherhood in their own lives and in the lives of other women.'(75–76)

Aditi has an overwhelming wish to resume her dance.

> I cannot stop now. I am seized by this madness," she says, putting on her dancer's jewellery, one by one. "I look at the mirror and see a beautiful dancer, flowers in her long, long hair. Not as slim as the Harappan dancer – one hand cockily placed on her hip – but glowing. The only time that beauty has ever mattered to me: during every appearance on stage. Passion and intensity, given unreservedly to the love of my life: *Dance*' (37).

She recalls the way her Guru taught her the Ganesha *varnam*.[6] It was as if he had "given each one of us a rare and precious jewel, very casually, without ceremony" and remarks: "One begins a varnam as one would a journey, knowing that there is a point of departure and a time of return. " (125–126) Next, she completely internalizes a beautiful *ashtapadi*[7] by giving us a feel of having gone beyond the physical expression of dance:

> Suddenly, I found a place for myself on that stage, in front of so many people, that was mine alone. I was lost, far away. Perfect, perfected, in time and yet out of it, aware of my limbs held in position, but lost to everything else. I had slipped out of myself, peace, great peace, a golden nothingness…And then the moment ended with the word being sung, the music flowed on and I returned to myself, relieved that I had not missed a beat, terrified that I might have.' (175)

After this exalted feeling comes a moment when Aditi is seized by a mood of chilling intensity when she wants to give up dancing:

> I want to extinguish it, jump on it, crush it. Wrap my hand around it and pull it out by its pernicious roots. At puja, I tell Him to withdraw my gifts from me, give them to someone else who can use them. I lay my ankle bells down at His feet, put aside the dreams of a book bearing my name on it. 'I submit', I tell Him. 'I surrender to your wishes. I accept that I may never dance or that when I do, it will be when You desire, O Nataraja, Lord of Dance. (185)

Hovering in the background of this book is a destitute woman, Thayee, literally thrown on the streets by her son and his family. She now lives on dole. From the material comfort of her home, Aditi is compulsively and inexplicably drawn to this woman and often provides her with food and water. She is unable to either ignore or forget her, even though her mother tries her best to drive her away from the vicinity of their house. Like Khendi, the beggar from whom young Naina Devi learnt a song, Aditi seems to be fascinated by the down and out Thayee. Once again, as Rao remarked about the different faces of a woman, one wonders if we are not just an inch away from Thayee, for it would take little to tilt the balance.

Aditi is deeply influenced by her father who is a philosopher by temperament and training. As a doting father, he spends hours explaining Swami Vivekananda's discourses to Aditi. "He was deeply concerned about his mother. That is the living Vedanta. Nowhere does it say that Vedanta and love of one's mother don't go together or for that matter, love of ice cream! Vivekananda loved ice cream.

Chocolate ice cream," explains her father, calmly. Given an atmosphere of that kind, even her small child stumps Aditi with a question when she squashes a head lice with her thumb nails.

> "So when the lice dies, it becomes atman?" asks little Sanju.
>
> "Er…yes."
>
> "And then it is born again as?"
>
> I decide never to kill one again, except by medication." (78)

Aditi grows up on various religious legends that influence and condition her thinking. There is Aaryamba, with her son the eight year old Shankara who would become the renowned Adi Shankara in a school of philosophy. And then, there is a vividly narrated story of Punitavati, a devotee of Shiva who is herself endowed with such divine power that her husband leaves her in fright to go in search of an ordinary woman who could be a wife. She would evolve later as the famed Karaikkal Ammaiyar. Aditi, like Naina Devi (seen through the point of view of Rao) negotiates her space through marriage without overturning accepted norms of femininity. For all three of them – Rao, Naina Devi and Badrinath – an intelligent and deep understanding of their own cultural and social context gives them the strength and resilience to answer the calling from within and pursue their art with passion.

It is, however, interesting to see that both Rao and Badrinath required a written discourse to share their journeys with the reader. About the act of writing, Margaret Atwood says, "Feminism has done many good things for women writers, but surely the most important has been the permission to say the unsaid, to encourage women to claim their full humanity, which means acknowledging the shadows as well as the lights." Radha Chakravarty in her book *Feminism and Contemporary Women Writers: Rethinking Subjectivity* says "If you Can't Say Anything Nice, Don't Say Anything at All" (144). In writing their books, both Rao on her guru Naina Devi and Badrinath on a significant phase in her life, have not just explored several issues for themselves, they have also contributed new dimensions to contemporary feminist philosophy.

NOTES

1. *Thumri-dadra:* Thumri, one of the three main forms of music in the North Indian tradition, is light, romantic, and is derived from 'thumak ke rijhana', meaning to 'delight and endear the audience' with a graceful movement. It has the feel of dance. Thumri developed through a sustained patronage in the late 18th Century, though scholars differ about the time of its origin. Lucknow's ruling nawab Wajid Ali Shah is considered to have played an important role in the development of this form. Dadra is also a part of the thumri repertoire, but is smaller and lighter and has a teasing mood. The term is derived from 'dadura' meaning 'frog' in its quick, leaping movements.
2. *Chilman:* A screen through which one can see without being seen by others.
3. *Sarangi:* A stringed instrument played with a bow in Hindustani classical music. It has a sound box made of tun wood and goat's skin.
4. *Gharana:* A style of singing that identifies a certain school founded by a guru and followed by his disciples.
5. *Ganda:* A ceremony of initiation in which a coloured thread is tied around the wrist of a disciple symbolizing his inclusion in the gharana.
6. *Varnam:* Means colour. It is central to a Bharat Natyam repertoire in which the dancer displays her command over both 'nritta' (pure dance) and 'abhinaya' (the poetry) and her caliber is assessed by the way she renders a varnam.
7. *Ashtapadi:* A poem in eight stanzas, the most famous being Gita Govinda, the Song of Krishna by the Oriya poet Jayadeva 12 AD. The poems speak of the love of Krishna (jeevatma) and Krishna (paramatma).

REFERENCES

Ahmed, Sara, Jane Kilby, Celia Lury, Maureen McNeil, Beverley Skeggs. *Transformations: Thinking Through Feminism.* Eds. London & New York: Routledge, 2000.

Atwood, Margaret. "If You Can't Say Anything Nice, Don't Say Anything at All" p. 24, in Libby Scheir, Sarah Sheard and Eleanor Wachtel, Eds. *Language in Her Eye: Views on Writing and Gender by Canadian Women Writing in English.* Toronto: Coach House Printing Press, 1990.

Badrinath, Tulsi. *Meeting Lives*, New Delhi: Niyogi Books, 2008.

Chakravarty, Radha. *Feminism and Contemporary Women Writers: Rethinking Subjectivity*, New Delhi, London, New York: Routledge, 2008.

Jain, Jasbir. *Indigenous Roots of Feminism: Culture, Subjectivity and Agency*, New Delhi: Sage Publications, 2011.

Lennon, John, Shinjuku-ku, Tokyo, Japan, *Soka Gakkai International Quarterly*: A Buddhist Forum for Peace, Culture and Education, January 2012.

Moschella, Melissa "Personal Identity and Gender: A Revised Aristotelian Approach" *Gender Identities in a Globalized World*, Ed Ana Marta Gonzalez, Victor J. Seidler, New York: Humanity Books, an imprint of Prometheus Books, 2008.

Rao, Vidya. *Heart to Heart: Remembering Nainaji*, New Delhi: Harper Collins Publishers India, 2011.

11

Alternative Discourses of Power: A Comparative Reading of Select Muslim Asian Texts

Ameena Kazi Ansari

I

The twentieth century saw the fading away of colonialism into myriad forms, phases, and contexts of postcoloniality. What emerged was a complex and complicated postcolonial scenario that evoked more questions than answers. The century saw the best of times when euphoria marked the liberation and freedom of erstwhile colonies. It also saw the worst of times when the same movements of independence engendered divisive nationalisms rather than cohesive nationhood, tumultuous contestations rather than negotiation and reconciliation.

From the Asian perspective, two distinct and significant postcolonial realities had emerged in the twentieth century. One had to do with the reality of the Cold War which had impacted the balance of power in Asia. At the height of the Cold War, erstwhile USSR and the US had competed for creating spheres of influence to further their hegemonic designs. When the USSR crumbled, the dynamics of the Cold War changed radically. There remained just one unchallenged superpower – the US. The new dynamics of this situation gave rise to aggressive assertion by the US since it emerged as the centre and agency of new/neo-colonialism. Backroom influence or direct interventions by the US invariably resulted in violent conflicts when peoples/communities perceived foreign intervention to be detrimental to their national interest, cultural identity, or political freedom.

Another noteworthy postcolonial reality that emerged was the sidelining or marginalization of communities/regions in the newly-independent nations. This was the handiwork of state apparatus or politicians to consolidate power. Once again, such stances engendered a sense of grievance. And grievance got exacerbated over time with state collusion, or intervention, with oppressive orthodoxies or state diktats, all of which resulted in violent backlash. There arose conflicts between the state, on the one hand, and people or community, on the other. While the state sought to gain the upper hand through devious legislation or brutal suppression, people and community questioned or often opposed these measures in a spirit of "getting back" at what they perceived to be the source of their torment or suppression.

Colonial concerns of empire and imperialism gave way to postcolonial machinations of intervention and aggression. In Asia, a contiguous region comprising Iran, Afghanistan, and Kashmir exemplifies the conflicts born out of colonial as well as postcolonial realities. This is a territorial belt that has seen the vagaries of time and tide. It is a region that has come to symbolize contrarieties of politics and political systems, the precept and the practice of faith, the imbroglio of tradition and modernity. The domain of colonial power came to be replaced by nationalist forces, professing and promising policies of inclusion and equitability. Ironically, this proved to be a façade of idealism which only concealed the new faces and powers of hegemonic control. Thus, great tumult and upheaval have marked the region's postcolonial history.

Let us first consider the case of Iran. It is a country that has witnessed colonial interventions and influence from Russia, Britain, and the US. It is a nation that has also had to come to terms with rapid changes which have marked its internal conflicts – military coups, monarchical dynasties, revolutions, and endeavours at counter-revolution. Each of these has been an upheaval accompanied by the rigours of the situation and circumstance. Afghanistan's history will tell a similar tale. It is a country that took on the might of the British Empire, the expansionist designs of the USSR, and the military intervention of the US. The country handed out convincing defeats to the first two; the third was compelled to review its presence there and to draw up a withdrawal plan from its territory. Internally, Afghanistan has also been witness to, and has experienced, dramatic changes in the governance in the twentieth century – monarchy, constitutional monarchy, coup, revolution, civil war, *loya jirga* gatherings, Talibanization, and puppet rulers propped up by the US. A glance at Kashmir's history will vouch for its turbulent past. As a territory, it has faced British rule and the oppressive policies of local rulers, seen a fragmented public opinion regarding accession to India or Pakistan, been the cause of tensions and wars with Pakistan and the conflict arising out of aspirations of self-determination, it has suffered insurgency, Indian military intervention, and violent protests against human rights violations by the armed forces.

On one level, these specific histories symbolize the political upheaval and social turmoil, the cultural variance and ideological contestation that define today's world. On another level, the regional belt comprising Iran, Afghanistan, and Kashmir resonates with its peculiar blend of unity and diversity. The common factor is Islam, the predominant faith in the region. This, however, does not at all imply a pan-Islamic uniformity. Instead, the region has diversities that arise out of different cultural, social, and political precepts and practices of a common faith. The term "Muslim" is used to foreground and emphasize this diversity, which is deeply rooted in the specifics of culture and language.

II

In the face of the onslaught of globalization and geopolitics, English has also carved out its niche as a language of literary expression emanating from the region. Consequently, the new literary discourse emerging from there foregrounds the specificities of the space that nurtures many a writer and his/her creative imagination. It is an imagination that is grounded in history and memory, nostalgia and re-creation, culture and anarchy. The creative trajectory of this discourse is socio-politically nuanced, assertive, and polemical, very much in keeping with the multiple dimensions of contemporary postcolonialities. The contextual specifics of this remarkable literary harvest are compared through three works of fiction that are respectively rooted in Iran, Afghanistan, and Kashmir. They are Azar Nafisi's *Reading Lolita in Teheran*, Khaled Hosseini's *The Kite Runner*, and Mirza Waheed's *The Collaborator*.[1]

Each writer shares the lived experience of residence in their own country – Nafisi in Iran, Hosseini in Afghanistan, and Waheed in Kashmir. To quote Amin Malak, each has "experienced Islam first hand" in a sense.[2] Their works appear as alternative discourses of power emanating from a region known more today for interminable conflict rather than literary expression. Each is written in English. Each is born out of the diasporic experience of its creators, all of whom are now settled in the West. Each work juxtaposes East and West with their specific markers of ethos, culture, and the precept and practice of faith and values.

One feature of this writing is the creation of literary historiographies that resonate with the flavour of region, culture, and faith. This is done through the commoners' perspective, a perspective that is distant and different from the mainstream perceptions of the powerful and the elite. The text becomes a symbolic testimony of ordinary citizens, the silent marginalized majority whose voice rarely finds a place in the annals of history.

Nafisi's text is overtly autobiographical. It takes its cue from Nabokov's *Lolita* which becomes the metaphor of forbidden fruit in the post-Islamic Revolution Iran. As a university teacher who cherishes academic freedom and engagement, Nafisi forms a reading club of chosen students in whom she sees the spark of critical analysis. The book's protagonists are young women who evolve from the art of literary critiquing to actively critiquing and contesting the repressive measures meted out to women in the Islamic Republic.

Hosseini's novel draws attention to the sub-human existence of the marginalized Hazara community[3] in Afghanistan. The novel's protagonist, kite runner Hassan, and his son, Sohrab, are the metaphors of Hazara humiliation by the Pashtuns.[4] Whether it is liberal monarchy or whether it is Taliban orthodoxy, sodomy is the favoured and frequent weapon of punishment for Hazaras. It is through Hazara eyes that Hosseini creates a narrative foregrounding the horrendous ethnic contestations that exist, and have long existed, in Afghanistan.

Waheed's narrative revolves round a protagonist who belongs to the nomadic Gujjars[5] of Kashmir. As the nomad is rootless, and always inferior to the settler/settled, it is entirely in keeping with things that the young hero of the story is assigned the job of retrieving documentary evidence that remained on the bodies of so-called "infiltrators" after being shot dead by the Indian army in Kashmir. The protagonist's terrifying and unwilling collaboration and compliance with army diktat brings to the fore the helplessness of individual when pitted against the power of the state.

III

Each of the three texts highlight the fact that contemporary Muslim Asian writing is inclined to challenge and critique state apparatus that tries to muzzle individual freedom. They are texts with remarkable contextual underpinnings of the politics and the ethos that have shaped the writers' lives and creative imaginations. Facts are transmuted into fiction, reality is conveyed through the realism of narrative, and the political is crafted into the polemical. The microcosmic world of the text comes to symbolize the macrocosmic world of lived regional realities.

Another feature of Muslim Asian writing is the conscious cultivation of Western idiom and image, as well as metaphor and symbol, to convey Eastern/regional realities. On one hand, the dynamics of commercial success dictate to a writer; on the other hand, the taste of prospective readership guides him/her. When writing is about countries and regions that have seen great turmoil, and when writers feel the need to give an inside/subjective view of that turmoil to a readership that is sceptical, then it makes good sense to adopt an idiom that such readership will easily take to. *Reading Lolita in Teheran*, *The Kite Runner,* and *The Collaborator* are about tumult and upheaval. Their creators also know that behind their fiction lie uncomfortable truths. Yet, their works endeavour to reach out to an audience that is critical, if not hostile, to the very region and political setup that the work portrays.

Nafisi, Hosseini, and Waheed have risen to the occasion by writing in English about spaces and peoples that are seen as threatening US and European interests and security. Their figurative use of language is more likely to provide the discerning reader alternative ways of perceiving text, contexts, and reality. When Hassan's skills with the slingshot save Amir from bloody retribution by a bully, Hosseini gently nudges the reader to hark back to the biblical David–Goliath encounter. The familiarity of the image simultaneously reinforces the Hazara's strength and helplessness. Another instance of reliance on Western symbols to convey Eastern/regional realities is Nafisi's reference to *poshlust*. While it was once Nabokov's special Russian term to underline the close relation between banality and brutality, in Nafisi's narrative it defines the "atmosphere of perpetual dread" that hung over women in Iran's Islamic Republic. The title of Waheed's novel finds its justification in the narrative's focus on insurgency in Kashmir. While reportage blames Pakistan for training insurgents, Waheed weaves a narrative that points to a collusion between all the players in the field of Kashmir affairs – India, Pakistan, and the insurgents. The text metaphorically suggests that militancy in Kashmir is an insidious collaboration between the very forces that seem to challenge and fight each other. It is a tale of how government presides over circumstances guaranteed to arouse militant backlash, how civilians unwittingly inspire militancy, and how the police and paramilitary forces collaborate in encounter deaths.

Another powerful dimension of Asia's Muslim writing is the premium placed on human relationships and age-old traditions, on cultural precepts, and practices. Eastern traditions honour both of these as they are seen to offer succour and sustenance during personal, social, or political upheaval. In their own specific ways, each of the works being analysed celebrates the father figure. In *Reading Lolita in Teheran*, Nafisi eulogizes her own father for daring to be different and unafraid of what this might entail. He entered politics, she writes, but despised politicians. For this, he was charged with insubordination and sent to jail. Insubordination, thus, became Nafisi's personal symbol in post-Revolution Iran. It evolved to symbolize her preferred way of life and became a watchword that defined her unconventional academic perceptions, her professional life, and also her fictionalized narrative. In *The Kite Runner*, Hosseini highlights some of the precepts and practices that define Afghan life. The tradition of *ihtiram* prevailed when the protagonist's father in the US goes to propose a match on his son's behalf. It involved the old man declaring before the girl's family and relatives that he came with the greatest of humility to put forth the proposal, that he had the highest regard for the girl's parents, family members, and ancestors, and that his prayer was his son proving himself worthy of the kindness of his proposal being accepted. Protocol and tradition dictated that acceptance of such a proposal be followed by *shirini-khori*, the ritual of the "eating of the sweets", to formalize the engagement. Another important custom – the tradition of the wet-nurse – is eulogized as a fraternal bonding that goes to the extent of obliterating the distinction between master and menial. A wet-nurse fed both protagonist and his Hazara servant's son who, it later turned out, was the protagonist's half brother. The knowledge of sharing breast milk established a brotherhood which the protagonist morally and physically honoured by whisking away his half-brother's orphan child from a Taliban paedophile. In touching upon such age-old conventions, these writers underline the bonding, obligation, and commitment that marks social interface in the region under analysis.

One of the most significant and interesting aspects of this writing concerns the portrayal of various facets of Islam. Post 9/11, this faith and its faithful have been viewed with great suspicion and even greater distrust. The changing contours and reception of Islam also get reflected in these writings. The chasm between Islam (perceived as precept and practice of religion) and Muslim (symbolizing the disparate cultures of Islam's adherents) gets clarified through three narratives. The term "Muslim" is deliberately chosen as it "allows for the individual writers conception, vision and rendition of the culture of Islam".[6] The narratives emphatically erase the perception of a single pan-Islamic history, culture, and ideology. More importantly, they reflect the changing contours of Muslim perceptions and actions in a world scenario that is constantly changing. The Muslim dilemma between the theory and practice of faith is sensitively brought out by Nafisi who offers a pithy comment on how things have changed within her own lifetime. It is an observation that is born out of comparative experience and analysis. It juxtaposes the last phase of Iranian monarchy with the period of Islamic republic. She writes:

> During the Shah's time…I felt I was in the minority and I had to guard my faith against all odds. Now that my religion is in power, I feel more helpless than ever before, and more alienated. (LIT 327)

In *The Collaborator*, Waheed re-creates the fire-and-brimstone rhetoric of clerical orthodoxy on the issue of visual entertainment. Heavenly reward or hellish punishment, it is suggested, shall be decided on the basis of TV or films that an individual views in his/her lifetime. The mullah in the novel thus proclaims:

> …Those who pray five times a day and forsake the ways of the kafir—all this *naach-gana* on TV and this dirty cinema thing that they arrange sometimes—will never come in harm's way, and will escape the high fires of Jahannum, the deep burning pyres of Hell! (TC 34)

Waheed describes such men as "God's own guerrillas" who go about smashing video rental shops, torching cinemas, dragging schoolgirl's from buses to check for nail polish, and sending them back home to wear floor-length burqas. In similar ironical vein, Hosseini describes a TV talk show scene being moderated by two bearded clerics who are asked if the teenaged son of the caller could go to hell for wearing his baggy pants so low that the seam of his underwear showed.

The writers' aim is not to mock or denigrate their faith; it seems more oriented towards perception, introspection, moderation so as to balance precept and practice.

It is also very pertinent to point out that this writing problematizes sexuality and celebrates womanhood. Both these facets of gender get highlighted through referential contexts that foreground the need for women's empowerment in a region that has been singularly oppressive to them. On one hand, the harsh realities of life that confront women are highlighted. For example, Nafisi writes of her own female compatriots who have a greater sense of freedom *inside* their homes and experience a sense of imprisonment when they step out from its confines. Hosseini speaks of rampant sexual perversions that exist due to political patronage, and despite the threat of horrendous punishment that awaits transgressors. Waheed underscores the brutal violation of womanhood that occurs when abduction and rape becomes the instrument of state punishment, perpetuated by the armed forces of that very state. Motherhood stands violated in his description of lactating mothers as the "milk beggars" or women who, due to lack of nourishment as a result of endless curfews to flush out Kashmiri militants, have been reduced to shrivelled wretches.

The powerful are shown to have literally and metaphorically sodomized the weak, especially women. In Kashmir, a governor was even called the "Curfew King" for misusing his authority to wreak vengeance on a populace for the violence perpetuated by a few. In Afghanistan, any Hazara who stood up for asserting his self-respect was condemned and banished to Hazarajat.[7] It is a hell on earth, a sub-human space that has moved backward in time. In Iran, women were condemned to death for wearing make-up or moving with men other than relatives.

Contemporary writing from Iran, Afghanistan, and Kashmir re-creates these past realities through the medium of fiction. In doing so, it evolves its own idiom, "crossing boundaries and expressing ethos in an adopted language"[8] (Malak 6); it forges a new historiography and ushers in a new canon of minority discourse. It is a canon that highlights the churning dichotomies which define the region – minority or majority, master or menial, elite or ordinary, secular or religious, guilty or innocent, orthodox or liberal, ever steeped in crisis or catharsis. In sensitively bringing out these dichotomies, the selected texts reflect environment and ethos in a state of flux. The tragedy is that this flux is viewed by the West as a symbol of what it conceives to be the Orient. Jorge Luis Borges succinctly summed up this view when he asserted that "Hearing the word *Orient*, ... we all think, first of all, of the Islamic Orient, and by extension the Orient of northern India".[9] It is a region where a standardized Islam is seen to prevail; it embodies an existence and ideology that is savage, uncivilized, hard-line, orthodox, and exclusivist. Such a view, writes Amin, is a "reductionist equation of the whole culture of Islam" (6); it is deliberately essentialist and condescending. But it must be asserted that politicization and polarization, as also contestation and reconciliation, have been inseparable from the making, unmaking, and remaking of community, society, nation, and region. It is also true that writers often aspire to create alternative discourses that bear upon or reflect these concerns. In a sense, theirs is a minority discourse which consciously endeavours to posit literary configurations that run parallel to the mainstream one. In the present day scenario, this is especially true of texts/writing that reflects Muslim Asian sensibilities and sensitivities. These texts have contexts that symbolize the intersection of the "world of ideas" and "world of practice"[10] from the contemporary, existential point of view. Metaphorically speaking, this writing subsumes for itself the role of presenting the other side of the picture, the seamier side of life. Consequently, there emerges a body of writing which seeks a place in literary canon as a literature of resistance as well as reconciliation. It is a discourse *of* the minority, *by* the minority, but certainly *not for* the minority. It would be pertinent to conclude with Azar Nafisi's quote in this context. She says that "Stories put us inside the experience of others and make us feel and see what we have not felt or seen before. Through this, you come to the shock of recognition that there is this universality of experience".[11] It is in the context of this universality that Muslim Asian writing has to be seen as alternative discourses of power.

NOTES

1 The representative texts selected for this paper are Azar Nafisi's *Reading Lolita in Teheran: A Memoir in Books* (Random House, 2003), Khaled Hosseini's *The Kite Runner* (Riverhead Books, 2003), and Mirza Waheed's *The Collaborator* (Viking, 2011). Quotations from them will be followed by LIT/KR/TC with page number.

2 Amin Malak, *Muslim Narratives and the Discourse of English*, New York: State University of New York Press, 2005. In the book, Malak speaks of Muslim writers consciously choosing to write in English, a tongue that is generally perceived to be hostile to Islam. Their agenda behind this, he suggests, is to appropriate the language of the master to convey the discourse of the menial and the dispossessed. Muslim writing can also be viewed as an endeavour to foreground the shift from "resistance to reconciliation" (11). Select novels in English by Muslim writers from different parts of the world are analysed and critiqued from multiple perspectives that have to do with Islam, Muslim identities and history, etc.

3 Hazaras are an ethnic group in Afghanistan with genetic roots in Central Asia. They are Shia Muslims, who have faced harsh repression in that country. Their rebellions have been crushed, and they have faced severe persecution by the dominant ethnic group, the Pashtuns.

4 Pashtun or Pakhtun are the dominant ethnic group in Afghanistan. Their ethnic origins are Iranian and they subscribe to Sunni Islam. Over the centuries, they have been the ruling class in Afghanistan. Prominent among them are rulers like Sher Shah Suri, of the Grand Trunk Road fame, and King Zahir Shah, Afghanistan's last monarch.

5 Gujjars are a pastoral community found in India, Pakistan, and even eastern Afghanistan.

6 Malak, p. 6.

7 An area in Afghanistan's Hindu Kush mountains where Hazaras reside. It is here that Hazaras were exiled for daring to stand up against their brutalization.

8 Malak, p. 6.

9 Jorge Luis Borges, *The Thousand and One Nights*, 1980, trans. Eliot Weinberger, The Georgian Review, 1984, 564–574 <www.oocities.org/tidbits4you/ArabianNights/Borges.html> accessed 6.2.2014

10 Matthew Arnold spoke of these two facets of civilization in his 1864 seminal essay 'The Function of Criticism at the Present Time'.

11 'AUTHOR Q & A: A Conversation with Azar Nafisi', Random House Readers Circle Interview <www.randomhouse.com/acmart/catalog/display.pperl?isbn> accessed on 7.2.2014

12

The Spiritual Economy of Caste and the Politics of Inversion: A Theme-Based Study of Three Dalit Narratives from Bangla

Sayantan Dasgupta

One of the most remarkable trajectories we have been witnessing in contemporary Bangla literature is the "sudden"[1] emergence and visibility of a body of what is called "Dalit Literature in Bangla". Over the last five years or so, we have seen a burgeoning academic engagement with this corpus, as indeed we have seen enhanced media coverage of writers and publications associated with it, and the dissemination of a small body of this literature in English translation as well.[2] It would probably not be unfair to venture that we are on the way towards recognizing this corpus as a distinct genre within Bangla literature in a way we have not yet done. This is a welcome development as it promises to open up newer perspectives and possibilities of social change. The incorporation and resurgence of newer trends within literary history is imperative for the further development and enrichment of the literature. It also promises to seriously challenge the traditionally held notion that there is no substantial body of Dalit writing in Bangla.[3]

Bangla Dalit literature seems to sport a political edge, which is indeed the case with Dalit literature in other bhasas; it also seems to take up as thematic preoccupation, more often than not the workings of caste in modern Indian society. In many cases, this oeuvre borders on the *testimonio*, incorporating real-life incidents and experiences. I shall try in this paper to look at a few representative short stories from this oeuvre and read them in terms of theme. Thematology, or *stoffgeschichte*, is a Comparative Literature methodology triad; as opposed to the other two, Historiography and Genology; it attempts to map disparate texts together in terms of content. I will try and see how certain thematic preoccupations allow us to map the texts concerned together within a comparative frame that can be productive for understanding this genre as a whole.

Bimalendu Haldar's "Chhobol", Jatin Bala's "Fatna", and Shyamal Pramanik's "Charanpurer Charandas" are the stories that may be identified as belonging to this genre of Bangla Dalit writing. These stories attempt, in different ways and to different degrees, to interrogate, or at least to problematize traditional notions of social hierarchy and repressive structures within society. The narratives sometimes end up highlighting the economic and caste repressions that feed off and sustain each other, and use space in innovative and distinct ways to highlight the bahujan Dalit realities. Again, the "body" seems to figure as an important *motif* in all these texts, as well as a site of contest, on which various repressive discourses are performed, and also through which the subjectivity of the repressed is often asserted.

Physical space is often used effectively and is often imbued with deeper structures of significance in Bangla Dalit writing. Often, writers situate their stories in isolated, rural, or suburban spaces, where one lacks the metropolitan anonymity that the city sometimes offers the Dalit. That is not to say, of course, that caste discrimination is absent or even less acute in the city; there are several stories in Bangla Dalit writing archive that testifies to this fact. However, the city, with its enhanced access to education, its promise of anonymity, and its plurality of spaces, seems to sometime offer options and sites of resistance that are absent elsewhere. This is so true of a story like Manju Bala's "Dain," for instance, where the city-bred Swapna tries to egg on *Ghanar Ma* or Ghana's Mother, to challenge the caste-based exploitation that reigns supreme in her village. Spaces like *Vanrajya* in Manoranjan Byapari's "Ribaj," isolated as they are from "civilization", seem to offer fewer options.

Bimalendu Haldar's "Chhobol" too is located in a space deep in the hinterland. The ambiguity of geographical knowledge on the part of the protagonist makes the repression particularly difficult to challenge, and the resistance all the more desperate and significant. Asmani, the protagonist of the story, lives somewhere deep in the Sunderbans. Her understanding of her spatial location and of alternative worlds is at best vague and incomplete as is highlighted right at the beginning of the story – "Asmani will leave. A shallow river flows in front of her, and modest forest on its other bank … and beyond that? She has no clue about what lies beyond. But she has heard that beyond the forest stretches out undulating paddy fields, and beyond that is the big dam. A long walk along the dam brings one to the jetty, and from there one can take the ferry to places like Sonakhali, Patharpratima, and Canning. And then…? Then Asmani will find her own way … But what if she can't?" The landscape of the Sunderbans and the dire poverty rampant in the region – a place where survival spells an everyday struggle against an unyielding natural world – are reiterated in the way the author sketches the lifestyle of the Asmanis: "Asmani probably did not have a morsel all day. There is nothing at home. That is the way things are most days. Sometimes she spends the whole day wading into ditches and marshes and gathering leaves and herbs. Sometimes she gathers waterlily stalks, boils them and salts them".

The *stoff* of "Fatna" is quite different from that of "Chhobol"; yet we see how space again figures as a potent entity in that story as well. "Chhobol" is at one level about an unequal marriage – Asmani is married to the old Kusho Buro, who seems to have taken advantage of her poverty and orphaned status to get married to her. Kusho Buro, many years older than Asmani, had given her shelter when her father had passed away and all his possessions were confiscated by those from whom he had borrowed money. Later, he had married her. During the course of the story, Kusho Buro, a poor snake-charmer, develops an intimacy with Gobindo, son of Naresh Chakraborty, the village chief, and sells her off to him for ten thousand rupees. The irony of the situation and the caste tensions are brought out in Asmani's wonder as she sees her husband and Gobindo sharing confidences and having a good time together: "A Brahmin son's befriending low-caste snake charmers like them!" The attempt to abuse caste-class privilege and sexually exploit Asmani provides the main *stoff* of the story. The story also ends up sketching a complicated politics of domesticity, with Asmani finally exacting revenge on Gobindo and fleeing the cursed space, carrying with her Kusho Buro, the very husband who had sold her into slavery. Is this a gesture of affection born out of an understanding of the circumstances that had forced Kusho Buro into such a situation, or is it an act of self-preservation committed with the understanding that Kusho Buro perhaps has something she does not have, that is, a knowledge of geography, of how to get away from that accursed place where "all the people have turned into snakes, leeches and bloodthirsty tigers?" There is a certain ambiguity here as the reader is left to draw her or his own conclusion in this matter.

There is no room for such a politics of domesticity to manifest itself in Jatin Bala's remarkable story, "Fatna." The story focuses single-mindedly on the life of a character called Rajen. Rajen wages an unending struggle for survival as he teams up with his mongrel in his everyday search for food. There is hardly any human interaction in the story; in fact, Rajen's life is predicated upon an engagement with the natural world rather than the human world, with beasts rather than human beings. Yet, what ties this story with "Chhobol" is, among other things surely, the important role that landscape plays in it. "Fatna" evidences an intense engagement with nature, bland and unforgiving. This story is no paean to the beauties of the natural world; Rajen's engagement with nature is an engagement of convenience – he is a scavenger, and the vultures in the sky and the mongrel, Tepi, by his side, share a peculiar bond with him purely because they are accomplices in their battle for survival. Thus, "…the first thing he does after waking up is look up at the sky. After rubbing his eyes a couple of times, he looks up into the vast emptiness, scanning the sky for vultures. He spends hours staring at the blazing blue sky".

Rajen, the scavenger, spends the whole day scanning the sky for vultures because from where they descend, and he can estimate which *bhagar* has a new body. He follows the trail of the vulture, aided by his dog, and locates the carcass. He flays it as the vultures wait patiently at his side; once he is done, the vultures do the rest of the job. He then sells the skin to the merchant; that is how he ekes out a hand-to-mouth existence. Rajen's absorption in the animal world and his near-excommunication from the human world are significant as this seems to highlight the bestial existence that the society has assigned to him. There is an almost symbiotic relationship that seems to accrue between Rajen and the scavenging birds. The sheer isolation in which the dwelling of Rajen, the "low"-caste scavenger, is located, and the utter lack of interaction with humankind (except the merchant to whom he sells the hide – Rajen's family is mentioned in the story, but we do not encounter any interaction of any sort between Rajen and the rest of the family) in the entire story gives it a particular and unique charge.

The story is set at a time when Rajen cannot seem to find any corpses. What the vultures finally lead him to is a living cow, old and ailing, tied to a tree in the middle of nowhere, with nobody around. Plagued by sheer hunger, he looks around furtively and flays the living cow hastily and makes off with the hide. The vultures then close in. For him, as for so many of those whom we have deprived and disempowered, this is a struggle for survival, no less. And it is this struggle for survival that Dalit writers like Jatin Bala seem to try and portray in their fiction.

The cow, of course, functions as a symbol of the Brahmanical order, and the dilemma that Rajen faces, and indeed, his decision to kill the cow so that he and his family can survive, is charged with a particular significance. The claims of the body come out on top here and trump any hegemonic ideologies that Rajen may have been up against. The necessities of the world here and now are clearly shown to be imbued with greater immediacy and power than the claims of a world after. There is, thus, a clear secular charge to this story – "secular" used here in the original sense of the world – and this seems to be largely true of a substantial body of Dalit literature written in Bangla.

The Dalit "body" figures as a site of contest in different ways in the archive of Dalit literature. In the stories we are looking at, it figures, among others, as a site of resistance – one that compels and makes it possible for the Dalit to challenge discourses of power. An example of the same is to be found in the treatment of this theme in "Fatna" as we have seen. But the body also figures sometimes as an object of "higher"-caste desire in a matrix that brings together the economics of caste, class, and gender. In such cases, too, the body is often turned into a site of resistance – the very intended site of repression is turned into the site where rebellion is manifested. This is the case with "Chhobol" as well. Gobindo's sexual advances on Asmani repel her at first, but she soon realizes that this provides her the perfect opportunity not just to extract revenge but to transgress the boundaries of the space within which she finds herself imprisoned. In a move that reiterates her claim to subjectivity, she seems to succumb to Gobindo's advances; indeed, it is she who seems to take the initiative and uses her body and her sexuality to punish her oppressors and decimate them, and in the process, opening up the possibility of a new life somewhere else for herself and her husband. An almost identical strategy is used by Seema in Mahitosh Biswas' story called "Hishab".

The body is again highlighted in Shyamal Pramanik's "Charanpurer Charandas" though in a very different way. The mother's sufferings and their physical manifestations make Charandas, the child, more palpably aware of the differences between the haves and the have-nots, and make him more determined to breach the caste-class barrier. The story encapsulates Charandas' life story and resonates with Ambedkar's call to educate, organize, and agitate. It highlights how education holds the key for breaking out of the circle of caste-based discrimination, and how "class" can empower one to fight the caste system in modern India.

This story is also important for other reasons. In Charandas' quest for education, and through it, for economic prosperity, lies another story. It provides the narrator the opportunity to lay bare the discourses of caste that often taint our education system. College and office spaces, in spite of their association with education, are not free from caste discrimination, Charandas discovers. And it is finally through another move that Charandas seeks redemption. The story ends with a mass conversion; Charandas and the other inhabitants of Charanpur convert to Buddhism as a mark of protest – the only way they can fight the workings of caste seems to be through a rejection of the very religion which engendered and sustained the discourse of caste. It is the ultimate act of rebellion through which the protagonist leaves his mark on history, a history that refuses to otherwise acknowledge the caste system, as it refuses to acknowledge the contribution of those who fought the caste system to build a modern India.

We can appreciate now that Dalit writing in Bangla seems to powerfully textualize themes of repression and resistance as it engages with the workings of caste in contemporary India in different ways. This body of literature seems to hold the potential of yielding more nuanced understanding of certain disconcerting aspects of contemporary India as well as of the relationship between society and literature in our times.

NOTES

1 There is, of course, nothing sudden about its emergence. This body of literature has been produced over a certain period of time in Bangla. However, it has remained largely outside the ken of academia, and largely marginalized in terms of the visibility it has commanded in mainstream media. There could be different explanations for this, but investigating those explanations lies beyond the purview of this paper.

2 *Survival and Other Stories: Bangla Dalit Fiction in Translation*, edited by Indranil Acharya and S. P. Singha, emerging out of a project initiated by Vidyasagar University, and published by Orient Blackswan in 2012, was probably one of the first such anthologies to command widespread visibility. Several such volumes are currently under preparation and are expected to be published soon by various publication houses.

3 While the concept of a Dalit literature has been in vogue for several decades, it has traditionally been associated with bhasas such as Marathi, Gujarati, Tamil, and Telugu but has seldom been used in the context of Bangla.

REFERENCES

Bala, Jatin. "Afloat." (translation of "Fatna"). Tr. Sudeshna Basak. Accepted for publication in Tutun Mukherjee et al. eds., *The Oxford Anthology of Dalit Writing from Eastern India.*

Bapari, Manoranjan. "Custom." Tr. Sayantan Dasgupta. *ibid.*

Biswas, Mahitosh. "Accounts." Tr. Sreejata Mazumdar. *ibid.*

Haldar, Bimalendu. "Snake-strike" (translation of "Chhobol"). Tr. Soumyadip Das. *ibid.*

Pramanik, Shyamal. "Charandas of Charanpur" (translation of "Charanpurer Charandas") Tr. Srabasti Dey and Rohit Dattaray. *ibid.*

13

L'Ecriture feminine: Writing from the Margins

Rachel Bari

My thought and my writing are one thing. It's like breathing. I don't re-breathe a breath ... Everything I have – my intellect, my experience, my feelings have been used ... Language is a very reflexive thing for me. So I don't know if I've broken them (rules)[1]

— *Arundhati Roy*

I

Speech, writing, images, myths, and rituals are signifying practices. Men and women appropriate the grammar of a language to express themselves differently from each other. Helene Cixous says that nearly "...the entire history of writing is confounded with the history of reason" (879). Unlike men, women are relegated to the realm of emotions and feelings, not reason. The argument, therefore, develops between the two: Reason and Emotion. The language learnt by a woman is a "given"; it does not emanate from her self. Her self is also a "given". So, what happens to language? She is distanced from her body, and if she cannot feel the presence of the body in her language, then how does she speak and what does she write? How many times does a woman feel the ground, and how many times her words give away when she is compelled to speak, yet cannot do so? As language is a medium fashioned for male purposes; it can at no point of time belong to a woman. She, thus, remains uncomfortable with its structure and usage. Why is a car always "she" and why is the river also always so? What is the rationale behind such constructions? Yet a woman learns to speak this language and live the body given to her. She is both Kristeva's *hysterix*[2] and Irigaray's *mysterix.*[3]

Helene Cixous challenged women to write themselves out of the world men constructed for them. Women need to re-frame language, push out rules, and rebel to allow the innate quintessential, pre-oedipal language to emerge. She first coined the word *Ecriture feminine* where she asserted that "women must write their self; must write about women and bring women to writing, from which they have been driven away as violently as from their bodies" (875). Elaine Showalter defines this movement as "the inscription of the feminine body and female difference in language and text" (249). Cixous claims that by writing their selves women will be able to return to the body which has been more than confiscated from her: "Censor the body and you censor breath and speech at the same time. Write your self; your body must be heard" (880). However, as Cixous explains, it is impossible to arrive at a neat definition, or to develop a theory relating to the term: "It is impossible to define a feminine practice of writing and this is an impossibility that will remain, for this practice will never be theorized, enclosed, coded – which doesn't mean that it doesn't exist. But it will surpass the discourse that regulates the phallocentric system" (883).

The French term *l'ecriture feminine* may thus be understood properly. In the French–English dictionaries, "writing" is equivalent to *ecriture.* The contemporary critical use of this term dates from Roland Barthes's extension of the meaning of the French term in *Le Degre'Zero'de l'ecriture* (1935), which in English translates into *Writing Degree Zero.* In an article on *ecriture,* Ann Banfield has named other texts which have contributed to the emergence of this term. The translators of Barthes point out that although in everyday French *ecriture* normally means only "handwriting" or "the art of writing", it is used here in a strictly technical sense to denote a new concept (7). This new concept has to be explained with reference to

Barthes' setting of *ecriture* in opposition to literature. This distinction is related to what is made out of the "lisible" and "scriptable", or as rendered in English translation, between "readerly' and "writerly" texts. Banfield points out that the distinction between *ecriture* and literature is more striking in French because prose fiction in French has appropriated to itself certain grammatical characteristics which distinguish it from other forms of writing. For Barthes, "writing zero degree is a colourless writing, freed from all bondage to a pre-ordained state of language" (83); it represents an attempt "to go beyond literature by entrusting one's fate to a sort of basic speech, equally far from living languages and from literary language proper" (83). Now, can this be applicable to non-French readers? Ann Banfield says that although the grammatical markers of *ecriture* are not so apparent in English, nonetheless the term points to a writing characterized by "absence" – an absence of the marks of literature, of human agency, which is not limited to French language or culture. She says further, "*Ecriture* as substantive is a product now divorced from the person and activity of its producer," it is "the name for the coming to language of a knowledge which is not personal" (13).

Theories of *ecriture* appealed to the Structuralists who were keen to stress the depersonalized systematics of Langue and eager to reject views which saw human presence and origins in language. To Elaine Showalter, *ecriture* feminine is "the inscription of the feminine body and female difference in language and text" (249) *Ecriture* feminine is more of a description of an ideal and future achievement rather than a particular type of writing. It is not that this is a new concept; there were a few precursors also. Virginia Woolf, for instance, in her essay "Women and Fiction" wrote way back in 1929:

> But it is still true that before a woman can write exactly as she wishes to write, she has many difficulties to face. To begin with, there is the technical difficulty – so simple, apparently; in reality, so baffling – that the very form of the sentence does not fit her. It is a sentence made by men; it is too loose, too heavy, too pompous for a woman's use.

Woolf says that a woman must "alter and adapt" the current sentence until she can write one that "takes the natural shape of her thought without crushing or distorting it" (145). The problem here would be that a woman must first be taught to think her thoughts. And thinking her thoughts is learning to re-condition a mind and thought process that has been conditioned since times immemorial. This is surely a tough job, but it is not entirely impossible. Even a cursory look at a few novels by women writers across continents will open up a vista of experience which would tell us that things are changing silently. As always, things have always been going on but little is noticed or highlighted.

II

I would like to focus now on this issue and engage with the problematic of language as used by these writers. For this purpose, I have chosen to consider three different texts – Arundhati Roy's *The God of Small Things*, Toni Morrison's *The Bluest Eye,* and Judith Katzir's *Closing the Sea*. Toni Morrison's *The Bluest Eye* opens as follows:

> Here is the house. It is green and white. It has a red door. It is very pretty. Here is the family. Mother, Father, Dick, and Jane live in the green-and-white-house. They are very happy. See Jane. She has a red dress. She wants to play. Who will play with Jane? ...
>
> Here is the house it is green and white it has a red door it is very pretty here is the family mother father dick and jane live in the green-and-white house they are very happy see jane she has a red dress she wants to play who will play with jane…
>
> here is the house it is green and white it hasared door it is very pretty here is the family mother father dick and jane live in the green-and-hey are very happy see jane she has a red dresss he wants to play who will play with jane...

The entire paragraph is not being quoted here because these few lines would suffice to lay before us the way language can be used, and handled to communicate what the writer wishes to communicate. Linguistic technicalities apart, what strikes one is the way in which a novel, as a text, attempts to strike a balance and reconcile with words, thoughts, feelings, and emotions. It would be noticeable that every speech/expression subverts the established rules of language. Take away, for example, the usual spacing pattern between two known words to see that they become unfamiliar. It is only when the mind adjusts itself to what one has learnt, one may read the words correctly and coherently. This implies that meanings change when the elements of unfamiliarity are made to creep in. If we keep repeating a word for a long time (take any word), we would find that a particular word sounds strange and unfamiliar, and it is then that we go into how this particular word could have come up with that kind of meaning. The rest becomes easy thereafter. In Toni Morrison's *The Bluest Eye*, however, the situation is different. The initial subversion of the accepted norms of language should prepare us for what has to follow in the pages to come.

The novel begins "Quiet as it's kept…" and Morrison herself says in the "Afterword" to the novel that this opening phrase "has several attractions" for her. It is not only "familiar" but also "conspiratorial". This takes on an added significance when we take into consideration the political climate of the times, that is, the mid and late nineteen sixties which happened to be a time of great upheaval in the lives of the black people. The publication of the book "involved the exposure: the writing was the disclosure of secrets, secrets we shared and those withheld from us by ourselves and by the world outside the community" (*The Bluest Eye* 169). Morrison further says that this phrase is also a figure of speech. It is deliberately chosen because it is "speakerly". It suggests the framework of black woman's writing which is a "whisper" that the teller knows which others do not know. "The intimacy I was aiming for, the intimacy between the reader and the page, could start up immediately because the secret is being shared..." (169) What she says next is quite significant: "Sudden familiarity or instant intimacy seemed crucial to me. I did not want the reader to have time to wonder". Further, "What do I have to do, to give up, in order to read this? Because I know (and the reader does not – he or she has to wait for the second sentence) that this is a terrible story about things one would rather not know anything about" (169). Here is a writer who writes not only as a writer but also as a reader, a writer who manipulates, quite masterfully, the received language to communicate a cultural context rendered in that very language. Is it that whoever spells out *ecriture* feminine is always biological?

If, on the one hand, Morrison does in a way succeed in subverting language, in yet another way, she voices her difficulties trying to portray something feminine. Let me quote an extract:

> The shattered world I built, is pieces held together by seasons in childtime and commenting at every turn on the incompatible and barren white-family primer, does not in its present form handle effectively the silence at its center: the void that is Pecola's "unbeing". It should have had a shape – like the emptiness left by a boom or a cry. It required sophistication unavailable to me, and some deft manipulation of the voices around her. She is not seen by herself until she hallucinated a self...
>
> Also, although I was pressing for a female expressiveness, it eluded me for the most part, and I had to content myself with female personae because I was not able to secure throughout the work the feminine subtext that is present in the opening sentence (the women gossiping, eager and aghast in "Quiet as it's kept') The shambles this struggle became is most evident in the section on Pauline Breedlove, where I resorted to two voices, hers and the urging narrator's both of which are extremely unsatisfactory to me. It is interesting to me now what where I thought I would have the most difficulty subverting the language to a feminine mode, I had the least, connecting Cholly's "rape" by the whiteman to his own of his daughter. This most masculine act of aggression becomes feminized in my language, "passive"...(172).

In "speakerly," "aural," and "colloquial" language, Morrison subverts the familiar to reveal something different in another cultural context. She attempts to "shape a silence while breaking it" and "transfigures the complexity and the wealth of Black American culture into a language worthy of the culture" (172).

Across the seas, we have yet another way of treating language. Arundhati Roy's *The God of Small Things* has these words on a single page: "For Mary Roy who grew me up..." The ease with language begins here:

> Gentle half-moons have gathered under their eyes and they are as old as Ammu was when she died.
> Thirtyone.
> Not old,
> Not young.
> But a viable die-able age. (3)

We might question: "Where are the rules of the language since it is partly poetry, partly prose, a mode of reflexive expression, like breathing. For the children, the funeral is "Dus to dus to dus to dus to dus" (7). And Estha spontaneously can utter "NAIDNI YUB, NAIDNI EB" (Be Indian, buy Indian) (58) Reading backwards, it is a child's world, detached and distanced from the absolute conditioning of the human mind. Mis Mitten had complained that the twins had nataS in therir seye (Satan in their eyes) (60). What happens next is equally interesting. They were made to write:

> *In future we will not read backwards. In future we will not read backwards.*
> A hundred times. Forwards.
> 'SsenetiloP,' he said. 'SsenetiloP, ecneideb**O**,'
> 'ytlayo**L**, ecnegillentn**I**,' Rahel said.
> 'ysetruo**C**.'
> 'ycneiciff**E**.'(**P**oliteness, **O**bedience, **L**oyalty, **I**ntelligence, **C**ourtesy, **E**ffeciency) In other
> words, POLICE.(60)

What is important is not what the Police stands for but the sheer novelty in having to write, or type words and letters which your fingers and mind are not accustomed to. In other words, it is unconditioning the conditioned mind and limbs. The sheer arrogance with which Roy uses language is surprising. Caution thrown to winds, the only need is to communicate, not just to create meanings, and to configure culture and the conditioning of the grown up people and children. *The God of Small Things* is a book that comes alive with a language unconditioned.

Yehudit Katzir better known as Judith Katzir's *Closing the Sea* is yet another work which needs a mention in this context. It is book comprising four novellas, *Schlaffstudne, Fellini's Shoes, Disneyel, and Closing the Sea. Schlaffstudne* begins:

> Once, when the summer vacation stretched over the whole summer and tasted of sand and smelled of grapes and a redheadsun daubed freckles on your face and, after Sukkot, the wind whistled into a gang of clouds and we galloped home through the ravine in a thunderstorm and the rain stabbed your tongue with mint and pine and the neighborhood dogs set up a racket, barking like uncles coughing at intermission in a

winter concert, and suddenly spring attacked with cats shrieking and the lemon trees blossoming and again a hamsin and the air stood still in the bus but we got up only for Mrs, Bella Blum from the Post Office, a dangerous-child-snatcher who comes to us in bed at night with the wild gray hair of a dangerous-child-snatcher and narrow glasses on the tip of the sharp-as-red-pencil nose of a dangerous-child-snatcher and who smiles with the cunning flattery of a dangerous-child-snatcher and poles dry-ice fingers into our faces, and only if we'd give her all the triangular stamps would we somehow be saved or if we prayed to God, who disguised himself as a clown in the Hungarian circus and rocked, balancing himself on the tightrope under the blue canvas of the rent, in high-heeled shoes and wide red-and-white checked pants and then he as terrible in school and the teachers called the father said to him, Albert, you're seventeen years-old now, not a child, what will become of you, but when he was twenty-six he met Lenin and Churchill and showed them the theory of relativity and there were a lot of discussions, and he became famous all over the world, so when I hear about abortions I say, Who knows what can come out of that child, why kill a human being. Misha sighed again and lit a cigarette... (*Closing the Sea* 5–6)

Creating a new language through which women can express themselves might sound very ambitious and could raise expectations, which if not fulfilled could have very disastrous effects. But (to borrow from Irigaray again) the aim is to utilize the existing systems of meanings or signification to exceed, or overflow the oppositional structures and hierarchizing the procedures of phallocentric texts. Through this, it is possible to create a new form of expression which will be able to express the inexpressible and also to create a female subject with the potential to create its own meanings rather than be caught in the masquerade of femininity.

Language need not bind. Yet that is exactly what it does to a woman. It binds and restricts. She cannot express in word what she feels. One cannot punctuate feelings and the words which emerge out of them. Rationality fails to express the inexpressible. In a way peculiar to others but natural to them, women tend to express themselves better and more effectively. *Ecriture* feminine may not have evolved yet the margin has shifted.

NOTES

1 As said to Jon Simmons on his "Arundhati Roy Web" "from within" quoted in Becky Smyrl – Biography of Arundhati Roy www.haverford.edu

2 For more details refer Anne Maria Smith's *Speaking the Unspeakable.* One may also refer to Sara French's *Re-imagining the Female Hysteric: Helene Cixous' Portrait of Dora at* www.gsa.unimel.edu.au , M. Hanrahan's *Cixous's Portrait de Dora. The Plays of Whose Voice. at* www.jstor.org

3 For more details read Luce Irigaray's *Speculum of the Other Woman* 191

REFFERENCES

Banfield, Ann. *Unspeakable Sentences: Narration and Representation in the Language of Fiction*. Boston: Routledge and Kegan Paul, 1982.

Barthes, Roland. *Writing Zero Degree (Le Degre Zero'de l'ecriture)* Trans. Annette Lavers and Colin Smith Jonathan Cape 1967.

Blanchot, Maurice. *The Infinite Conversation* trans. Susan Hanson Minneapolis and London: University of Minnesota Press 1993.

——— *The Space of Literature*, trans. A Smock Lincoln University of Nebraska Press 1982.

Cixous, Helene. *The Laugh of the Medusa Signs, 1 (4)* trans. Keith Cohen and Paula Cohen 1976 875–93 www.dwrl.utexas.edu.

Foucault, Michel. *What is an Author?* trans. Donald F. Bouchard and Sherry Simon in *Language Counter-Memory, Practice* ed. Donald F Bouchard, Ithaca, New York: Cornell University Press 124 – 127.

French, Sara. *Re-imagining the Female Hysteric: Helene Cixous' Portrait of Dora* www.gsa.unimelb.edu.au.

Hanrahan, M. *Cixous's Portrait de Dora. The Plays of Whose Voice.* www.jstor.org

Irigaray, Luce. *Speculum of the Other Woman* trans. Gillian C Gill. Cornell University Press New York 1885.

Katzir, Judith trans. Barbara Harshav *Closing the Sea and Other Stories.* London: The Toby Press, 2006.

Kristeva, Julia. *Revolutions in Poetic Language* trans. Margaret Waller New York Columbia University Press, 1984.

——— Tales of Love, trans, Leon S. Roudiez. N. Y. Cornell University press 1987.

——— *Desire in Language: A Semiotic Approach to Literature and Art.* ed Leon S.Roudiez, trans, Thomas Gora, Alice Jardine and Leon S. Roudiez, Oxford: Blackwell, 1980.

Morrison, Toni. *The Bluest Eye.* New York: Vintage Publications 1991.
Roy, Arundhati. *The God of Small Things.* New Delhi: India Ink, 1997.
Showalter, Elaine. *New French Feminisms: Essays on Women, Literature and Theory ed.* London: Virago, 1986.
Woolf, Virginia. *A Room of One's Own.* London: Hogarth, 1929.

14

Political Intervention in Minority Discourse: *Storm in Chandigarh* and *India: A Million Mutinies Now*

Maninder Pal Kaur Sidhu

The ramifications of minority issues in literature through political and cultural discourses have gained high visibility with the works of Michael Foucault and Edward Said. The Punjab problem, a typical case of the rising democratic aspirations of the minorities, messed up by the number game of electoral politics, has been probed by Nayantara Sahgal and V. S. Naipaul in their well-acclaimed literary texts. The murky politics behind the demand of the state of Punjab on linguistic basis in 1966, handled by Sahgal in *Storm in Chandigarh*, and the concomitant disillusionment leading to a communal rage in the 1980s, visited by Naipaul in a section of *India: A Million Mutinies Now*, signify the sensitivity of ethnic and political issues, and how they impinge upon the national discourse. An articulation of this minority issue, in retrospect, underscores the exigency of politically handling the grievances and the democratic demands of religious minorities with fairness, in order to prevent the creation of ugly and unalterable historic precedents. In this process, the variation in the standpoints of diaspora writers, as also those writing from within India, also gets highlighted in a comparative perspective.

The demand for re-structuring the boundaries of provinces on a linguistic basis rocked the foundations of the newly formed Indian nation, which had just been divided on the basis of religion in 1947. As the Indian government, yielding to public pressure, reorganized the states in the 1950s on the basis of language, the demand for the state of Punjab with a Punjabi-speaking majority by the Akali Dal was in perfect consonance with the prevalent spirit of ethnicity. It became a problematic category for it underlined, along with the claims of language, the background of the pre-independence history of the religious aspirations of the politically conscious Sikh minority. Understanding this bifurcation of the state on linguistic basis, as a victory of parochial politics, Sahgal forewarns against fuelling-up the combustible communal ideology, and retrogressing to fundamental religiosity by the political leadership of the state in *Storm in Chandigarh*. Gyan Singh, the chief minister of truncated Punjab, the central character in the novel, comes across as a conniving merchant, selling dreams of political identity to fulfill his political ambitions, well-timed to coincide with the resettlement of the post-colonial territorial mélange of the nation. The vision of a "Sikh Utopia", in the mind-scape of the bruised and piqued Sikh masses, was resuscitated post-partition with the demand for Punjabi *Suba* by Gyan Singh. He is grateful to the stroke of good luck when "the language issue had blended in his mind with his religion. But how could it ever have been otherwise?"(145) It contained enough propagandist possibilities to swing the collective radar of the masses in favour of division, leading to the further mutilation of whatever remained of a once geographically organic Punjab. His appeal was a blend of truth and imagination with the enchantment of a revival of a practically twice-truncated Punjab to its past glory as a land of five rivers. Dubey, a senior bureaucrat, is quick to realize the scale of the political aspirations of the CM and makes the following assessment: "Gyan had stepped onto the heights below which lay a kingdom… A sense of imminent peril gripped him. It was Delhi, not Gyan, that needed warning if India was to stay united" (76).

Sahgal's deep insight into political issues and sharp analysis of history makes her novel almost prophetic in its analysis of the provincial side of the story. Her perception of motives behind the hocus-pocus raised for public consumption by politicos is fairly noticeable. In 1981, when the religio-political forces in Punjab turned increasingly secessionist rather than secular, the Sahgalian insight was echoed by the political scientist, Paul Wallace, in *Political Dynamics of Punjab* as he posited that "language, religion and regionalism combined into a potentially explosive context" (2), and this, as history testifies, led to unprecedented happenings in the Hindu-Sikh chapter of Indian history. The eminent historian, Bipan Chandra, too, prescribes to the subtext of Sahgal's text in his explicit reading of contemporary India: "Majority communalism inevitably leads to fascism, while minority communalism leads to separatism or separatist sentiments" (163). Khushwant Singh in his monumental work on Sikh history makes a more politically realistic observation: "The demand for the *Suba* was in fact one for a Sikh majority state; language was only the sugar coating" (292).While this was a legitimate political strategy of having some share in the power within the federal system, nothing has been suggested by Singh about a separate Sikh state.

There are minor misconceptions about historical facts in the novel which are passable since they could be fictional contrivances or personal perceptions of the author. But the following observation in the novel about Gyan Singh makes a direct reference to real political events in the India:

> More fateful was the conference that had carved out the new state of Hariyana, giving him the leadership of Punjab. It was a truncated Punjab, but his to rule. He had gone to Delhi to argue for a state where the Punjabi language would have a place of pride, and *astonishing* he had been given it. He wondered if the protagonists of Pakistan had been equally astonished, even dismayed, when a country had been dropped in their laps (142).

This significant observation in the novel is not corroborated by the historical data available on this period of Punjab history. The historical recordings of the frustrating struggle involving Master Tara Singh, Giani Kartar Singh, Hukam Singh, Sant Fateh Singh, the suspended IAS litterateur Kapur Singh, Darshan Singh Pheruman, Justice Gurnam Singh, and many others from overseas are contradictory to this assessment of an easy victory of the demand for the Punjabi *Suba*. Ramachandra Guha's observation, in his monumental account *India After Gandhi*, too, substantiates the fact of the exasperating fight for the *Suba*: "It had taken twenty years of almost ceaseless struggle to compel New Delhi to constitute a Sikh majority province within India" (557). The high profile and politically aware characters in the novel are tight-lipped about the linguistic re-organization precedent set by the formation of the states on the basis of the following languages in the country: Oriya, Telegu, Tamil, Malayalam, Kannada, Marathi, and Gujarati.

The entwinement of minority aspirations with political degeneration has been highlighted by Sahgal but only from the provincial end – the unfair skepticism and political intrigues of the central government escape the writer's critical interrogation. Sahgal does not touch the issue of the unfair linguistic enumeration done by the Central Government, taking the large post-partition *tehsil* as a unit, rather than the more linguistically organic entity of the village. The systematic alienation of the Sikhs in the 1951 and 1961 census in which "following the intense Arya Samaj campaign, Punjabi Hindus disowned Punjabi as their mother tongue" has not been alluded to in the text, even tangentially (Singh and Malik: 36). There are silences and gaps on the issue of the discriminatory treatment meted out to the proponents of the Punjabi *Suba* and the betrayal and hood-winking by the Centre in the final dispensation of the promises initially agreed upon, as revealed by Hukam Singh, the former speaker of the Lok Sabha in the *Indian Express*:

> In her dealings with the Punjab and the Sikhs, Mrs. Gandhi practiced a kind of duplicity more becoming a small-time politician than a farsighted statesman. While appearing to concede the *Suba*, she first deprived it of its capital Chandigarh and then made its transfer to the Punjab conditional on the Punjab giving up Fazilka and Abohar, which were predominantly Punjabi speaking, to Haryana, even though they were not contiguous with it ("Other Side" 1983).

A. G. Noorani had, then, made a startling observation on Mrs Gandhi's intransigence, manifest in the bizarre terms proposed through a commission: "The tribunal Mrs. Gandhi envisages will necessarily have the terms of reference unheard of in the *entire history of boundary-making in the world.* It will have to be directed explicitly to ignore the basic, universally accepted principle of contiguity" ("White Paper": 1984).

The Sikhs on their part fought both the wars in that decade for the nation and the Sikh peasantry suspended its agitation for the Punjabi *Suba* and rallied to support the fighting forces in the 1965 war against Pakistan. It is this smoldering fire of the built-up angst, which gets easily fanned from time to time to suit different political motives that goes without representation in Sahgal's text. While Gyan Singh's use of regionalism to stir up the emotions and prejudices of the people of Punjab remains the core issue, the centre leaving the capital city of Chandigarh, built for Punjab, hanging as a bone of contention between the two states, keeping its interventionist powers intact, finds no mention in *Storm in Chandigarh.*

Nivedita Menon attempts an in-depth analysis of the diverse nuances of post-colonial nationalism by highlighting its inherent hegemonic tendencies, and revealing the compulsive oppression involved in keeping it one piece: "No project of nationalism is ever "completed"– it is [merely] frozen at some point or the other through a coercive apparatus…" (223). Due to the strategic position of Punjab as a border state and the religious identity of the Sikhs, the Indian Government eyed with suspicion the otherwise legitimate demand for a Punjabi speaking province. Finally, it acceded to the demand but not in all geo-political fairness. In retrospect, territorially, the state of Punjab has lost much more than it has gained, by pressing the demand to its logical conclusion, as Sahgal has portrayed. But what goes without a mention is the hegemonic political game played in the national capital – the centre riding roughshod over the inexperienced Punjabi leadership and mishandling the situation, sometimes a bit slyly.

In a major section of his book, Naipaul picks up the strands of the Punjab imbroglio where Sahgal had left them in her prescient text. *India: A Million Mutinies Now* is an incisive questioning of Sikhs with diverse mindsets that brings to the fore some pertinent human compulsions and monumental political blunders committed in the case of Punjab. An eerie sense of the wayward historical push that the reader gets from following Naipaul, through the by-lanes and village-lanes, on the highways and in the metros, is somewhat akin to the awareness aroused after traversing the terrain of Sahgal's Punjab. The account of each witness in the book is countered with many an alternative tale, keeping the narrative open to multiple interpretations; the extremely subtle and gently suggestive authorial comments push the account to becoming an unprecedented historical/literary force within diasporic writing. The realistic quotient in the work of both the contemporary writers, owing to their strong literary connection with non-fictional writing, is strikingly high. Most of the telling symbols of mental and material change in modern India, which have spawned innumerable contradictions in politics and society, have remained their intellectual concerns.

While Sahgal structured her prescient novel on the (mis)handling of the grave political issue in the higher echelons of power, Naipaul traveled in 1990 to the live playground of terror, Mehta Chowk in Amritsar, to a small farmhouse, where a militant group had just killed two older sons of a family along with the mother, father, grandmother, and a cousin. He traverses the state to meet an IAS officer who resigned in protest against the discrimination with respect to the Sikhs, a college lecturer turned a fundamentalist, correspondents, intellectuals, farmers, and businessmen for eye witness accounts of a situation, far too complex to be simplistically explained. Naipaul questions a reporter called Dalip about the disturbed look on the faces of the militant leader, Bhindranwale and his followers, and quotes his reply to psychoanalyze the frustration all around: "It's a minority fear, the persecution complex, the death wish. It's a new religion" (479). There is a need to probe the situation a bit more realistically by focusing on the role of the political parties in the imbroglio. "Bhindranwale's rise and fall was symptomatic of leaders of diabolic cults. He was promoted by Giani Zail Singh in a bid to contain Akali influence" wrote Chandan Mitra in the recent anniversary issue of the *India Today* voicing the sentiments of most historians of the present day. The evolution of the Bhindranwale phenomenon has gone down the pages of history as a paradigm of the sly moves of the power clinging politicians in the democratic game of numbers in the post-Nehruvian era.

In "Communalising Punjab", Dipanker Gupta analyses the minority complex theory to implicate the whole nation in the emergence of the minority consciousness amongst the Sikhs: "None of the demands made by the Akalis were ethnic or communal. They were straightforward regional and secular issues…The Congress insisted on communalizing these demands by raising the bogey of Sikh separatism. This immediately struck a responsive chord in Hindu hearts uneasy with forebodings of another partition". Unveiling the hideous role played by the national media, especially the leading dailies, *Times of India* and *Hindustan Times,* Patwant Singh writes, "Instead of investigating the political failure of those in power, the media, while seemingly critical of the communal passions building up, in effect, fanned them" (17).

The Punjab problem was symptomatic of many more "mutinies" simmering under the uneasy quiet in India, politically pressing for expansiveness and inventiveness in the nationalist discourse. Naipaul perceives in the retaliatory mood of the post-colonial renaissance, an aggressive re-connection of communities with their pre-colonial histories as he noted: "every group thought itself unique in its awakening; and every group sought to separate its rage from the rage of other groups" (420). At the same time, Naipaul regrets the inability of the Sikh religion to revitalize itself in the changing times to surge forward; he laments the stagnation, and much worse, the turning back of the clock, for the brave enterprising group, already hit by the exodus of 1947:

> To most people what happened in Punjab was a pure tragedy, and not easy to understand. From the outside, it seemed that the Sikhs had brought this tragedy on themselves, manufacturing grievances out of their great success in independent India. It was as if there was some intellectual or emotional flaw in the community as if in their fast, unbroken rise over the last century there had developed a lack of balance between their material achievement and their internal life, so that, though in one way adventurous and forward looking, in another they remained close to their tribal country origins. (424)

Naipaul's observations of the Sikhs remain psychoanalytical, monolithic, superficial, and critically lethargic as he evades the issue of the deceitful, meddlesome, bad politics unleashed by the Central government that boomeranged to consume the prime minister of the country as well as thousands of Sikhs in a horrendous carnage in 1984. In an in-depth analysis of the unfortunate link between electoral politics and the rise of communalism in India, Rajni Kothari traces the "planned destabilization of the Akali Dal in Punjab" by the Central government, to the phenomenon of "ethnicization" of politics in his search for answers to the pertinent question of "how the twins of a single community – Hindus and Sikhs – could be made to feel alien to each other, how a basically democratic struggle for autonomy and justice within a federal set-up [in Punjab] was communalized and came to be looked upon as 'anti-national'"(Singh 78).

Without the shackles of the mythical responsibility of a native, Naipaul races through a religio-socio-economic commentary on Punjab, carefully evading the politics that had failed the minority, while Sahgal, personally and publicly, attached to the generation that mid-wifed the nation's labour-pangs at the time of freedom, in her well-meaning fervour for a holistic vision of India, naively presents a one-sided argument. Both writers opt to ignore the fact that the retrogression to religious parochialism began with the subtle communalization of the 1951 and 1961 census by the visionless power-mongers and religious hegemons who had nothing to do with the Sikh minority at large.

It must also be said that in times when most writing is of an ephemeral quality, and the writers either sit on the fence or take refuge in imaginative fantasy and ambiguous symbolism, the frank engagement of thinkers like Naipaul and Sahgal with grave political dilemmas in their own characteristic manner endows their aesthetics with substance and merit. Trying to know India with a purpose of connecting with his ancestral roots makes Naipaul a slightly detached observer, who has never lived or may not ever live in India. In the case of Sahgal, however, it is different as she is an active participant and has watched and lived with the country's growth and development, as also its geographical and political climes. As a result, Naipaul's approach is clinically objective and at times philosophical, while Sahgal takes into accounts the cultural propensities and political idiosyncrasies to portray a more nuanced picture of the Punjabis. Time and again, Sahgal has clearly enunciated the difference that is bound to stay between home-grown stories and diasporic writing by engaging with this on-going debate: "The daily business of living in India makes for its own kind of writing. Those who live here are joined by the gut to the nitty gritty of this particular social and political environments...The ultimate battles for a new world are fought on one's own soil, and part of the battle is putting it into words" (Address: 2007).

Over a period of time, the appropriation and assimilation of regional languages/cultures into the mainstream Indian culture through "constructive channels" has been carried out with astute political planning, veneration, and reward-ceremonies to strengthen the unity of the nation. Moreover, the Indian psyche now appears at ease with a dual sense of identity. The force of regionalism was contained timely by some amount of fairness in its democratic practices, and it has now evolved into a more sophisticated form of power negotiation called coalition politics. The regional parties justify their existence only *vis-à-vis* an opposition from the Centre – the Centre and the states are perpetually sweating it out in a political wrestling match for the health and vibrancy of the democracy.

It can be posited that the complex imbroglio of socio-religio-political events portrayed in *India: A Million Mutinies Now* is not easy to unravel, but the bleeding wounds from the Partition, unethical politics, a pastoral disquiet, historical nostalgia, a general intellectual wilderness, manufactured opinion, implanted fundamentalism, and the subsequent yearning for a religious utopia, may have been the sparks which lit up the mindless inferno of terrorism in Punjab. Generally assessing, *Storm in Chandigarh* is conceived as a social artifact of an era of tribulation in a sensitive area within the Indian boundary, lamenting the political onslaught on the primordial Indian tradition of syncretism and cultural layering. Edward Said surveys the misfortunes of post-colonial nationalism in *Culture and*

Imperialism, and like Sahgal, deplores the infinity of pretexts on which humanity can be divided:

> True, there has been a disturbing eruption of separatist and chauvinistic discourse, whether in India, Lebanon, or Yugoslavia…In our wish to make ourselves heard, we tend very often to forget that the world is a crowded place, and if everyone were to insist on the radical purity or priority of one's voice, all we would have would be the din of unending strife, a bloody political mess…(xxxiii)

In the case of Punjab, Sahgal and Naipaul see no unmanageable contradictions in the Centre–state relations or aspirations – when the knots of "culture" are unfastenable, where is the question of "imperialism"? It remains to be seen if political statesmanship will continue to prevail, and if history in the coming times will lay the matter to rest.

REFERENCES

Chandra, Bipan. *Essays on Contemporary India.* 1993; rpt. New Delhi: Har Anand Publications, 1999.

Guha, Ramachandra. *India After Gandhi.* London: Picador, 2007.

Gupta, Dipanker. "The Communalising of Punjab, 1980–85." *Economic and Political Weekly.* 13 July 1985.

Kothari, Rajni. "Electoral Politics and the Rise of Communalism." 78–100, Singh and Malik. *Punjab: The Fatal Miscalculation.* New Delhi: Patwant Singh Publications,1985.

Malik, Harji. "The Politics of Alienation." 33–62, Singh and Malik. *Punjab: The Fatal Miscalculation* New Delhi: Patwant Singh Publications,1985.

Menon, Nivedita. "Between the Burqa and the Beauty Parlour? Globalization, Cultural Nationalism, and Feministic Politics". *Postcolonial Studies and Beyond.* Eds. Loomba, et al. Durham: Duke University Press, 2005.

Mitra, Chandan. "The Suicidal Missionary". *India Today.* Anniversary Issue. 26 Dec. 2011.

Naipaul, V.S. *India: A Million Mutinies Now.* London: Vintage, 1998.

Noorani, A.G. "White Paper on a Black Record." *Illustrated Weekly of India.* 22 July 1984.

Sahgal, Nayantara. *Storm in Chandigarh.* 1969; rpt. Delhi: Penguin Publishers, 1988.

"The Ink is Soiled." Sahitya Akademi Awards Function. Sahitya Akademi, New Delhi. 20 Feb. 2007. Address.

Said, Edward W. *Culture and Imperialism.* London: Vintage, 1993.

Singh, Hukam. "The Other Side." *Indian Express.* 11 April 1983.

Singh, Khushwant. *The History of the Sikhs, Volume II: 1839–2004.* 1999; rpt. New Delhi: Oxford University Press, 2010.

Singh, Patwant, and Harji Malik, eds. *Punjab: The Fatal Miscalculation.* New Delhi: Patwant Singh Publication, 1985.

Wallace, Paul. "Religious and Secular Politics in Punjab: The Sikh Dilemma in Competing Political Systems," *Political Dynamics of Punjab.* Eds. Paul Wallace and Surinder Chopra. Amritsar: GND University, 1981.

15

Subaltern Voices in Indian Epic Recitals

Rashmi Mathur

I

"In India and South-east Asia, no one ever reads the *Ramayana* or the *Mahabharata* for the first time. The stories are there, always already," (132) wrote A. K. Ramanujan. His statement very categorically sets out the fact that the two fundamental mythological pillars of Indian society – the *Ramayana* and the *Mahabharata* – continue to engage the Indian imagination to such an extent that they have found their extensions in various literary and extra-literary texts. Calling the two texts ancient in the traditional sense would be inappropriate since they have ever invoked our consciousness and have survived as living creations. They have superseded the epic genre, and have now been re-created as political treatises, warfare discourses, religious illustrations, film and television shows, as well comic books. Having said that, I would make an effort and engage with select modern renderings of Ved Vyasa's *Mahabharata,* which has been executed in more than a lakh of shlokas in rhyming couplets and in the same meter all through. It has the distinction of being the longest poem in history, more than seven times the length of Homer's *Iliad* and *Odyssey* taken together.

Obsession with this *magnum opus* whose title has sometimes been interpreted as being the "Story of Bharata" has led to the creation of innumerable versions. In the sixteenth and seventeenth centuries, it took the form of religious and mystical commentaries by monastic scholars. In the twentieth and twenty-first centuries, creative writers made attempts to re-interpret the mythological themes in order to pose literary and ideological questions. A long and impressive line of writers like R. K. Narayan, P. Lal, William Buck, C. Rajagopalachari, Ramesh Menon, Irawati Karve, Shashi Tharoor, and several others have appropriated *Mahabharata* to configure modern predicament in a variety of forms and genres. Apart from English, *Mahabharata* has been written and re-written in various other languages also. Some of these include Shivaji Sawant's *Mrityunjay* in Marathi, Pratibha Ray's *Yajnaseni* in Oriya, P. K. Balakrishnan's *Ini Njan Urangatte* in Malayalam, M. T. Vasudevan Nair's *Randaamoozham* in Malayalam, and Krishnaji Khadilkar's *Kichaka-Vadha* in Marathi. Even non-native writers like Elaine Aron in *Samraj* have attempted to capture the essence of the epic by appropriating the technique of magic realism. Recently, Maggi Lidchi-Grassi's *The Great Golden Sacrifice of the Mahabharata* has come up as a re-interpretation of Vyasa's epic from Arjuna's point of view, with Arjun and Ashwatthama sharing the limelight as narrators. This shows that the *Mahabharata* has the colossal potential to span thousands of readings and interpretations since in one of its renditions, it boasts: "Whatever is here may be found elsewhere; what is not here cannot be found anywhere else" *(yadihasti tadanyatra, yannehasti na tatkvacit)*. The twentieth and twenty-first century writers have found solutions for management deadlocks in the epical narrative. For example, Gurcharan Das's *The Difficulty of Being Good*, brings the lessons of Vyasa's epic to bear upon such aspects of modern life like corporate governance and the problematic of ethics.

For an avid *Mahabharata* fan, one of the best ways of appreciating the epic's complexities is to read perspective retellings – centred on the lives and experiences of specific characters. Such works (whether narrated in the first or the third person) affix us to the consciousness of a single protagonist and can be very effective when the reader is already familiar with the story told in the conventional way. The retelling and the narrative shift from the infallible and omniscient Ved Vyas to one of the more fallible, human, involved narrators also leads to a resultant shift in interpretation, as illustrated by John Hellweg:

> In terms of our focus on intercultural and intersemiotic translation, it is relevant to point out that there are many Mahabharatas, that there is an extraordinary plurality of texts and tellings, and that it has been transmitted and transformed through a bountiful array of performance genres both within and beyond South Asia. It has been transmuted as it passed from being recited by sutas (bards) to kshatriyas (warriors or rulers), as it came under the custody and influence of brahmins (priests), as it was transported between rituals, festivals, palaces and villages and as it was disseminated into Southeast Asia. It has been transmitted and transformed—intersemiotically translated—from many performative genres into textual versions and from textual versions into performative genres.

One such perspective which can be unveiled for us through these commentaries and ever new *avatars* is of recognizing the ordeal of the Subaltern which has for so long remained submerged within mainstream perceptions of the epic.

The Subaltern School of Historiography emerged in the 1980s. Initiated by Ranajit Guha, it is a critical movement attempting to read history from below. With the growth in subalternism, Indian History found a new and a perceptive approach that was critically needed. The term "Subaltern" came from the writings of Antonio Gramsci and it refers to the subordination in terms of class, caste, gender, race, language, and culture. Gayatri Chakraborty Spivak in her essay titled, "Can the Subaltern Speak?" wrote "the historiography of the Subaltern Studies group has concentrated on recovering the voice and agency, largely erased from traditional historical accounts, of members of Subaltern groups including peasants, tenant farmers, urban workers, tribals, shudras, untouchables, and women in these groups". Subaltern historiography is an attempt to allow people to speak between and through the pages of elitist historiography and in so doing, to speak for, or to sound the muted voices of, the truly oppressed. As a movement, subalternism has been more prominent in politics, history, economics, sociology but it has its votaries in literature and creative writing too.

II

For the purpose of tracing the growth of Subaltern voices in mainstream Indian mythological literature, three modern versions of the self-same *Mahabharata* have been chosen here. The texts have attempted to give voice to the voiceless in a society bridled by all kinds of caste, race, gender, social issues. The three renderings are Shivaji Sawant's *Mrityunjay* published in Marathi in 1974, now available in Hindi and English versions, Chitra Banerji Divakaruni's *The Palace of Illusions* published in 2007, and Devdutt Pattanaik's *Jaya*, published in 2010. The three works respectively depict the important events in the epic from the perspective of Karna, Draupadi, and an omniscient narrator, Vaisampayana, who narrates the entire tale retrospectively to Pandavas' great grandson King Janamejaya.

Shivaji Sawant's *Mrityunjay* is an epical rendering of the great epic inspired partly by Ramdhari Singh Dinakar's famous *Rashmirathi*. His narrator and protagonist is Karna, a divine child born out of wedlock to the regal Kunti, simultaneously blessed for great deeds but cursed for the decisions he takes and the path he traverses. Sawant presents Karna as an unsung hero, the epitome of all positive qualities like courage, bravery, skill, magnanimity, and honour. Sawant puts a veritable stream of metaphors in Karna's mouth to voice his admiration for the beauty of nature, a cascade of words to voice his continuous moments of self doubts where he keeps suspecting the possible motive behind his supernatural gifts, a flood of litany to describe every feeling and emotion throbbing in his heart from youthful love to extreme indignation. Beside the linguistic skills of the text, its narrative technique also needs commendation. Sawant has employed multiple narrators, Karna, Kunti, his wife Vrishali, his brother Shona, his friend Duryodhana, and the divine Krishna to unravel layers in Karna's multi-faceted personality. The magnanimous Karna who, in more conventional renderings of the epic, emerged as a shadow or pseudo spirit of Duryodhana, is here fleshed out by Sawant. His character is redeemed, his great sacrifice in giving up kinship, and elder brotherhood for the sake of his word to Duryodhana ranks him in the category of foremost heroes of India.

Throughout the text, Sawant ruminates upon Karna's obsession with his low caste. This gets apparent in the welling up of self-abhorrence when his caste was mentioned. The constant humiliation by all and sundry, even the grandfather Bheeshma calling him a petty chariot rider amplifies his existential angst. In this process, he emerges as a Subaltern figure seeking his right place in the historiography of Indian epics. He sympathizes, with the plight of another fellow Subaltern, the tribal chief Eklavya who also smolders under the same neglect from his teacher Drona, and who also realizes that the right lineage along with meritorious qualities can only ensure success in this fallible and superficial world. As a Greek tragic figure, in spite of his many noble and meritorious virtues, his *hamartia* remains the secret of his birth and Duryodhan's friendship, which he is not willing to forsake. Even when he gets the chance to redeem himself and occupy the Panadava throne, he turns down the offer and prefers to identify himself as a "chariot rider's son and not as an offspring of the Sun God, as Radheya rather than Kaunteya" (Sawant 590).

Chitra Banerji Divakaruni, in keeping with the literary trends of her times, weaves a tale of magic realism with Panchaali alias Draupadi in *The Palace of Illusions.* Her first person narrator is a headstrong young girl of divine origin, emerging out of fire with the double edged boon of being and becoming a "queen of queens, envied even by Goddesses but also a maid servant and the mistress of one of the most magical palaces on earth but also remembered for causing the greatest war of her time" (39). What is remarkable about Divakaruni's overtly feminist rendering is the silent obsession her protagonist bears for Karna in spite of being a polyandrous woman envied by many. Divakaruni doesn't deify her protagonist as an incarnation of Kali and Shakti but portrays her as a headstrong being, sometimes even a violent woman with a lashing tongue which goads her husbands towards revenge. The author writes: Her face was as striking as the full moon after a cloudy month of nights. But her gaze was that of a swordsman who sees a chink in his opponent's armor and does not hesitate to plunge his blade there. And every man in the assembly, even as he desired her, thanked his fate that it was not he who stood before her (95).

Illustrating the dichotomy between her looks and her acerbic tongue, she herself realizes that the other women around her are much more docile.

While Mahashweta Devi's *Draupadi* is a modern rendition of the epic theme, Divakaruni, churns at length the conventional epic tale imparting it a unique flavour and perspective. The author tones down Draupadi's scathing insult of Duryodhana in Indraprastha and shows her as Krishna's *Sakhi*. Being her childhood friend and confidante, he gives negative shades to her character by showing her petty rivalries with mother-in-law Kunti and co-wives of her other husbands. He projects her as an omniscient viewer of the Great War and shows her as a careless but eventually repentant mother of her five sons. He also gives voice to her mystical/religious experience, as well as her self-confession that the entire tragedy was spawned to a certain extent due to her own fool hardiness and vindictiveness and shows her dying an inglorious and neglected death, forsaken by her five husbands in the name of worldly renunciation. In spite of her name, fame, and front rank lineage, Divakaruni's protagonist is a Subaltern as she finds a hitherto denied vent to her ire, angst, and humiliation after the act of her disrobing and dishonour. The writer has also created a character who is fallible and imperfect, acting thereby as an iconoclast in breaking the mould of Draupadi as perfect. Her feminist agenda seems to be lying in bringing out the fact that women are not mistresses of their destiny. Her many roles demand attention and emotional juggling.

> The princess who longed for acceptance, the guilty girl whose heart wouldn't listen, the wife who balanced her fivefold role precariously, the rebellious daughter in law, the Queen who ruled in the most magical of palaces, the distracted mother, the beloved companion of Krishna, who refused to learn the lessons he offered, the woman obsessed with vengeance– none of them were the true Panchaali (229).

The third writer Devdutt Pattanaik has gone back to the ancient title of the epic *Jaya* with its deeper emphasis upon spiritual conquest rather than worldly victory in the form of Vijaya. His narrator is Vaisampayana who narrates his tale retrospectively long after it all happened. While Sawant and Divakaruni unheeded events are not directly related to their respective protagonists, Pattanaik's mastery lies in bringing each small incident to the fore and like a jigsaw piece, fitting its meaning within the larger picture of the cosmos. Pattanaik voices his concerns over the belittling of its epic stature in contemporary times, "Its wisdom has often been overshadowed by its entertainment value, its complexities over-simplified by well-meaning narrators, leading to ruptures in the traditional discourse" (xiv). He has painstakingly narrated each small legend, folk tale, belief, and then tried to weave it within the complete motif of good and evil to produce a tapestry of utmost invincibility. He has threaded together diverse incidents and showed them as a part of the greater design. He also eulogizes unsung warriors like Arjun's son Iravan, Bheem's son Barbarik, Draupadi leading an army of women and routing the Kauravas, the warrior woman Chitrangada and her son Babruvahana.

The author revives a number of prevalent and forgotten folk tales. When talking about the polyandrous Draupadi, he says that in their previous lives the Pandavas were Indras and Draupadi was Sachi, their common wife. He discusses Draupadi as the demure Gauri and the naked Kali, the ultimate Goddess who reigns over nine lakh deities (184), recounts the repeated attempts to conquer Draupadi by Duryodhan, Jayadhrata, Keechak who embodies physical perfection but leads to spiritual disillusionment. He also recounts the legends associated with Krishna and his various manifestations, Nala and Damyanti, Satyavan and Savitri, Brihanalla and Uttara. A little known anecdote related to the widow Gandhari marrying Dhritrashtra and her maternal family suffering the consequences, and the resultant pitiful rise of the diabolically crooked Shakuni, pinpoints to the tiny bit of worldly wisdom that demons are not born but made.

Pattanaik raises some very pertinent questions when he ruminates why Krishna doesn't participate in Draupadi's *swayamvar* and then answers his own query by writing:

> Draupadi had forbidden the very capable Karna from participating in her swayamvara on grounds that he was raised by charioteers. Through this display of caste prejudice, she inadvertently rejected Krishna who was raised by lowly cowherds. Draupadi embodies a world full of prejudice. This world may turn away from God and therefore suffer, as Draupadi inadvertently does, but God will never turn away from the world (111).

The five Pandavas, in the course of their travels and travails, encountered a number of adventures and experiences, forged a number of relations which in small ways reflected upon the larger picture of their lives and their destiny. Pattanaik here spawns the Subaltern narrative by expressing the regional and folk variants of the tale and its omnipresence in various parts of the country in different garbs. His focus on regional interpretations of epic actions makes it particularly riveting to know how epic villains and minions have been transformed into local deities. The Subaltern emerges in the form of Eklavya who is suppressed so that Arjun is crowned the greatest archer, Vikarna (Duryodhana's younger brother) is silenced so that Duryodhan can complete his dishonourable scheme of disrobing Draupadi, Hidimbi the great tribal chief cannot remain by her spouse Bhima's side due to her *rakshasa* origin, Seekhandi is ousted from family and society for his abhorred ambitions.

Subaltern whispers also appear when the Pandavas go into hiding for the final year of their exile and learn to acknowledge and respect the servants, the vast mass of people who are totally ignored in Mahabharata (202). Pattanaik uses the Subaltern lens to see Yudhistir garbed as a poor Brahmin, Bheem as a cook, Arjun as a transvestite, Nakul as a stable boy, Sahadev as a cowherd, and Draupadi as Sairandhari, hairstylist to the Queen, struggling with the inflated egos of their employers and gaining insight into the cornered position of the chaff and scum of society which will help them better appreciate their contribution at the time of the Great War. Pattanaik also comments upon the Vyas's depiction of the dichotomy of values in Karna, "Through Karna, Vyasa presents many conflicts of life: friendship or family, personal ambition or universal good, loyalty or opportunity. This makes him the tragic figure of the Mahabharata, almost a Greek hero, striving single-handedly to create a place for himself in the world that rejects him" (221).

III

After a brief analysis of the three texts through the Subaltern lens, we can safely deduce that the *Mahabharata* remains an engrossing epic and one cannot understate the worth of this old story that follows the "show, don't tell" principle popularized by Henry James, and poses more questions than it answers. Ramanujan had rightly pointed out the lasting impact of the text when he observed, "Every author, if one may hazard a metaphor, dips into it and brings out a unique crystallization, a new text with a unique texture and a fresh context. In this sense, no text is original, yet no telling is a mere retelling—and the story has no closure, although it may be enclosed in a text" (135).

The three authors Sawant, Divakaruni, and Pattanaik have given a free rein to their imagination and creative impulses. They have also not abided by the spirit of the master text in totality. Sawant has idolized and deified Karna to such an extent that all the other heroes of the epic are dwarfed in comparison. He ends his narrative after the end of war and doesn't show the post-war scenario even to the extent that he doesn't discuss Duryodhana's death at the end. He also depicts the Krishna–Karna relationship as that of a mesmerized devotee–lord relationship, whereas there doesn't seem to be much factual basis for this description. Divakaruni employs magic realism to give an ethereal tone to her text. Her Draupadi is not an ideal being; she messes up and is headstrong, doesn't recognize the devotion of Bheem, nourishes her forbidden love for Karna, belatedly realizes that the fruits of the tree of anger are extremely bitter. Pattanaik has tried to maintain the objective tone of the original text by not choosing a subjective narrator and has also incorporated the necessary moral lesson which is often lost behind the riveting tale. He has also attempted to establish an inter linkage between all actions, showing thereby the wheel of Karma in motion. Both Sawant and Pattanaik make excessive use of forest imagery which is the play field for the Subaltern while Divakaruni's Draupadi dreams and desires a palace of her own, again aspiring for a permanent shelter which is the first desire of the ravaged Subaltern.

Questions relating to what is fact and what is fiction intermingle in the three works. More than judging literature from the yardstick of truth employed for history, it would be quite appropriate to quote C. S. Lewis in this context who had said, "Literature adds to reality, it does not simply describe it. It enriches the necessary competencies that daily life requires and provides; and in this respect, it irrigates the deserts that our lives have already become". (23). It would be equally appropriate to refer to Sri Aurobindo in this context:

> The Mahabharata is the creation and expression not of a single individual mind, but of the mind of a nation; it is the poem of itself written by a whole people. It would be vain to apply to it the canons of a poetical art applicable to an epic poem with a smaller and more restricted purpose, but still a great and quite conscious art has been expended both on its detail and its total structure. The whole poem has been built like a vast national temple unrolling slowly its immense and complex idea from chamber to chamber, crowded with significant groups and sculptures and inscriptions, the grouped figures carved in divine or semi-divine proportions, a humanity aggrandized and half uplifted to super-humanity and yet always true to the human motive and idea and feeling, the strain of the real constantly raised by the tones of the ideal, the life of this world amply portrayed but subjected to the conscious influence and presence of the powers of the worlds behind it, and the whole unified by the long embodied procession of a consistent idea worked out in the wide steps of the poetic story. (Ramayana, Mahabharata)

REFERENCES

Divakaruni, Chitra Banerji. *The Palace of Illusions.* UK: Picador, 2008.

Pattanaik, Devdutt. *Jaya: An Illustrated Retelling of Mahabharata.* USA: Penguin, 2010.

Ramanujan, A. K. *The Collected Essays of A. K. Ramanujan,* ed. Vinay Dharwadker. USA: OUP, 2012.

Sawant, Shivaji. *Mrityunjay.* Bharatiya Gyanpith, 27th edition, 2003.

WEB REFERENCES

Dinkar, Ramdhari Singh. 'Rashmirathi' www.kavitakosh.org

Gramsci, Antonio. <http://www.postcolonialweb.org/poldiscourse/subaltern.html>

Hellweg, John. 'Peter Brook's The Mahabharata: The Exigencies of Intercultural and Intersemiotic Translation' Metamorphoses, Spring 9.1 2001 <http://www.smith.edu/metamorphoses/issues/links/hellwegpeter.html>

Lewis, C.S. <http://www.thesundayindian.com/en/story/beyond-boundaries/23/26279/>

Ramanujan A. K. <http://www.mahavidya.ca/wp-content/uploads/2010/08/Hallman-Katelyn-Variations-of-the-Ramayana.pdf>

Singh, Jai Arjun. "The Caravan." August, 2011. <http://caravanmagazine.in/Story.aspx?Storyid=1022&StoryStyle=FullStory>

Spivak, Gayatri Chakravorty. 'Can the Subaltern Speak?' http://www.mcgill.ca/files/crclaw-discourse/Can_the_subaltern_speak.pdf

Sri Aurobindo. "The Foundations of Indian Culture- Mahabharata, Ramayana." September, 1920. <http://intyoga.online.fr/indlit03.htm>

16

Of Possession and Dispossession: Narayan's *Kocharethi: The Araya Woman* and Mohanty's *Paraja*

Charu Mathur

Nirad C. Chaudhuri, the provocative analyst of the Indian social scene, wrote way back in 1965:

> In an industrialized India the destruction of the aboriginal's life is as inevitable as the submergence of the Egyptian temples caused by the dams of the Nile . . . . As things are going there can be no grandeur in the primitive's end. It will not be simple extinction, which is not the worst of human destinies. It is to be feared that the aboriginal's last act will be squalid, instead of being tragic. What will be seen with most regret will be, not his disappearance, but his enslavement and degradation. (*The Continent of Circe*: 77)

This gloomy forecast has turned out to be a progressive reality for more than forty million aboriginals in India. Also referred to as *atavika*, *vanavasi* (forest dwellers), *girijan* (hill people), or *adivasi*, they carry a special implication for being the original and autochthonous inhabitants of a given region forming sustainable societies that evolved a harmonious relationship with the ecosystem. This connotation of autonomous existence was greatly disrupted in the colonial times, and has not been restored even in independent India. The forces of colonization, industrialization, and globalization ever since the nineteenth century, have undermined the indigenous way of life and the hierarchal dominance of the so-called *civilized* society, converting a sizable population into a minority. Modernism, with its transformative agenda, brought about dramatic changes, forcing thereby the aboriginals to discard their age-old social patterns, cultural practices, and traditional political set up without providing functional substitutes.

The novels *Paraja* (1945) by Gopinath Mohanty and *Kocharethi: the araya woman* (1998) by Narayan, chronicle the pain of transition of the tribal people of southern India even as the country moved from colonial domination to a sovereign status. Mohanty's Oriya novel portrays the life of the Paraja tribe that inhabit the densely wooded forests of Eastern Ghats in Orissa. The first Malayalam novel to be written by a tribal about his people, Narayan's work reveals the pathetic predicament of the Malayarayar tribe that populate the pepper rich hilly terrain of mid-eastern Kerala. This study seeks to engage with these two texts from a comparative perspective, and to examine how the social positioning of the two authors influences the depiction of the many struggles of possession and dispossession of governance, land, culture, ethnicity, and identity of the indigenous groups, as they reconcile their pristine past with a troubled present.

Though both the works trace the dynamics of an indigenous community's shift in moorings, the location of the two authors, inevitably, shapes the tone of their narrative. Mohanty, an elite literary figure draws material for his writing from his observations and interactions with the Kondh and Paraja tribes in the undivided Koraput district, as an officer in the administrative machinery. Narayan, a humble employee in postal services, himself belongs to the Malayarayar community which he has chosen to represent in the novel. Since both the writers tap first-hand experiences to garner material for their work, they are both what Robert Scholes terms as "eye witness" narrators (256). The difference however is that Narayan's eyes turn "inward" so that the "self" and his own community become his subject matter, while in the case of Mohanty the gaze is directed "outward" so that the "other" and the socio-political scene itself becomes the dominant point of interest. Mohanty, therefore, sets up a master narrative that engages with developing a minority discourse. Narayan's perspective, on the other hand, is one of a subaltern that projects the consciousness of the prejudiced hierarchies of mainstream narratives. "Through *Kocharethi,*" the translator Catherine Thankamma states, "Narayan 'writes back' at all the misrepresentations of the Araya tribe in popular fiction and popular cinema" (*Kocharethi:* 208). While Mohanty's text is an attempt to understand the tribal position, Narayan's text is an act of subversion.

Paraja and *Kocharethi* open as ethnographic treats that minutely detail the beliefs and rituals related to birth, death, marriage, and the intimate eco-vision of the Paraja and Araya tribes, respectively. Though the ethnic practices of the communities vary considerably, what is common is the expression of strong in-group bonding which are both a manifestation of identity, as well as, a strategy for survival. As a cultural "insider", Narayan's inclusion of community specific words and expressions evoke the indigenous setting of the narrative. At the same time, he consciously avoids romanticizing his milieu. "The language is stark, to the point of being bald", and "the narrative often has a telegraph-like abruptness," Thankamma posits (*Kocharethi:* xi). Elaborate descriptive passages, recourse to poetry and song, and other structural and stylistic markers of literary writing that are so much a part of Mohanty's novel, are rarely found in *Kocharethi*. But it is this lack of style and craft in the first generation literate tribal people that lend the narrative its authenticity. In this connection, Scholes points out that the: Eye witness narrative in which the focus is outward rather than inward also has its factual and fictional polarity . . . . The impulse to shape, to improve, . . . inevitably makes itself felt . . . . and the more literate and sensitive a man is, the more he feels the creative pressures which drive him to seek beauty or truth at the expense of fact (258).

In any case, both the works reveal how the forces of acculturation disturb the cultural insulation that the tribes enjoyed in the past and these, initially, delightful narratives of ethnic richness turn to narratives of confused ethno-social practices. According to Bhabha: "The social articulation of difference, from minority perspective, is a complex, on-going negotiation that seeks to authorize cultural hybridities that emerge in moments of historical transformations" (2). The indigenous communities are under constant pressure to communicate with an alien and unfamiliar cultural terrain, to confront difference and negotiate with the reality of difference.

In an uncorrupted state, the adivasis were generally friendly and hospitable communities that were strong, hardworking, and honest, a glimpse of which is offered in the initial expositions of the novels. Their needs were simple and their desires limited. In spite of the difficulties they faced in surviving in forests while being totally dependant on the forces of nature, they were, by and large, a contended lot. They were close to what Sahlins describes as the "original affluent society", not for their material wealth but for their lack of want (85). The basis of Sahlins argument is that the tribal societies are able to achieve affluence by desiring little and meeting these needs with what is available to them (85–89). Irrespective of their humble belongings and at different stages in their lives, Sukru Jani in *Paraja* and Kochuraman in *Kocharethi* are almost boastful of their possessions. This state of self-sufficiency is severely compromised when the modernizing process introduces them to the Western ways towards affluence which Sahlins terms as the "Galbraithean way" where man's wants are great, not to say infinite, whereas his means are limited (85–9). It is a gap between the wants and the means that occasions their vulnerability. A generation of this gap creates threat to the elemental existence of the tribal population. The slide towards dispossession, for the protagonists of both the novels, is initiated with an expansion of their needs which they are unable to address.

The process of globalization and industrialization initiated in the colonial regime and carried forward in the post-independence era encouraged interconnection and interdependence of groups across boundaries. The introduction of cash economy, the compulsions of trade, a strong missionary presence, and demographic and geographic compulsions made it impossible for the tribal people to isolate themselves from other communities. It is here that the usual exploiters, masquerading as benefactors and state appointed guardians, step in. This is, in Bikram Das' words "in reality the entire ethos of a materialistic civilization seeking to encroach upon and engulf a primordial and elemental way of life" (*Paraja:* vi). For the tribal people, the "contrast between natural and man-made calamity is glaring" (*Paraja:* vii). In this novel, we are told how Sukru Jani's wife was dragged away by a man-eating tiger as she went to collect dry wood in the forest. "Sukru Jani suffers", Das elaborates, "but for him this event is comprehensible: it is part of his life. What he cannot comprehend, however, is the infinitely convoluted process by which he and his children are transformed from free men into *gotis* or surfs bound to the Sahukar (moneylender) for ever" (*Paraja:* vii). Similarly, Narayan in *Kocharethi* shows how all heroic attempts to resist the forest inspector and his associates meet with tragic failure and loss of land and dignity. They also fall victims to the cheating strategies of the tradesmen from nearby villages.

The agency of exploitation is multilayered and gradually works its way towards a reduction of tribal identity. Yet, Narayan's "insider" positioning grants them the dignity of solidarity and continuing resistance. The agency of exploitation in *Paraja* is embodied in the unified and unidimensional image of the Sahukar, and more often than not, Mohanty shows the deception and lack of loyalty of the Parajas towards their own people as contributing factors that lead to the plight of Sukru Jani and his family. Das, in the translators introduction to the novel claims, "Sukru Jani is not merely the primitive tribesman ensnared by the predatory moneylender from the city; he is also the quintessential man, waging heroic but futile war against a hostile universe struggling ceaselessly to accept and adjust" (*Paraja:* vi). The inability to empathize with the specific tribal situation and the novelist's sympathetic yet "outsider" perspective transforms the tribal predicament into a universal subaltern one. While Mohanty generalizes the tribal situation, Narayan resists the tendency to even club the experiences of the tribal people with those of the "untouchable" Dalits. "The difference between the two," claims Narayan, "the dalit who was subjugated and degraded within the caste system and the tribal who lived a difficult life but retained a definite identity is as glaring as day and night" (*Kocharethi:* 213). Moreover, Mohanty's use of expressions like "the ignorant tribesman" or "their heads were like stone" draw attention to his location among the bourgeois class (*Paraja:* 104, 33). Narayan, in contrast, while referring to his people in the novel even avoids the use of the word "tribe" on account of its colonial homogenizing connotation of the "uncivilized".

Development is a multidimensional concept that involves a progressive transformation of the social, economic, political, and cultural structures of a community. Tribalism and ethnocentrisms with its orientation towards group identity and rigid parameters of inclusion, resists development. This, however, may not be looked upon as disagreeable because the defining characteristic of tribal life is that it is an open, egalitarian, classless, and cooperative community which, in fact, is the natural state of human existence. Yet, the Eurocentric civilizing mission and its vision of a unilinear cultural evolution impacts the tribal lives and provides them with stepping stones to civilization. These evolutionist views that have survived colonialism and the state machinery in independent India have made implicit appeals to the adivasis to either adapt to the change that modernization demanded, or perish. Narayan's *Kocharethi* parodies this process of modernization. The ones who adapt to the changes, like Savitha and her husband, escape an imminent catastrophe while her parents Kochuraman and Kunjipennu, unable to do so, are left stranded in a hopeless situation. The state as an agency of development, therefore, carries forward the colonial civilizing mission. The nuances of thriving adaptation with reference to development are left unexplored by Mohanty as the Parajas are only shown as victims of a singular, and all-engulfing system of debt and borrowing.

The adivasis share a special relationship with land. Both Mohanty and Narayan sensitively delineate the tribal's changing perceptions towards land ownership. For Sukru Jani, we are told, land "was not merely a patch of earth – it was part of his body. He knew every contour and depression in the land; every thorn, every ant-hill has a history" (*Paraja*: 193). In the introduction to *Kocharethi*, Jayashree describes the tribal philosophy towards land possession: "He does not own any land, but the land is his as much as it belongs to anyone else in the community" (*Kocharethi*: xvi–xvii). Kochuraman and Sukru Jani, as shown in the novel, become owners by simply clearing and cultivating areas of forest land. Depending on the region, the adivasis evolved a mixed hunter-gatherer and farming economies, and enjoyed autonomy, controlling their lands as a joint patrimony of the tribe. This relative self-sufficiency and collective ownership of land by adivasis was disrupted by the advent of the Mughals in the sixteenth century. The British added to the consolidation of feudalism in India. Forest land belonging to the adivasis was rapidly made the legal property of the British in colonial India, and thereafter that of the state in independent India. It is this period in the nation's tribal history that the two novels capture. The Parajas and the Arayas are unable to comprehend why a man should be arrested and fined for felling trees in the forest, or even for cultivating a piece of land. Deprived of resources they traditionally depended on, and sometimes coerced to pay taxes, they are forced to borrow money at high interest rates. Caught in a vicious circle, they end up losing their land which is the essential source of their sustenance.

In this compulsive move towards civilization, religion for the adivasis becomes another site of ugly contestation. Essentially, adivasis were ethnic groups who were animists and spirit worshipers, and did not subscribe to any religious faith. Forces of acculturation visited the adivasis in different guises to drag them within the religious fold. Narayan is forthright in his comments when he says:

> The Christians came and started English medium schools. They said worshipping stones and trees was wrong. Then the Rashtriya Swayamsevak Sangh (RSS) and Vishwa Hindu Parishad (VHP) came and did the same – replaced Puliambulli and Marutha with Vishnu and Durga: ochre robes replaced the gowns of the priests and nuns. No one was really interested in us as people. (*Kocharethi*: xviii)

The Hinduization of names in the younger generation in Narayan's work – "Parvathy", "Madhavan", and "Narayanan" – all upper caste Hindu Gods, in contrast to the names of the older generation – "Kunjadichan", "Kunjipennu", "Ittyadi", and "Chirutha" – speak of silencing of a culture on account of religious appropriation. In his novel, Mohanty refers to the Christian presence amongst the Paraja and Kondh tribes of Orissa. The Christian converts called Dombs and the Parajas lived in two separate "streets" and they looked at each other with suspicion. Outsiders, like the forest guard, took advantage of these fractured relations within the community to serve their own interests. The creation of religious identities and their politicization emerge as dominant discourses of divisiveness within the tribal groups.

The pre- and post-independence periods saw the construction of the nation space and the fervour of nationalism permeate the imagination of tribal minorities. Pillai comments that "the arrival of nationalism and its accompanying cultural fictions proved effective in erasing those signs and symbols that problematise modernity and its project of homogenisation". (n.p.) The novel, *Kocharethi* encloses a space of transition from the colonial to the post-colonial within the imagined boundaries of the nation-state. Narayan gives voice to the grand narrative of nationalism through the trickle of ideologies of Gandhi and the Congress amongst the Arayas. The newly formed religious identity of tribal population is further tested through the debate and attempt at understanding the unfortunate religio-political dynamics that led to the partition of India. Madhavan and his fellow tribal comrades foreground their nationalist identity and commit themselves to the cause of the nation. Mohanty, in *Paraja,* on the other hand, surprisingly ignores the tribal encounter with a crucial phase in the nation's history. Either, he believed that the tribal people enjoyed an insular position with reference to the nationalist discourse, or he perceived their inconsequentiality in relation to the master narrative of the Independence Struggle.

The novels also create an alternative discourse on gendered subalternity. Veering away from the stereotypical women in mainstream Malayalam writing, Kunjipennu, the female protagonist of Narayan's novel, is portrayed as possessing a strong individual and sexual identity. She inaugurates the key theme of cultural change by refusing to commit herself to a custom-ordained endogamous marriage, and marries the man of her choice. Also, declining to confine herself to gender-specific roles, she writes herself onto the text through her participation in life's decisions and struggles. Even her representation in the paradigm of sexual/maternal body is empowering. In contrast, women in *Paraja* are used as analogues for the violation of land and other kinds of economic and political exploitation. The erosion of the Paraja identity by the outsider is evident in the migration of Jili and Bili as labourers at the road construction site where they fall victims to the sexual advances of the recruiting agents and construction supervisors. The exploitation is symbolically complete when Jili also succumbs to the sexual demands of the Paraja's most potent enemy, the Sahukar. Woman's body, in the novel, thus become the site where greater economic, territorial, and cultural battles are fought.

In its larger sweep, modernity brought forth the wave of formal education for all. In *Kocharethi*, the arrival of a teacher in the settlement marks another transformation as the Araya children now begin to attend school. Parvathi gets through college and finds a job for herself in Kochi. Against the wishes of her parents, she marries a man who belongs to her own community and who holds a government job. In doing so, she emerges as a child of the globalized world. Though her parents, Kochuraman and Kunjipennu, nurture the subaltern dream of a government job for their children all along but when this moment comes in the life of their daughter, it brings no jubilation to them. The dream itself is a signifier of a shift in the indigenous perspective and the embrace of modernity. In *Paraja*, Mohanty does not directly address the issue of education, but he repeatedly points at the consequences of illiteracy as the tribal people become easy victims to the machinations of the exploiters from the outside world. To fight those who belong to the world of letters, the tribal people need to equip themselves with the weapon of education. Yet, Mohanty does not trace the enabling movement towards the edification of the subaltern, as Narayan does. Narayan, himself a product of such a performance, envisions it as a source of hope for his community.

For the indigenous in India, the process of transition from a pristine existence of self-sufficiency and comparative autonomy to one that negotiates the pulls of modernity and globalization has been a corrosive one. It has wielded a multi-pronged attack at the very foundations of their existence and livelihood. Both the novels, *Paraja* and *Kocharethi* map out the trajectories of possession and dispossession for the tribal people within the power structures that relegate them to the position of minorities. Mohanty's delineation of the tribal position is through his imaginative participation with the indigenous subaltern, but he perceives them as passive victims incapable of affirmative action. Narayan, as a partaker of the tribal dilemma, grants his community the dignity of agency through empowerment by drawing on the very instruments of domination of the master discourse.

REFERENCES

Bhabha, Homi K. *The Location of Culture*. London, New York: Routledge, 1994.

Chaudhari, Nirad C. *The Continent of Circe: An Essay on the People of India*. New York: OUP, 1966.

Mohanty, *Paraja*. Trans. Bikram K. Das. New Delhi: OUP, 1987.

Narayan, *Kocharethi*. Trans. Catherine Thankamma. New Delhi: OUP, 2011.

Pillai, Meena T. "Translating the Nation, Translating the Subaltern." *Translation Today*. 1.2 (Oct. 2004): n. pag. Web. 18 Feb. 2012.

Sahlins, Marshal. "Notes on the Original Affluent Society." *Man the Hunter*. Ed. R. B. Lee and I. DeVore. New York: Aldine Publishing Company, 1968. 85–9.

Scholes, Robert. "Point of View in Narrative." *The Nature of Narrative*. Ed. Robert Scholes, James Phelan, Robert Kellong. 1966. New York: OUP, 2006.

17

History of Race: Islands in the Nation

S. Asha

I

Modern India represents a unique society and social structure. Several external influences, interacting with diverse social pressures, have made way for the existence of some minority communities. Minority Discourse has, therefore, become a subject of larger interest in the modern Indian context. This is significant in view of the fact that we have a high density of minority communities who constitute separate islands within the Indian nation. Along with other silenced communities whose origins could be traced outside India: the Jews, Parsis, and the Anglo-Indians have carved a niche for themselves in contemporary India. The Anglo-Indians, as well as the Bene Israel community have had a long history of struggle for assimilation, and both have risen to positions of prominence in India like the Parsis who have assimilated quite comfortably into Indian society. It needs to be probed, however, whether these communities that have been able to maintain their identities, have suffered discrimination at the hands of the Indian majority in spite of their commitment to the Indian nation.

The Anglo-Indian and the Jewish Community in India offer unique points of comparison in terms of history of acculturation/assimilation. This study seeks to take into account the historiography of the two communities as presented in Allan Sealy's *The Trotter-Nama: A Chronicle* and the select works of Esther David, particularly *Book of Esther* and *The Walled City*, as these are definitive documents of their respective communities. Considering the two texts as the compendium of lived experience, I wish to examine as to what insights into history and culture of these communities do these texts offer, and whether it is possible to locate them against the background of binary oppositions of the self and the other.

Before developing a view on Sealy's text, let me engage with the very words *nama* itself. *A Dictionary of Urdu, Classical Hindi and English* defines the word *Nāma* as a noun referring to Name. Broadly speaking, the name can be a letter, an epistle, a record, a written document, a treatise, a book of history, or deed (e.g. *Iqrar Nama*). Although *nama* is not a genre in itself, it has acquired various meanings during the course of changing cultural and political patterns of society. They are writings which range from the personal experiences to travelogues and chronicles. Meisami's observation that the historian is interested "less in recording facts of history than in construction of a meaningful narrative" brings out the characteristic feature of the *nama* as a document in which there is interplay of the factual and the fictional. *The Trotter-Nama: A Chronicle* was Allan Sealy's first successful book. Dedicated to "the other Anglo-Indians" minority community in India, the book brings out a vivid picture of the community's involvement in the plurality of Indian culture which Frank Anthony believed to be a "forgotten feature" (37). It represents a rare combination of history and fantasy, covering seven generations, two cultures, and two centuries.

In many texts, the Anglo-Indians have been described as "strange, sad, monadic people" who "live in a kind of bubble or many bubbles", who "speak a kind of English" and who "fantasise about the past" (560). Sealy also represents this stereotype but he presents a picture of the same through humour and caricature, thus giving the novel the genre of "historiographic metafiction" as Linda Hutcheon puts it. She states that historiographic metafiction denies the natural, methods of distinguishing between the facts of history and figments of fiction. This fiction does not accept that history alone is real and that history holds monopoly to truth. In this manner, both history and fiction reach up the level of discourses, constructed by humans, signifying systems. In this process, there is a conscious attempt to problematize the process of recording history.

II

With reference to the above, I might posit that Sealy plays upon historical facts by problematizing the notion of the origin of "Trotter". The first Trotter's father was of Franco-Swiss origin. He perhaps changed his name from Trotter to Trottoire to escape some religious persecution. His son, Justin, however, changed his name from Trottoire to Trotter, to appease the British for he had aligned with the East India Company. The Trotter family has been given a base of elite power as against the narratives which project the Anglo-Indians as economically deprived. Sealy sketches his family tree in keeping with historians like Sumita Chakravarty and Romila Thapar who have referred to the elitist writing of history. Justin, the Great trotter is rich and has amassed assets through indigo, gunpowder, saltpetre, and ice. Sealy's text can thus be seen as one that acknowledges the unique role and perspective of the Anglo-Indian community who are ethnically and culturally a hybrid people of mixed Indo-European origin. They have been referred to variously as Eurasians, half-castes, and half-breeds, apart from being identified as diasporic, and a small community of people. Their peripheral position also underlines the insensitivity on the part of society. The great Trotter's fall from the Balloon may be seen as the downfall of Sans Souci and the community; it is a long struggle to find solutions in the identity which is mugged.

Sealy's chronicle has a crafted sequence so that in the selection of events, there is an interplay of facts with emphasis on dislocation and digressions. Allan Sealy presents a history of India unreliably narrated by Eugene, the Seventh Trotter, who is a painter, and a chronicler of his family history, from its founding to the present day. Sealy's work is set in Nakhlau, a fictional town, clearly reminiscent of Lucknow. The fact that the house is named Sans Souci, which is not an Indian name, asserts the nostalgic spirit of the Anglo-Indians. On the one hand, there is an authentic account of monuments – Imambaras, Turkish Gate, Chowk, Clock Tower, Kadam Rasul, Moti Mahal, Martiniere – but on the other there is a clever attempt to cast doubt on the whole line of the Trotters. The lineage of many of them is questioned. Sealy's narrative is more than a historical record. History takes in the various intervening generations of Trotters, participating in wars, trades, politics, covering events such as the Mutiny of 1857 and the rise of the Congress Party. It celebrates the infinite richness of human existence against the Indian backdrop.

The narrative crosses social and cultural boundaries cutting across a huge span of time. It presents a wide range of characters who contribute to the great cultural assimilation projected in the novel. Sealy's family tree includes characters from a wide range of professions, contrary to the notion that they are equipped only for the profession of "kiranis", that is copiers (55). The characters are clerks (Thomas Henry, railway officials (Phillip), teachers (Luis Vivian and Theobald Montagu) which is quite typical of the Anglo-Indians. But there are artists (Charles), policemen (Eustace) telegraphists (Cyril Brendish), film stars (Suchita, Pearl, Queenie), historians (Theobald Montague), politicians (Jacob), radio-broadcasters(Elwin), photographer (Alex), and adventurers (Justin and Mike). The characters like Montague, Thomas Henry, and Alex are even a part of the Indian nationalist movement. The Great Trotter has wives from variegated ancestries. Sultana is a Muslim, Farida Wilkinson, daughter of a partly Muslim and partly European origin, Jarman Begum, casual daughter of a foreign ink vendor and a local courtesan, and Rose who is English.

Sealy confirms the fact that "English look less favourably upon alliances with native women than we do in our territories, though at one time they paid a sum of one pagaoda for every child brought for christening out of such a marriage so that their soldiers might be encouraged to take Indian wives" (118). Sealy's concern is the Anglo-Indian hyphenated identity. He imparts a new dimension to the concept of single identity by projecting the life of Justin Trotter and his seven generations. Justin Trotter is representative of the first Europeans who arrived and subsequently settled in India. His character is drawn from Claude Martin and Emperor Akbar. Major General Claude Martin[1] (4 January 1735–13 September 1800) was an officer in the French, and later the British Indian Army who rose to the position of Major General in the British East India Company. The question of identity becomes more prominent in Trotter's character. He is French by birth, English by choice, and Indian by circumstance.

The chronicle includes characters from the domain of religion as well. We have one Munshi Nishan who knows Muslim texts in spite of being a staunch Hindu. Justin's love for religions can be discerned from the fact that he learns Islam, Buddhism, and Sanskrit, and employs cooks from all religions, castes, and regions. The novel offers a humorous critique of Justin's imitation of Akbar in this regard. Like Akbar's *Din-e-Ilahi*, Justin Trotter contemplates laying foundation of a new faith *Din-e-Hawai*. Akbar, it may be recalled, was the descendant of Babur who had the paternal lineage of Timur and Changez Khans on the maternal side. Akbar has never been identified as Mughal Indian. Eugene, the seventh Trotter, confesses "I'm half Anglo, you know" (3). It was customary to differentiate men on the basis of colour as "Gora" and "Kala" which were familiar terms, and interestingly, recruitment in the British armed forces was also determined by colour consideration. In *TrotterNama* Justin called Mike a "country born" (319). Their identity remained Indo-British who subsequently became Eurasians. The term "Anglo-Indian" was sanctioned by Viceroy Lord Hardinge in 1911. As the first Anglo-Indian, Mike becomes the symbol of the community's miseries. He is the soldier who fought for the rulers in alliance with the British and had to abandon the regiments when loyalties changed. Sealy has modelled his characters on historical counterparts. Mike's son, Charles, is an artist unlike his father who is an artillerist. He has been drawn upon the Anglo-Indian artist and free thinker called Charles Pote, rated as the greatest artist of the community by Frank Anthony (62). Another character John Kahn Trotter is modelled after John Ricketts who presented a petition to the Duke of Wellington against the treatment by the British. Other Anglo-Indians too campaigned against mistreatment and racial intolerance by the British. Cyril Brendish has been named after George Brendish, a telegraphist, who sent an important message during the Mutiny (338). According to Frank Anthony, Thomas Henry Kavanagh, after whom the middle Trotter, Thomas Henry, is modelled, was the first identifiable Anglo-Indian winner of the Victoria Cross for his heroic contribution in the Mutiny. Henry Louis Fonseca-Trotter's character resembles that of the famous poet Henry Louis Vivian Dorezio. Gradually, the thought of Britain as "Home" is dismissed. Early British settlers were fascinated with Indigo and became successful Indigo planters, having Indian wives. The story of their oppression of workers resulted in "Blue Mutiny" in Bengal in 1861. Theatrical performances of *Nildarpan* in 1872–73 and agitations continued till Gandhi's fight for the cause of the workers in 1917.

The post-independence exodus of the British reduced the Anglo-Indians to a minuscule community fearing, disliking, and attempting to assimilate with the natives. Eugene sees the earth of India as "a miniature painting bordered with blue and indigo and dusted with gold". This is an extension of his perception of Sans Sauci which was the home of his ancestors. He adds more colour to the Indian landscape by including the greens, the blues, and the khakis for the Anglo as well as the Indians (559). Eugene makes an attempt to explore new vistas to move ahead and further his career as an artist with a call to others too to dispel all apprehensions, and intermingle with the people of their adopted land.

III

The question of acculturation by the Jewish community in India can be examined through varied narratives particularly by women, which function as windows to different Jewish Communities in India. These include *Bread Butter and Chutney*: *Growing Up Between Cultures: A Memoir of an Indian Jewish Girl* by Carmit Delman, *Ruby of Cochin: An Indian Jewish Woman Remembers* by Ruby Daniel and Barbara Johnson, *Jewish Portraits: Indian Frames* by Jael Silliman and *Book of Esther* by Esther David. This study, however, focuses on the

Bene Israel community which has been portrayed by Esther David in her writings. *Book of Esther* chronicles the experiences of four generations of a Jewish family in India and *The Walled City* traces the lives of three generations of women of the same extended family of the former novel.

The Jewish community has been living in harmony in India for over two thousand years. India has had a legacy of three distinct Jewish groups, The Bene Israel, the Cochin or the Malabar Jews, and the White Jews from Europe. Other smaller groups include the Baghdadi Jews, the Bnei Menashe, and the Bene Ephraim. According to Biblical history, ten tribes of Jews were exiled from Samaria. They undertook a sea voyage but were shipwrecked and washed ashore the Konkan coast, south of Bombay, India. There were seven men and seven women survivors, believed to be the true ancestors of the Bene Israel community. They buried their dead near Nawagaon which later became the Bene Israel cemetery. As the local habitants offered them shelter, they decided to stay permanently in the Konkan villages, instead of trying to make a place in the Indian political scenario at large. They adopted the surnames like their Hindu counterparts "Nawgaonkar," "Penkar," "Wakrulkar," and "Dandekar". They adopted the occupation of oil-pressing and came to be known as "Shaniwar Telis" as they abstained from work on Saturdays which was their day of "Sabbath". They adopted Marathi language; in fact, they resembled the Marathas in customs and appearances and could hardly be discriminated from them. They, however, adhered to some practices of Judaism like dietary laws, circumcision, and strict observance of Sabbath, marriages at the synagogues, while observing their fasts and festivals. The subject of caste, as discussed by G. S. Ghurye, can be applied to the Jews in this regard who states that the Bene Israel Jews attained the caste identity of "Shanivar Telis". "They were expected to marry within their caste, follow their own practices of worship, and keep themselves separate from the rest of Indian society, except in the realm of business" (31–42). Nathan Katz too, in his book *Who are the Jews of India?* discusses the castes created by the Jews in their adopted society, and their further divisions into sub-castes. He observes that it was the Sabbath that helped the community retain its identity. The adoption of local names and Marathi language can thus be regarded as the initial process of their assimilation. In *The Walled City*, Esther observes that Jewish origins "hang somewhere in the inner world of my memory", the tales of the shipwrecked ancestors, gradually adopting Indian clothes, languages and the name of the village which they inhabit (22). Esther repeatedly questions the extent to which her family has maintained the Jewish identity and adapted the one of their new homeland which includes the way women dress, maintain their hairstyles, wear anklets and nose-rings. Resemblance with Hindu friend Subhadra, the inability to recite Hebrew prayers, and fascination for the tinkling temple bells, are yet other attempts that underline the process of assimilation. As a child, Esther wonders why the women in the family do not wear bindi on their foreheads. *Book of Esther* further gives an interesting insight into the origin of the Bene Israel community. It records that the story of the origin of the community was passed from one generation to another in the oral tradition. They were escaping the Greek ruler Antiochus Epiphanes. The shipwreck story also has the inference of the Puranas according to which the seven men and women, found dead by sage Parshuram, were resurrected by him through chanting of mantras. Esther observes that the Chitpavan Brahmins in Maharashtra too have a similar story but they perhaps adopted the story to "find acceptance in the communities around us" (30).

IV

Both the writers record their communities' participation in historic wars. There is a vivid description of the Bene Israel community actively participating in wars, particularly the Mysore Wars leading to the death of Tipu Sultan. Solomon who as subedar of the 16th regiment of the Bombay native infantry of the East India Company, inadvertently considers himself to have been party to Tipu Sultan's death. The first Mysore War was fought during 1766–9. Haidar Ali was attacked by the Marathas, the Nizam, and the English. Haider Ali had an upper hand. Many lost territories were restored to him. The second Mysore War was fought between the English and Haider

Ali's troops. Haider Ali died and was succeeded by Tipu Sultan who fought valiantly against the English and Maratha forces through the third Mysore War of 1790–2 to the fourth Mysore war of 1798–99 in which he was killed. Subedar Major Samuel Ezekiel Divekar had been captured by Tipu Sultan's forces after the second Mysore war. However, due to the queen mother's intervention on hearing him and his fellow captives pray in a strange language, Tipu Sultan pardoned them. Samuel Ezekiel Divekar built the first synagogue in Bombay in 1796, a fact recorded faithfully by Esther David. It is revered by Hindus and Muslims too. The Bagdadi Jews also built a synagogue in 1861. The Magen David Synagogue built by David Sassoon stands in Byculla which is a popular area for the Baghdadi Jews. It is interesting to note that the two communities were rather on the same side in the wars they were involved in.

Like *The Trotter-Nama, Book of Esther* also draws upon the factual history for its narration. David Solomon Dandekar who met Tilak in Yerwada Jail in 1898 and smuggled sheets of paper and pouches of supari prepared by Shebabeth for Tilak who was addicted to Supari, is modelled after eminent nationalist Abraham Solomon Erulkar. The novel includes distinguished personalities of the community as characters. Jerusha, the gynaecologist, is Jerusha Jacob Jhirad, who was awarded the Padma Shri in 1966 for her work in gynaecology and for her services in social welfare; (3) Dr. Reuben David Dandekar, was awarded in 1975 for his outstanding work and originality as superintendent of the Ahmedabad Zoo. Another Indian Jew to receive the *Padma Shri* award in 1970, Mr. Ezra Mir, is a member of the Baghdadi Jewish community of Bombay. He features as Ezra in the novel. Esther David gives a faithful account of the Ahmedabad Zoo by mingling the real and the fictional. Right from its inception to Jawaharlal Nehru's visit is recorded in detail. Two characters from real life Shri Mehdi Nawaz Jung[2] and Jivraj Mehta[3] make the narrative of Nehru's visit very authentic. The zoo and Balvatika of Ahmedabad visited by Nehru in these years owe their existence to the hard labour put in by Reuben David, Esther's father (Joshua), and it still stand as testimony to the Jewish community's contribution to Indian social life.

The Jews have made attempts to assimilate into the Indian society in many ways. Apart from the dresses, customs, culinary habits, and language, we have a vivid account of their participation in Indian festivals like Diwali, Holi, and Navratri. As a child, Esther often wondered why only her house remains unlit during Diwali, why does the pujari not accept anything to eat at her house, and what is unjewish about celebrating Holi? The best way to answer these questions was to draw parallels between the two cultures. She wonders whether it is possible to correlate Lakshmi's visit on the night of Diwali to Prophet Elijah's appearance during the feast of Passover.

The community celebrates several festivals with enthusiasm, as do the other communities in India. The most important among these are Rosh Hashanah,[4] Yom Kippur,[5] Simchat Torah, Passover[6] and Purim.[7] Between the first two, they visit their friends and relatives, prepare elaborate meals which include Maharashtrian dishes like puran poli too, dance merrily, and seek forgiveness on the Day of Atonement. They also do special cleaning and polishing of utensils to welcome prophet Elijah. The community also has accepted inter-community marriages over the years in an attempt to assimilate into Indian society at large. In a community where marriage between Bene Israel and Baghdadi Jews, Jerusha-Ezra was looked down upon, there are instances of Julie (Julekha)–Iqbal and Sinora–Peter's marriage in *The Walled City* (p.99).

The Bene Isreal community too have made for their "promised land". Their attempts to assimilate have received a jolt from time to time with losses in plagues and riots. The Bene Israel population steadily increased from 6000 in 1830s to 10000 by the turn of the century. Their number increased up to 20000 in 1948 but by 1961 the number reduced to 16000 because of emigration to Israel at a large scale. Their identity has thus become as Esther David states in the introduction to *The Walled City*, "diminishing minuscule minority community" (ix). Yet her thwarted attempt to "uproot myself from my surrogate motherland and replant myself in the land of my ancestors" (p.371) is a confirmation of the community to its Indian identity. Yet, greater efforts are required to come closer and constitute a whole, than live in separate islands within the nation.

NOTES

1 Major General Claude Martin (4 January 1735–13 September 1800) was an officer in the French, and later the British, army in India. He rose to the position of Major General in the British East India Company. Martin was born in Lyon, France, into a humble background, and was a self-made man who has left a substantial lasting legacy in the form of his writings, buildings, and the educational institutions. His different facets include soldier, collector and connoisseur, nabob, self-surgeon, hot air balloonist, philanthropist and educationist.

2 Shri Mehdi Nawaz Jung was into social work and co-operative movement after retirement from service in 1949. He was persuaded to join Indian National Congress. He contested a general election in 1952 from the Hyderabad constituency and won the election with a very big majority. From the year 1952 to January 1960, Shri Mehdi Nawaz Jung was a Minister in the former Hyderabad State and then in Andhra Pradesh Government, holding various portfolios such as Public Works Department, Roads & Buildings Department, Irrigation & Power, etc. and Governor of Gujarat (1960–65).

3 Jivraj Mehta was briefly the personal Doctor to Gandhiji after returning to India and joining the freedom movement. He was twice incarcerated (1938 and 1942) by the British government for his role in Gandhiji's Satyagraha movement. After independence in 1947, Dr. Jivraj graced public office in various positions. He devotedly served people as the first "Dewan" (Prime Minister) of the erstwhile Baroda state in free India sworn-in on 4 September 1948, director general of health services and held many other portfolios. He was the first Chief Minister of the newly formed Gujarat state from April 1960 to September 1963. Later he has also served as the Indian high commissioner to the United Kingdom (1963–66).

4 Rosh Hashanah is the Jewish New Year, according to oral tradition day of memorial and the Day of Judgment, in which God judges each person individually according to their deeds, and makes a decree for the following year. The holiday is characterized by the special mitzvah of blowing the *shofar*. According to the Torah, this is the first day of the seventh month of the calendar year that marks the beginning of a ten day count to Yom Kippur. According to an opinion in Jewish oral tradition, the creation of the world was completed on Rosh Hashanah.

5 Yom Kippur is the holiest day of the year for most Jews (Karaite Jews regard Passover as the holiest day of the year, as do Samaritans). Its central theme is atonement and reconciliation. This is accomplished through prayer and complete fasting – including abstinence from all food and drink (including water), unless fasting is prohibited for medical reasons. The fast and other prohibitions commence on 10 Tishri at sunset – sunset being the *beginning* of the day in Jewish tradition. Yom Kippur is considered, along with 15th of Av, as the Happiest days of the year (Talmud Bavli – Tractate Ta'anit).

6 Passover is one of the three pilgrimage festivals (*Shalosh regalim*) ordained in the Torah. Pesach commemorates the liberation of the Israelite slaves from Egypt. The Counting of the Omer is a count of the days from the time they left Egypt until the time they arrived at Mount Sinai.

7 Purim commemorates the events that took place in the Book of Esther. It is celebrated by reading or acting out the story of Esther, and by making disparaging noises at every mention of Haman's name. In Purim, it is a tradition to masquerade around in costumes and to give food and drink to the poor and the needy. In Israel, it is also a tradition to arrange festive parades, known as *Ad-D'lo-Yada*, in the town's main street. Sometimes the children dress up and act out the story of Esther for their parents.

REFERENCES

Anthony, Frank. *Britain's Betrayal in India: The Story of the Anglo-Indian Community*. Delhi: Allied Publishers, 1969.

Daniel Ruby, Johnson Barbara *Ruby of Cochin: An Indian Jewish Woman Remembers,* Jewish Publication Society of America, 2002.

David, Esther. *Book of Esther,* New Delhi: Penguin Books, 2002.

——— *The Walled City.* Chennai: Westland, 2009.

Delman, Carmit. *Bread, Butter and Chutney: Growing Up Between Cultures-Memoir of an Indian Jewish Girl,* New York: Ballantine Books, 2002.

Ghurye, G. S. *Caste and Race in India*, Bombay: Popular Prakashan,

Hutcheon, Linda. 'Historiographic Metafiction', *The Poetics of Post Modernism: History, Theory and Fiction,* New York, 1988

Katz, Nathan. *Who are the Jews of India?* Berkeley, Los Angeles, London: University of California Press, 1999.

Meisami, Julie Scott. 'History as Literature', *Iranian Studies*, Winter/Spring Vol. 33, Nos 1–2.

Sealy, Allan. *The Trotternama: A Chronicle,* New Delhi: Penguin Books, India, 1990.

Silliman, Jael. *Jewish Portraits: Indian Frames Woman Narratives from a Diaspora of Hope,* Hanover: NH University Press, New England, 2001.

Section 3

Co-Text

18

Marginalizing Rural Life: Tolstoy and the World Literature Anthologies

John Burt Foster, Jr

Tolstoy's long career as a fiction writer bears witness to his growing concern for the ordinary lives of Russian peasants, even for peasant life generally throughout the world, and also for writing about that subject in ways that could connect with peasant readers. This is a goal that merits being considered as an effort to create a "minority discourse", given that at the time Russia was still a country with widespread illiteracy. Certainly, Tolstoy thought in these terms when he started making this major change in his way of writing, some years after becoming deeply involved in the early 1860s and again in 1872 with literacy projects on his country estate (Maude 1987: 250–78, 333–5, 344–7).

This trend in Tolstoy's career reveals that a "minority discourse" can aim to speak to and/or to represent a group that in fact constitutes a numerical majority. Indeed, literature's exclusivity as a written medium in cultures with a large number of illiterates is probably the classic example of this apparently paradoxical situation. Groups that, when measured solely by quantity are in the majority, can be minoritized when the application of some qualitative standard prevents them from fully participating in their society or culture. We should also allow for the point that although "minority discourse" will usually mean a communication *by* a member of that minority, the writer does not *have* to belong to a minority. Tolstoy, who was born into the middle levels of the Russian nobility, would again be a leading example of this kind of writer. Notwithstanding the potential for ignorance or bad faith among even well-meaning writers who try to speak for others, his example deserves to be taken seriously due to the sincerity, intense commitment, and verbal power with which he pursued this goal.

Tolstoy's concern with these issues began with some brief, but structurally important episodes in his two most famous works, the long novels *War and Peace* (1869) and *Anna Karenina* (1878), both of them aimed at well-educated readers far removed from the life and the world of the peasantry. Still, in the first novel there is the peasant soldier called Platon Karatayev who accompanies Pierre, one of the book's three male protagonists, as a prisoner-of-war during Napoleon's disastrous retreat from Moscow (*War and Peace* IV. i: 12–13).[1] In the other novel, the main male character, Levin, experiences a final moment of spiritual/philosophical enlightenment during a chance talk with a labourer. That man tells Levin about an upright peasant, also named Platon, who refuses to "skin a man alive" in his business dealings (*War and Peace* VIII: 11–12). That both peasants' names converge with that of the Greek idealist philosopher may suggest Tolstoy's reluctance at this time to face the full truth about peasant life, despite his effort to give serious attention to peasants in his fiction. However, *War and Peace* does include the stark scene in which Pierre ignores Karatayev's execution as a straggler because lack of food and the bitter cold have drained Pierre himself of normal human feeling (*War and Peace* IV, iii: 12, 14). The dire situations of both the characters could be taken to hint at problems of poor nourishment and inadequate shelter among the peasantry at other times than during Napoleon's catastrophic retreat. One should also recall the very different and more explicit implications of the scene in *Anna Karenina* when Levin, in an unusual action for a landowner, joins a group of peasants to mow a field of hay (*War and Peace* III: 4–6). The scene stands out for its fidelity to the physical effort, to the natural flow of a day outdoors, and especially to the satisfying feelings of solidarity created, at least temporarily, by working and eating together.

This concern for peasant life culminated with Tolstoy's "povest'" (or long story) titled "Master and Man" (1895) and with short stories he wrote for peasant readers like "God Sees the Truth, but Waits"[2] (1872). Tolstoy would eventually credit the latter, which had been developed from an anecdote first told by Karatayev (*War and Peace* IV, iii:13), with being his best work of fiction (*What is Art*? 182).[3] Another, non-fiction writing of this trend during the second half of Tolstoy's career was the set of goals laid out in his treatise *What is Art*? (1898), which connected his efforts to create a minority discourse with a larger, cross-cultural vision for universal or worldwide literature.[4]

Tolstoy's perspective on peasants and on life on the land had altered greatly by the time of "Master and Man", two decades and more after the great novels. He had now made a full transition to writing about rural life after serfdom, the system of bondage that dominated the Russian countryside until it was abolished in 1861. The focus has shifted from traditional landowners like the extravagant elder Rostov in *War and Peace*, or the conscientious Levin in *Anna Karenina*, to a more practical, down-to-earth social order. Brekhunov, the master in this story, is a hard-driving rural businessman, not at all like the morally upright Platon in *Anna Karenina*. Nikita is a landless labourer, who fatalistically does not question his boss's orders when they set out to close a deal despite an impending blizzard. "God Sees the Truth, but Waits" tells a story that Nikita could have followed and appreciated, about a merchant unjustly convicted of murder and exiled to Siberia. As the title implies, the story hinges on what happens when this man happens to meet the real murderer. In the end that man cannot help confessing his guilt, first to the merchant and then to the authorities, yet he only does so when it is too late for the innocent man to be freed before his death. Harsh injustice, patient suffering, and the drama of an awakened conscience are conveyed in simple, forthright language suitable for beginner readers.

What is Art? generalizes on this story's example, as it argues for a worldwide literature based on ordinary life experiences and communicated to readers through its "infectious" emotional content (*What is Art?*: 163–4). By this term Tolstoy means an ability to awaken in readers the same basic emotions that the author felt while writing the work. Ideally this "content of feeling" would be so strong that no "superfluity of detail" of the kind that Tolstoy had come to reject in nineteenth-century Western realism, and even in his own novels (*What is Art?*: 179–81), would be required to make the story resonate with readers across classes, cultures, and ages all over the world. In this spirit, Tolstoy can imagine an audience that would include "a Russian peasant, a Chinese, an African, a child, an old man, educated, or uneducated" (180), where the reference to Chinese and African readers shows his strong interest in a possible world audience.

What is Art? was too controversial to escape unscathed from the Russian censorship of the time. To make up for the deletions and substitutions that had been ordered, Tolstoy asked his friend Aylmer Maude to translate the book in its original form into English. Then, at the very time that Constance Garnett was translating the great novels that Tolstoy had rejected in this treatise; Maude translated a group of his stories that accorded with its criteria for good art. That book appeared in 1906 with Oxford University Press under the title of *Twenty-Three Tales*; it eventually reached India. As Harish Trivedi's translation of Amrit Rai's biography[5] of Premchand makes clear, Premchand was reading this book, which included "God Sees the Truth, but Waits" but not "Master and Man" by March 1914 (Rai 1990: 80). Later the biography makes an intriguing comment about the impact of this reading on Premchand: "He, too, had read the moral tales of Tolstoy and been influenced by them in his writings. He had also adapted twenty-three of these stories to the Indian context and published them in a volume under the title *Prem Prabhakar*" (Rai 1990: 113).[6] Needless to say, it would be interesting to learn exactly what this adaptation to the Indian context might have involved. For example, what would have been the Indian equivalent to the Siberian exile in "God Sees the Truth, but Waits"? I should add that these stories, which do merit being called "moral tales", also demonstrate Tolstoy's interest in writing a world literature that, drawn from ordinary experience, would go beyond what he saw as the "provinciality" of Western realism (*What is Art?* 181). In particular, such a literature sought to do justice to the qualities of peasant life, above all to the "feel" of that life as guided by a theory of art whose emotional infectiousness would hold Platonic idealization to a minimum.

A century after Tolstoy's death in 1910, this trend in Tolstoy's career raises the question of its continued relevance. Now that world literature has again become an academic subject, not only in the United States but elsewhere as well, how much attention do Tolstoy's experiments in minority discourse receive in the anthologies seeking to enlarge this field's place in the college curriculum? An allied issue would be how little impact *What is Art?* has had on the world literature movement compared to Goethe's comments on *Weltliteratur*. Indeed, the new anthologies have found it difficult to give adequate representation to any stage in Tolstoy's career. Even the great novels, despite their fame worldwide, are so long that they would have to be excerpted, a practice that editors have undertaken with ancient epics and the *1001 Nights*, but not with novels.

To understand why several of the anthologies chose to represent Tolstoy with another of his long stories, "The Death of Ivan Ilych" (1886), we need to consider Tolstoy's place in the more narrowly conceived anthologies of Western literature that existed when the world literature trend began around 1995. Here two Slavists with broad interests in European literature had key roles to play. One was the well-known comparatist René Wellek, originally from Czechoslovakia, who had taught Russian literature before he founded Yale's department of Comparative Literature. For the unit covering realism in Maynard Mack's pioneering *Norton Anthology of World Masterpieces* (a title at odds with its focus on the Western tradition), Wellek relied *only* on Russian fiction, with "The Death of Ivan Ilych" joined by Turgenev's *Fathers and Sons* and Dostoevsky's "Notes from Underground". Later editions replaced Turgenev with Flaubert, and there things remained when this widely used anthology brought out a global edition, edited by Sarah Lawall. The other Slavist was the Russian-American novelist Vladimir Nabokov, who as professor of Russian at Cornell gave a popular course that featured *Anna Karenina* along with novels from Dickens to Proust, as well as several shorter works of fiction. Sometimes Nabokov would assign "The Death of Ivan Ilych", which he called Tolstoy's "most artistic, most perfect, and most sophisticated achievement," and "a forerunner of Russian modernism" (*Lectures*: 238). This judgment would get added authority from Nabokov's growing celebrity as a fiction writer.

When anthologies with a global reach began to appear, the Bedford (Davis), which had originated in a national grant to encourage the teaching of world literature, followed the Norton's lead by using "The Death of Ivan Ilych". Other ways to sample Tolstoy's work were tried, however. Thus the Harper-Collins chose the six-page fable, now out of print, called "God Sees the Truth, but Waits" (*Caws and Prendergast* 1994: 2067–73). The Longman, under the direction of world literature theorist David Damrosch, also used a short story to present Tolstoy (Damrosch 2004: 593–600). But "After the Ball," written in the author's final decade, is not a peasant fable. Instead, as an anecdote told by a narrator from Tolstoy's social milieu, it could be said to hark back to Kitty's shock at being ignored by Vronsky at her first ball, a critical incident early in *Anna Karenina* (I: 23). In the story, a young man has happily danced the night away with a colonel's daughter; but then, when he wanders out the next morning in a mood of restless euphoria, he faces an even harsher experience of lost illusions. He watches, horrified, as the father oversees a soldier's brutal punishment.

Still another introduction to Tolstoy, this time from a contemporary fiction writer in a volume more likely to be used in creative writing courses, appears in *You've Got to Read This*, an anthology of thirty-five favourite short stories with appreciations by the writers who picked them. Ron Hansen, who is one of the editors, chose "Master and Man". His praise for this long story, which is so strong that Hansen can remark that it "annihilated a great deal of fiction for me" (Hansen 1994: 516), inadvertently echoes a Russian tribute to Tolstoy just before his death, recorded in Nabokov's autobiography, *Speak, Memory*. The author remembers having seen an oddly literal memento in a rural schoolhouse: 'a so-called "typographical" portrait,' in which a "complete Tolstoy story ('Master and Man') had gone to make its author's bearded face" (Hansen 1994: 154). To understand why this story, rather than "The Death of Ivan Ilych," might have been selected to sum up Tolstoy will require further attention to both works.

The difference between Wellek's view that "The Death of Ivan Ilych" typifies realism at its best and Nabokov's contention that it looks ahead to modernism indicates an intriguing versatility. But this story most likely earned its place in anthologies for a more specific reason. With a power and originality of its own, it draws on the same inspiration as two major scenes in Tolstoy's novels. In *War and Peace*, it recalls Andrew Bolkonsky lying wounded among the dead and dying after Napoleon's triumph at Austerlitz and finding new meaning in gazing at the lofty sky (*War and Peace* I.iii.16). There is also the account in *Anna Karenina* of the last days of Levin's tubercular brother Nicholas, leading up to "Death," the only named chapter in that novel (*War and Peace* V: 20). "The Death of Ivan Ilych" constitutes a part of these stark, even relentless visions of mortality, but unlike the many-sided novels, the story keeps this side of Tolstoy in sharp focus. By opening with Ivan Ilych's funeral, it closes off any uncertainty about where his mishap while hanging a curtain in his new, "just-right" apartment will lead. Indeed, the dry formality of his career as a judge and the monotony of his citified existence could give the impression that he perished long before his actual death.

This is where the story misrepresents Tolstoy. Its urban setting and the legalistic routine of Ivan Ilych's work are familiar features of the modern world, but they fail to reflect the full range of Tolstoy's work. In its satirical tone, "The Death of Ivan Ilych" relates back mainly to his portrayals of Russia's capital Petersburg, with its courtiers and top officials like the Kuragins in *War and Peace*, or like Vronsky and Karenin in *Anna Karenina*. But in those novels the capital city's stifling atmosphere regularly gives way to the countryside's expansiveness, which scarcely appears in "The Death of Ivan Ilych."

In this regard, "Master and Man" offers a significant counter example, so much so that it reads like a companion piece to the earlier story. Its rural setting of villages, open fields, and woods brings forward into the next generation the freshness of outdoor experience, the directness and simplicity of manners, and the practical concern with land management that marked the gentry estates in the two novels. Though the circumstances in this story changed drastically from the time of those novels, this rural environment, unlike the urban, or suburban ones that increasingly dominate the English-speaking world, was the norm in both Tolstoy's Russia and many other nations worldwide at that time. By this point he knew this life better and had greater confidence in writing about it, so that characters who were once episodic or marginal could take the centre stage. This is a decisive shift in the decade since "The Death of Ivan Ilych", where the peasant Gerasim, who comforts the dying man by holding up his legs, is still a minor figure on the order of Karatayev or Levin's hay crew. Thus, if the earlier story showed Tolstoy's skill at updating a socially privileged type, "Master and Man" brings a major shift in outlook, resulting in a work that illustrates "minority discourse" in the sense of giving a voice to characters and situations otherwise excluded from literature.

The blizzard in the second story, in which the men get lost and the master freezes to death while finding unexpected satisfaction in saving his labourer's life, parallels Ivan Ilych's mysterious, cancer-like disease as an image of mortality. But even as "Master and Man" stresses life's precariousness as forcefully as "The Death of Ivan Ilych," it does so in an elemental natural setting, not in a confined domestic space. The latter site, again, conforms more closely to modern life as experienced by the likely users of the anthologies; but the storm in "Master and Man", with its buffeting wind, its erasure of familiar landmarks, and its deepening chill possesses a stark directness missing from the disease. Rather than a personal misfortune, it represents an immemorial threat to human existence in general, rendered in local Russian terms, to be sure, but with obvious parallels in the cyclones, earthquakes, floods, volcanoes, or tsunamis that strike elsewhere. Shared awareness of a danger before which everyone is vulnerable even brings unsolicited offers of shelter when Tolstoy's travelers make a stop in a peasant village. This hospitality contrasts with the self-serving thoughts of Ivan Ilych's fellow jurists, who worry that his funeral might interfere with an evening of cards. Because bitter cold and loss of one's way threaten everyone in the story, while a disease like Ivan Ilych's picks people off randomly, the master images for mortality in the two stories set a visceral feeling of solidarity before an existential danger against a rationalized and legalistic egotism. Indeed, given the place that emotional infectiousness would later hold in Tolstoy's theory of art, a key feature of Ivan Ilych's illness may lie in its incommunicability in this figurative sense as well as in the literal, medical one. A blizzard's perils, however, should be obvious to everyone; and Brekhunov's error, which resembles Anna Karenina's on leaving for Italy with Vronsky after nearly dying, lies in his failure to profit from a second chance. Even after he has circled back to the same village after getting lost the first time, he insists on setting out again.

In an urbanized, high-technology world, however, Tolstoy's quasi-Kafkaesque treatment of Ivan Ilych's bitter isolation, face to the wall while suffering in his fashionable apartment, has gotten a better hearing than the master's resolve, after several false choices, to save the life of a man he led into danger. Thus, despite "The Death of Ivan Ilych's" partiality within the sweep of Tolstoy's career, this is the story that has gained fuller exposure in the English-speaking world. In a bibliography of Tolstoy criticism in English up to 1978, the index gives "The Death of Ivan Ilych" almost three times as many entries as "Master and Man"; and the ratio widens to more than fourteen to one over the next quarter century (Egan and Egan, 1979 and 2005).[7] That typographical portrait remembered by Nabokov, which linked author to story in a rural setting, emblematizes this discrepancy between source and target cultures. In the creation of an English-language world literature, "The Death of Ivan Ilych" has travelled far better than "Master and Man".

At stake in the scholarship, as well as the anthologies, is a cross-cultural filtering process that has favoured the story that is closer to current experience in the English-speaking world. The effect of this policy is to marginalize the trend in Tolstoy's later career that, in addition to developing a minority discourse tied to peasant life, he thought was best suited to be the basis for world literature. Even if current trends suggest an accelerating turn away from agriculture as humanity's dominant way of life, should every record of rural existence and, more important, of its characteristic conflicts and values be excluded from anthologies that aim to represent the world's literatures in all their breadth and historical depth?

This is not, however, my ultimate position on this subject. As already suggested, the short stories "After the Ball" and "God Sees the Truth, but Waits" have their own claims to mirror Tolstoy's career. The first one evokes and repudiates, rather simultaneously, the world of the great novels, thus epitomizing the dramatic shift in Tolstoy's later goals as a writer, while the second one was his favourite example from his own writings of the world literature he wished to substitute for those novels. When described this way, however, the two stories go together so well that they raise the question of why these anthologies couldn't find space for all twelve pages of Tolstoy – or for even more. "How Much Land Does a Man Need" (1886), a somewhat longer short story that was admired by James Joyce, who also praised "Master and Man" (Ellmann 247), describes a Russian peasant who strikes a deal with a nomadic tribe to buy all the land he can circle on foot in one day. When he gets greedy, makes too wide a circuit, and then has to run to reach his starting point by nightfall, he dies of over-exertion, so the only land he needs at the end is a six-foot grave. The story evokes mortality with the same starkness and freshness of conception as "The Death of Ivan Ilych" or "Master and Man", but the peasant's land hunger also addresses the imperialism of the late nineteenth century from a different angle (the nomad/farmer split rather than racial difference) and in another setting (the Eurasian steppes instead of Africa) than Achebe's dissenting judgment on Conrad, which is a staple in several anthologies.

What is missing, even in relying on these two or three well-chosen short works, would be Tolstoy's skill at interweaving such small building blocks to produce novels. Here it is useful to recall his self-styled "peepshow" approach to narrative, which relied on stringing together a multitude of short, sharply focused scenes (*Tolstoy's Diaries*: 333). As a result, the more than eight hundred pages of *Anna Karenina* can consist of almost 240 chapters averaging less than four pages each. The short story, far from miniaturizing Tolstoy, is actually his normal unit of composition. This would be one reason for choosing *Hadji Murad*,[8] as both his most representative work and his best work of world literature. This is a short novel that he wrote between 1896 and 1904 but chose to set aside, and it could be published only after his death. At first, again due to censorship in Russia that was only lifted after 1917, the full work had to appear in a 1912 English translation by Aylmer Maude.

Consisting of twenty-five chapters, averaging five pages each, this novel combines the perspectives of "Master and Man" and "The Death of Ivan Ilych"[9] by giving sharply focused vignettes both of peasants working on the land, and of leaders at the centres of power. Moving back and forth between Russians and Muslims during a long war of territorial expansion in the Caucasus, it ends with the brutal, disturbing death of its protagonist. As a result, even as *Hadji Murad* shares the great novels' social breadth, historical subject-matter, and subtle interplay among a large cast of characters, it also stresses the precariousness of existence and the value of simple solidarities over the egotism of power, both of them with themes central to the shorter works discussed in this essay. In addition, unlike "God Sees the Truth, but Waits" which anticipated Tolstoy's interests in world literature, *Hadji Murad* was completed after he wrote *What is Art?* It thus responds more directly to the ideas in that treatise, even as it stays in closer touch with Tolstoy's earlier achievements. And it does so in the deceptively simple style that he developed for his stories of minority discourse, a style that this work, which went through multiple rewritings, packs with meaning and implication. Yet it also features a cross-cultural content that, even as it bridges the social divide between the Westernized Russian elite and the mores of peasants still living under serfdom, can provide a sympathetic portrayal of several Muslim groups on Russia's border with the Middle East.

To conclude, "The Death of Ivan Ilych" promotes the image of a Tolstoy who speaks most directly but quite narrowly to North American and Western European readers. As a result, its use in several anthologies suggests that their sense of world literature continues, like other views on world literature that have emerged elsewhere, to show a clear partiality for writings nearest to their own place and situation.[10] "Master and Man" comes closer to the Russian realities of Tolstoy's time, as well as to those of a non-Western world that was still mainly rural and ruled from abroad or above. But it is *Hadji Murad*, with its manageable length for surveys of world literature that gives the best sense of Tolstoy's full career as a fiction writer. It displays a complexity of character, of narrative perspective, and of structure not allowed for in *What is Art?*, with its wholesale rejection of Tolstoy's earlier writings. In addition, its cultural and religious breadth, its deep emotional appeal, and its concise, direct style bear strong witness to Tolstoy's goals for world literature. At the same time, in the brief but moving chapters that pay sympathetic attention to the work and mores of peasants on both sides in the war (*Hadji Murad*: 21–7, 50–4, 90–1), this short novel also illustrates the later Tolstoy's project of creating a "minority discourse" that would correct one of literature's major blind spots – its inattention to the life-worlds of the illiterate.

NOTES

1 I cite volume as (IV.i.12–13) referring part, and chapter numbers for passages from *War and Peace* and *Anna Karenina,* since these novels have been translated so many times into so many languages that specific page references would not be very helpful. Wording follows the English translations listed in the References.

2 See *Twenty-Three Stories*. Trans. Louise and Aylmer Maude. 1906; Oxford: Oxford UP, reprinted in 1934, includes 'God Sees the Truth, but Waits' and 'How Much Land Does a Man Need?'

3 *See What is Art?* ed., introd., and notes by W. Gareth Jones. Trans. Aylmer Maude. London: Bristol Classical Press, 2007. Reproduces the Maude translation of 1898.

4 Tolstoy often uses the adjective 'vsemirnyj,' whose literal meaning would be 'all world' or more idiomatically 'worldwide,' where English translations of *What is Art?* have 'universal,' a term widely critiqued by postcolonial criticism. This slippage in implication surfaces very clearly at a point in Maude's translation where Tolstoy ties his goals for minority discourse (in the sense of writing attentive to the ordinary experience of minoritized groups) to his conception of world

literature. Thus he praises art which transmits 'the simplest feelings of common life, but such always as are accessible to all men in the *whole world* ('vsego mira') – the art of common life – the art of the people – *universal* ('vsemirnoe') art' (177; italics added).

5 Rai was Premchand's son.

6 The 'he, too' in this citation alludes to Premchand's interest in Gandhi, thus suggesting that Gandhi also read this collection of tales with interest, though I have been unable to confirm this point.

7 To be specific, the proportion shifts from 28 to 11 in favour of 'The Death of Ivan Ilych' in the earlier period to 216 to 15 in the later one.

8 This title often appears as *Hadji Murat,* in accord with the Russian spelling of the protagonist's Turkic name. Reproduces the 1912 version.

9 See *Tolstoy's Short Fiction*. Ed. with trans. by Michael R. Katz. 2nd ed. New York: Norton, also includes 'The Death of Ivan Ilych' and 'Master and Man.'

10 Sarah Lawall, who has herself edited a world literature anthology, points out that 'there is no single canon of world literature, nor is there likely to be one. As Brandt Corstius has shown (6) in studying canons around the world, different countries always give special weight to their own or familiar traditions' ('Canons' 39).

REFERENCES

Brandt, Corstius, J. C. "Writing Histories of World Literature." *Yearbook of Comparative and World Literature* 12 (1963): 5–14.

Cawes, Mary Ann, and Christopher Prendergast. *Harper Collins World Reader: The Modern World.* New York: HarperCollins, 1994.

Damrosch, David, et al. *The Longman Anthology of World Literature, Volume E: The Nineteenth Century*. New York: Longman, 2004.

Davis, Paul, et al. *The Bedford Anthology of World Literature, Book Five: The Nineteenth Century, 1800–1900.* Boston: Bedford/St. Martins, 2003.

Egan, David R., and Melinda A. Egan. *Leo Tolstoy: An Annotated Bibliography of English-Language Sources to 1978.* Metuchen NJ: Scarecrow, 1979.

——— *Leo Tolstoy: An Annotated Bibliography of English-Language Sources from 1978 to 2003.* Lanham MD: Scarecrow, 2005.

Ellmann, Richard. *James Joyce*. 2nd ed. New York: Oxford UP, 1982.

Hansen, Ron, and Jim Shepard, eds. *You've Got to Read This: Contemporary American Writers Introduce Stories That Held Them in Awe.* New York: Harper Collins, 1994.

Lawall, Sarah. "Canons, Contexts, and Pedagogy: The Place of World Literature." *The Comparatist* 24 (2000): 39–56.

——— et al. *The Norton Anthology of World Literature, Volume E: 1800 to 1900*. 2nd ed. New York: Norton, 2002.

Mack, Maynard, et al. *The Norton Anthology of World Masterpieces, Volume 2: Literature of Western Culture since the Renaissance*. New York: Norton, 1956.

Maude, Aylmer. *The Life of Tolstoy: The First Fifty Years.* New York: Oxford UP, 1908 rep. 1987.

Nabokov, Vladimir. *Lectures on Russian Literature*, ed. and introd. by Fredson Bowers. New York: Harcourt Brace, 1981.

——— *Speak, Memory: An Autobiography Revisited.* New York: Vintage, 1966.

Rai, Amrit. *Premchand: His Life and Times*. Introd. Alok Rai. Trans. Harish Trivedi. 1982; New Delhi: Oxford UP, 1990.

Tolstoy, Leo. *Anna Karenina*. Trans. Richard Pevear and Larissa Volokhonsky. New York: Viking, 2001.

——— *Hadji Murad.* Introd. John Burt Foster, Jr. Trans. and pref. Aylmer Maude. Washington DC: Orchises, 1996.

——— *Tolstoy's Diaries*. ed. and trans. R. F. Christian. 1985; London: Flamingo, 1994.

——— *Tolstoy's Short Fiction*. Ed. with trans. by Michael R. Katz. 2nd ed. New York: Norton, 2008.

——— *Twenty-Three Stories*. Trans. Louise and Aylmer Maude. 1906; Oxford: Oxford UP, 1934.

——— *War and Peace*. Trans. Richard Pevear and Larissa Volokhonsky. New York: Vintage, 2007.

——— *What is Art?* ed. With an introduction and notes by W. Gareth Jones. Trans. Aylmer Maude. London: Bristol Classical Press, 2007.

19

Communist Autobiographies and Minority Discourses: Leon Trotsky and Alexandra Kollontai

Kunal Chattopadhyay

FROM WORKERS' DEMOCRACY TO PARTY-BUREAUCRATIC DICTATORSHIP

In 1917, the October Revolution was started under the assumption that it would usher in a more democratic regime for and by the majority, since the dictatorship of the proletariat was identified with the widest flowering of democracy (Trotsky 2013; Mandel 1983, 1984; Marik 2008). By the time Lenin died, the Soviet Union had already become a one-party state, even if the horrors of the 1930s were still some distance away. Increasingly, the lines between dissent in the state, minority position within the Communist Party, and counter-revolution, would start getting blurred (Farber 1990; Marik 2008; Pirani 2008).

In 1936, Nikolai Bukharin, a veteran Bolshevik, made a long trip abroad in order to purchase for the Soviet Institute of Marxism-Leninism certain original writings of Marx and Engels, held by the German Social Democratic Party (SDP). As the SDP had been dissolved by Hitler, its material was put in the custody of its co-thinkers in other countries, and the Russian Menshevik Boris Nicolaievsky was one of the people Bukharin had to negotiate with. During his long stay, he had extended discussions with Nicolaievsky (Nicolaievsky 1965; Tucker 1992), occasionally with Fedor Dan, another Menshevik (Radzhinsky 1997), and others. He painted a grim picture of Stalin's politics and economic policies, and seems to have predicted at least imprisonment for himself. Yet, when Nicolaievsky asked him why he did not stay on in the West, he rejected the option.

Most communist dissidents in the USSR were caught in this trap. They could not seek refuge in the West, for they saw in it imperialism, trying to overthrow the first workers' state. They did not wish to be defectors to capitalism. They were minority, dissident communists, but communists nevertheless, most of whom had taken part in the creation of a discourse that made honest communist dissent an increasingly deadly oxymoron. Stalinist discourse from the late 1920s insisted that communists had to support the socialist fatherland at any cost, suppressing any criticisms. Critical voices were swiftly conflated with counter-revolution and vassalage to imperialism.

The idea of workers' democracy was not merely rhetorical. The October Revolution had been made through a mobilization process that was far more democratic than anything its opponents had to offer. Such a view has been long contested by right-wing scholarship (Schapiro 1966; Pipes 1990; Figes 1996). The call for a Soviet seizure of power had been openly debated. Wherever there was a possibility, the Bolsheviks tried to minimize violence and to take power peacefully. It is also clear that this confidence was based on a rising tide in the Soviets, factory councils and trade unions, even more than in the municipal bodies. Throughout Russia, from late August, new elections to Soviets were being organized. The Bolsheviks made significant gains. Thus, at the Second Congress of the Soviets of Workers' and Soldiers' Deputies of Urals, representing 505,780 workers and soldiers, which met on August 17–21, the Bolsheviks had 77 deputies against 23 for the Mensheviks. (Kutuzov 1957: 226). On 9 September, the presidium of the Petrograd Soviet lost by

414 votes to 519, with 67 abstentions. In August, work had barely begun in the rural areas. But by 21 September, the Saratov Soviet had 320 Bolsheviks against 103 SRs. 76 Mensheviks, and 34 non-party deputies. (Andreyev 1971: 263). The final stage of the conquest of power saw limited violence, because the armed forces as well as the masses of workers had actually been won over.

Even after the insurrection, there was ample democracy. The crisis came with the beginning of the civil war (Bruce Lincoln 1989). Not only the open right-wing, but also the biggest of the socialist opposition parties, the Socialist Revolutionary Party, took up arms. Civil War was not conducive to the flowering of democracy. The counter-revolution was actively aided by both imperialist camps. The German ambassador, Count Mirbach, on arriving in Moscow, met a number of members of the Imperial Family. (Mandel 1992: 22). By April 1918, the Entente had come to the conclusion that they would have to invade Russia and overthrow the Bolsheviks. (Bruce Lockhart 1933: 253–4, 265, 273, 283–5). White Terror was a brutal anti-poor peasant, anti-worker, and anti-communist policy. The aim of the officers was not to establish parliamentary democracy, but a dictatorship. White ruled territories were either run as military despotisms or were given in charge of discredited bureaucrats of the Tsarist era. In May 1918, the Eighth National Council of the SR Party resolved that in order to get rid of the Bolshevik government, it was permissible to allow the entry of Allied troops in Russia (Serge 1992: 288).

It was this context that saw a gradual restriction of democracy. Yet, till 1921, that was tempered by recognition that this was not the goal. Party members comprised only a small part of the elected soviet leaders at the lower levels (Vladimirsky 1920; Abrams 1968). The struggle against the counter-revolution led to the creation and institutionalization of the Cheka. But many Bolsheviks attacked it harshly, and shortly after the end of the Civil War it was abolished, and its successor, the GPU, initially had very limited powers. It was actually towards the end of the civil war and foreign interventions that the transformation was finally accomplished. In 1921, the Kronstadt revolt, and the fear of renewed invasion by the Whiteguards, led to the ban on opposition parties, as well as the ban on factions (organised currents) within the Bolshevik party.

Up to 1921, party membership was not chiefly a matter of privilege. Members had to be in the forefront of struggles. Thus, in 1920, during the Red Army's march towards Warsaw, the total loss to the army was 33% of its forces committed, while the loss of Bolsheviks in the army was 90% (Bruce Lincoln 1989: 416). At this point, with the wars finally over, if there had been a return to the first period of the revolution, there could have been more positive developments. Instead, between 1921 and 1939, the one-party state and its bureaucratic elite emerged in their complete shape. The end of war meant that economic reconstruction had to be carried out. But the critical economic situation and the lack of democracy at the economic level (the end of workers' control, the introduction of cost accounting in factories with the New Economic Policy) and the return to free trade in agricultural production meant acute pressures. There was an attempt to tackle these by administrative-bureaucratic means, which led to a burgeoning party and state bureaucracy. And it was in this period that the dogma began to grow that absolute party unity was essential, as well as the idea that it was the party that would command in all areas. Bukharin had originally been one of the architects of this new power structure. In the mid-1920s, he had remarked that the place for a second party in the USSR was in jail (quoted in Nahaylo 1989: 58). After 1921, dissenting views came from many Communists themselves (Daniels 1960). Between 1921 and 1938–9, such dissent was treated in a sequence of ways. In the first phase, 1921–3, dissent meant being considered a minority. This meant being excluded from certain important policy making areas. Between 1924 and 1927, being a minority meant one was considered a deviationist from authentic communism. This authenticity was being constructed with reference to a Lenin cult and the creation of an official version of party history and the history of the revolution. Between 1927 and 1934, opposition increasingly meant a political crime. Finally, 1935–9 saw the crime as systemic, with roots back through party history. Party history itself was re-written to show leaders like Zinoviev, Kamenev, Bukharin, all as traitors. But the roots of this went back to 1923–4, when these very people had collaborated in rewriting history to start painting Lev Trotsky as a villain.

THE FUNCTION OF THE PARTY AUTOBIOGRAPHY

While much of this is old history, there have been important studies in recent times. The Israeli historian Igal Halfin has broken new ground by examining officially sponsored autobiographies (Halfin 2003, See also Halfin 2009). People applying for party membership, or for re-admission after having once lost membership, had to write an autobiography, as well as a declaration. The autobiographies did not narrate their entire life at an even pace. Their task was to highlight the role of the party, and show the journey of the individual's consciousness from a realist self, where the self is controlled by environment, to a revolutionary self, where the self controlled the environment. This journey was accomplished under party guidance.

Drawing on material from Leningrad and Tomsk, Halfin shows that autobiographies were encouraged to follow a set structure and include:

- General information
- Social status
- Family influence
- Education
- Profession
- Spiritual development, including the break with one's old world view
- Role in the pre-revolutionary period
- Role in revolutionary
- Role in civil war

"Lapsed" communists seeking re-entry, or those facing likely exclusion from the party, had to explain in addition:

- Why the lapse had occurred
- Was the soul of the lapsed communist capable of being saved?

So the autobiography was not a bland chronicle of all events. It had a function. As suggested by Hayden White, a narrative account is always a "figurative account":

> To leave this figurative element out of consideration in the analysis of a narrative is to miss [...] the performance in language by which a chronicle is transformed into a narrative [...] In the process of literalization – reduction of the narrative into sets of discrete propositions, for which the simple declarative sentence served as a model – what gets out is precisely those elements of figuration – tropes and figures of thought, without which the narrativization of real events, the transformation of the chronicle into a story, could never be effected. (White 1987: 48)

It is therefore necessary to work out the figurative rules by which the individual events in a writer's life become part of the totality of her or his autobiography. Halfin argues that there is a shift, where, in the pre-communist self, it is the external environment that controls or determines the self, whereas once one becomes a communist, or is imbued with proletarian class consciousness, the self controls the environment. Even though one invokes the diachronic line, the aim is to support the synchronic line, i.e. to show that in the present, the author is in harmony with the party. The class origins are also significant and one had to handle them properly. Thus, in 1925, a Leningrad student named Andronov wrote an autobiography which showed how a petty bourgeois individualist was transformed into a conscious proletarian. It opened with an acknowledgement that his father was the assistant director of a railway station. But, Andronov wrote, "I did not know him, and he played no role in my life". He is depicted as a drunkard who used to beat his wife. The point is to acknowledge this past and show how one had to overcome it (Halfin 2003: 72–6). Halfin's study shows that the function of the autobiography also shifted over time, as the regime became increasingly dictatorial, and as dissent became more and more coterminous with counter-revolution. Initially, the party denounced dissenters, especially those who had sided with Trotsky, as people who had fallen. They could be considered degenerates, who were however not fundamentally rotten. As the parry regime tightened and as the conception of building socialism in one country became more and more pronounced, this changed. In the 1920s, the function of the autobiography was to compel the applicant for membership to show what she or he had done in vital periods. Thus, one Klein, an applicant for membership, who was a student at Tomsk in 1925, was sharply questioned for not having applied for membership during the Civil War. The conclusion that was drawn by many, including the district committee that torpedoed the application, was not that he had been hesitant, but that he had wilfully not applied because he sympathized with the enemy. His application now, when the party was firmly in power, was seen as an opportunist action. (Halfin 2003: 61–3). In the 1930s, the situation had changed. Deviant communists were now viewed as virulent, malicious counter-revolutionaries, with the roots of counter-revolution going back to before the revolution in many cases. In the final period, 1935–9, it was argued that communist party membership meant one had received Enlightenment. It was assumed (or claimed) that such a person was incapable of committing errors. Like Lucifer, deliberate crime alone explained their behaviour.

But why were the recantations necessary? And why in such extreme form in the years of the Great Purges? Perhaps for the show trials, Stalin needed to completely discredit former rivals. But even low-level party members convicted in secret were forced to confess to outlandish crimes such as plots to assassinate Stalin, conspiracies with Lev Trotsky to dismember the Soviet Union, espionage for Nazi Germany. Given the unchecked power of the Soviet secret police, why did its agents not simply shoot alleged oppositionists? Many were shot in such a way. But why did they spend countless hours interrogating purge victims? Why did they force so many victims to confess to a vast range of crimes? Halfin argues that secret police interrogations were performances of Stalinist authority and that their transcripts should be read not as (distorted) records of events but as sites of discourse. These transcripts thus reveal little about the guilt or innocence of the accused but a great deal about the logic of Stalinist ideology.

Halfin can be supplemented by looking at texts where Christian rhetoric of salvation and damnation do appear. The concept of building a "new, socialist man", was turned into a concept of building perfection into men and women. Lenin, after his death, was canonized as the most saintly of all men. Funeral speeches of Old Bolsheviks (i.e. those who had become members before 1917) termed them "purest of the pure". It is however possible to question Halfin's suggestion that this was built into the foundations of communist politics itself. He produces no textual evidence from Marx, Engels, the German Social Democracy or Lenin. So our suggestion is, this relates specifically to Stalinism. In earlier essays, the present writer as well as Michael Lowy (Chattopadhyay 1997; Lowy 1984) have suggested that the estate-like nature of the party-state bureaucracy shows a kinship with the medieval Church as First Estate. Membership of an ideological group was key to the privileges, rather than socio-economic location or class being the foundations of political power or ideological domination.

Autobiographies showed a distinct pattern. In the 1920s, after the civil war, fear that non-proletarians would swamp the party led to tightening up of membership norms. The Trotskyist opposition of 1923 was very strong among the youth. So university students had to undergo re-registration. At that stage, they were still being considered souls that could be saved. So autobiographical recantations stressed their attachment to the revolution, the fact that it was the party that had taken them from darkness to light, and acknowledged that they had committed an error, from which the party had saved them. By 1927–8, persistence of oppositional moods and currents among students was treated much more sternly, though it was still the goal to win them, or some of them, back to the right path. By then, however, many students could be suspected of being deeply degenerate and not worth retaining in the party.

A second area where a party-state strait-jacket was imposed was on sexuality. War, revolution, and civil war had led to a break-down of the old sexual norms. By 1924–5 a backlash was to set in. Party conservatives, supported by conservative psychologists and educationists like Aaron Zalkind, wanted the restoration/imposition of what they felt was the true proletarian morality – strict monogamy, curb on abortion (in a country where other birth control measures were still limited), curbs on divorce.

WRITING MINORITY AND OPPOSITIONAL AUTOBIOGRAPHIES

Alexandra Mikhailovna Kollontai and Lev Davidovich Trotsky, two oppositionists, would question the party line both on issues of women's emancipation and on democracy and socialist construction. They both wrote substantial autobiographies that provide us with minority discourses.

A leading woman activist in the Russian Social Democratic Labour Party, Kollontai had sided with Lenin during World War I. Returning to Russia in 1917, she was again an early and strong supporter of Lenin when he proposed in his April Theses that the task in Russia was not a "bourgeois democratic revolution", but that of the working class taking power and beginning socialist construction. She was also a major orator, an organizer of working class women, and one of the central figures behind the Bolsheviks' journal for women workers, the *Rabotnitsa*. On 12 and 18 November 1917, at the initiative of Kollontai and a few other leading women, a conference of women workers was held in Petrograd, representing 80,000 women and having 500 delegates. Kollontai was also elected to the Central Committee of the Bolshevik Party as well as made, at the Second Congress of Soviets (which seized power in the name of the working class), the Peoples' Commissar for Social Welfare. A radical in matters of women's rights as well, Kollontai argued that there was a need to proceed in a direction that would ensure the break up of the traditional family. But prior to the X Congress of the by then renamed Russian Communist Party (Bolsheviks) she became a part of the leadership of an important minority calling themselves The Workers Opposition, and wrote a pamphlet defending their standpoint, as well as giving a speech at the Party Congress.

For Kollontai, as for Rosa Luxemburg, democracy was not a gift to be handed to the working class at some future date, and democracy could not sanction force in the construction of the future, though it might do so in eradicating the forces of the past. The Workers Opposition demanded a Workers' Congress, which at one level could be called impractical, because industry was virtually collapsing and the devastations of the past years had depoliticized a large part of the remaining workers, while the most conscious elements were the ones who had either gone to fight the civil war or had tried to join the administration. At the same time, these demands were based on a realization that unless the essential power of the working class was based in factory level organizations, large sections of less organized workers, including many novice women workers who had learnt to identify with the party would be turned into mere executors of decisions taken in their name by a newly emerging elite. Kollontai also felt that there could be no genuinely revolutionary changes in family and sexual relationships without a politics that was rooted at the point of production. When the New Economic Policy was introduced, restoring the market to a certain extent, and insisting on financial accountability of individual concerns, the Workers' Opposition demanded better security for workers. By 1922, a growing intolerance could be seen, and Kollontai became silent on questions of democracy. In 1923–4, she tried writing novels and short stories, like Bolshaia Liubov (A Great Love) and Liubov Pchel Trudovykh (Love of Worker Bees). Through these she tried talking about revolution, working class, socialist construction, and women. By 1925–6, her story Liubov Tretii Pokolenii and the short novel *Vasilisa Malygina* were under attack. She was accused of having written "solid feminist trash". Her idea, that the "new woman" should be constructed by rejecting traditional family norms, as well as traditional views on sexuality, were portrayed as petty bourgeois degeneration.

The autobiography was her final attempt to speak. Right from the title, it was an attempt to propagate her view on party, revolution, class struggle, and women's liberation. The title was *Autobiography of a Sexually Emancipated Communist Woman*. She had earlier expressed her strong views on morality, sexuality, and women's liberation. In *Make Way for Winged Eros* and *The New Morality and the Working Class*, she had stressed that love should not tie a woman in such a way that her commitment to work, revolution, and other areas of life were de-prioritized, and also that love should not be a code word to impose an authoritarian petty bourgeois moral standard on women.

This had resulted in sharp disputes. When she gave the autobiography its title she was still stressing the same elements. But in the galley proofs, she was compelled to make massive cuts (Kollontai 1971). These would be found only in the 1970s. A few cuts show one major area that she wanted to stress but could not:

> I have succeeded in structuring my intimate life according to my own standards and I make no secret of my love experiences any more than does a man. Above all, however, I never let my feelings, the joy or pain of love take the first place in my life in as much as creativity, activity, struggle always occupied the foreground. http://www.marxists.org/archive/kollonta/1926/autobiography.htm

Similarly, her assertion that her appointment as a senior diplomat had breached the double standard that permeated the diplomatic caste was deleted. Still, she was able, simply by an apparent neutral narration, to overturn the emerging codes. She records that she had married out of love, rejecting marriage of convenience for money, but felt this was not enough. Her interests turned to the revolutionary working class. "These were the years of the flowering of Marxism in Russia (1893: 96). Lenin at that time was only a novice ... Gorge Plekhanov was the leading mind of the time". So, coolly, she tells the reader that Lenin was not the "beacon" that drew her to Marxism. In 1903, she records, appeared her book on the Finnish Working Class. This again records that her work has to be seen as parallel to Lenin's works, such as *The Development of Capitalism in Russia.*

Yet we find another significant deletion. Talking of the revolution of 1905 she wrote (and crossed out in proof) "I realized for the first time how little our Party concerned itself with the fate of the women of the working class." In 1906–14 she was a left Menshevik more often than a Bolshevik. Here, we find her putting forward a complicated argument, which suggests that her alignment with the Mensheviks was due to Bolshevik sectarianism about participation in the Duma (a pseudo parliament with very limited rights) and that she was otherwise opposed to Menshevik political strategy. Since this did not amount to a confession of error, the entire passage was again crossed out. In 1911, in exile, she was associated with the Party

School organized by Maxim Gorkii, by dissident Bolsheviks and dissident Mensheviks. This was recorded in careful language, without highlighting the orientation of those members.

Kollontai's record of 1917 is significant. Within the Bolshevik party there was a pro-Lenin and an opposite current. Without stressing this (Trotsky had been violently attacked in 1924 for doing that) she however attempted to show how she had been associated with Lenin in the public mind in that year – a doggerel that linked the two of them, the fact that she voted for the insurrection in a meeting where several Central Committee members voted against, etc. Interestingly, both the foregoing were crossed out.

Finally, and most damningly, there were six references to Trotsky in the book, five of them strongly positive and one neutral. The obligatory denunciation in place by then, was totally absent. In other words, Kollontai was willing, or compelled, to delete views found too radical or oppositional by the ruling bureaucracy, but she would not rewrite her life or party history to tell outright lies in service of the official discourse. And so, after 1926, the book remained unpublished till its recovery in 1971.

Trotsky's autobiography (Trotsky 1930) was written under very different circumstances. He had by then been thrown out of the USSR but had received no visa from any Western democracy. By this time also, the official discourse was taking final shape (Stalin 1939 for the final shape of the official discourse). There was the apostolic succession – Marx–Engels–Lenin–Stalin. Trotsky was the arch-evil. He had opposed Lenin in 1903. He had opposed Lenin in 1907–14 over party building as well as revolutionary strategy. He had opposed Lenin in 1914–6 over international questions and the attitude to war. He had opposed Lenin in 1918 over the Treaty of Brest Litovsk. He had opposed Lenin in 1921 over the "trade union question". He had questioned the correctness of the party in *Novy Kurs* [*The New Course*] (1923) and had disputed the emerging official discourse in *Urokii Oktyabrskaia* [The Lessons of October] (1924). He had questioned the correctness of the claim that socialism could be built in one country (1924–7) and had challenged the using of the Communist International as essentially an instrument of Soviet foreign policy to the detriment of revolutions in other countries (1924–8). Expelled from the party in 1927, he had, unlike Zinoviev and Kamenev (two other leaders likewise expelled) refused to recant. Instead, he wrote an appeal to the Sixth Congress of the Communist International, challenging Stalinist theories and recent role, and published, after being thrown out of the USSR, diverse material, including a collection of documents called *The Stalin School of Falsification* that attempted to overturn the official discourse through detailed documentation.

His autobiography, written in 1929 (English translation published 1930), takes on the official mode of autobiography writing head on. He shows that he came from a kulak or rich peasant background and then became a part of the student intelligentsia. There is a straightforward narration about his father, neither apology nor hostility.

> My father was a farmer, first on a small scale and later on a larger one. As a little boy, he had left with his parents the Jewish town in the Province of Poltava, where he had been born, when they went to seek their fortune on the free steppes of the South. There were at that time about forty Jewish agricultural colonies in the provinces of Kherson and Ekaterinoslav, with a total population of about 25,000 souls. The Jewish farmers were on an equal footing with the other peasants not only as regards their legal rights (until 1881), but also as regards their property. By indefatigable, cruel toil that spared neither himself nor others, and by hoarding every penny, my father rose in the world.... The October Revolution found my father a very prosperous man. My mother had died in 1910, but my father lived to see the rule of the Soviets. At the height of the civil war, which raged with especial fury in the South and was accompanied by constant changes of government, the old man of seventy was obliged to walk hundreds of miles to find shelter in Odessa. The Reds were a menace to him because he was rich; the Whites persecuted him because he was my father. http://marxists.anu.edu.au/archive/trotsky/1930/mylife/ch01.htm

In sharp contrast to the emerging Lenin cult according to which Lenin had become imbued with revolutionary ardour at a very young age, Trotsky has a much more limited presentation of his own evolution:

> My political frame of mind while at school was vaguely oppositionist, but no more than that. In my day, revolutionary questions were still unknown among the students. It was whispered that certain groups met at the private

gymnasium maintained by the Czech, Novak; that there had been arrests; that Novak, who was our instructor in athletics, had been dismissed and replaced by an army officer. In the environment surrounding the home of the Schpentzers there was dissatisfaction, but the regime was held to be unshakable. The boldest dreamed of a constitution as possible only after several decades. As for Yanovka, the subject was unmentionable there. When I returned to the village after my graduation from school, bringing with me dim democratic ideas, Father, immediately alert, remarked with hostility: "This will not come to pass even in three hundred years."…. I faced the first crossroads on my path, poorly equipped politically even for a seventeen-year-old boy of that period. Too many questions confronted me all at once, without the necessary sequence and order. Restlessly I cast about me. One thing is certain: even then life had stored within my consciousness a considerable load of social protest. What did it consist of? Sympathy for the down-trodden and indignation over injustice the latter was perhaps the stronger feeling. Beginning with my earliest childhood, in all the impressions of my daily life human inequality stood out in exceptionally coarse and stark forms. Injustice often assumed the character of impudent license; human dignity was under heel at every step. It is enough for me to recall the flogging of peasants. Even before I had any theories, all these things imprinted themselves deeply on me and piled up a store of impressions of great explosive force. … In Nikolayev I met, in addition to the young people who were drawn toward Marxism, several former exiles who were under police surveillance. These were secondary figures of the period of the decline of the populist movement. At that time Social Democrats were not yet returning from exile, they were going into it. The two cross-movements gave rise to whirlpools of theory. For a time I too was drawn into them. There was an odor of putrefaction emanating from populism. Marxism repelled by its so-called "narrowness."…. I became intimately acquainted with the gardener, Shvigovsky, who was a Czech by origin. He was the first working-man I had known who subscribed to newspapers, read German, knew the classics, and participated freely in the arguments between the Marxists and the populists. His one-room cabin in the garden was the meeting-place for visiting students, former exiles and the local youths. One could obtain a forbidden book through Shvigovsky. The conversations of the exiles were punctuated with the names of the populists, Zhelyabov, Perovskaya, Figner, who were treated not as legendary heroes but as real people with whom the older friends of these exiles if not they themselves were familiar. I had a feeling that I was joining a great chain as a tiny link. http://marxists.anu.edu.au/archive/trotsky/1930/mylife/ch06.htm

While he traces his evolution, there is no acknowledgement of the role of the party in effecting a break, nor does he record a rupture with his family in a big way. He does say that he refused to take family finances since his father did not want him to get involved in politics, but that was all. Indeed, despite his political differences, an admiration for his father comes out quite clearly. Since he and his first wife, Aleksandra Sokolovskaia Bronshtein, were both full time activists, their two daughters were in fact brought up by the Bronshtein family. He also wrote that he subsequently lived with Natalia Sedova. It was however Aleksandra who formally retained the name Bronshtein, and she also was to be a leading "Trotskyist" till her death. As for becoming a Marxist, Trotsky shows this as a process reached through trial and error. He began as a populist sympathizer:

> I wrote a polemical article for a populist periodical in Odessa, taking issue with the first Marxist journal. The article had more epigraphs, quotations and venom than it had content. I mailed the article and a week later made a trip to find out its fate. The editor, through large glasses, eyed with sympathy an author whose head displayed an enormous mop of hair but whose face did not show a trace of beard. The article never saw the light. No one was the loser, least of all myself. http://marxists.anu.edu.au/archive/trotsky/1930/mylife/ch06.htm

> With the last autumn steamer, I left for Nikolayev, and resumed my quarters with Shvigovsky in the garden. And the same old business started in again. We discussed the latest numbers of the radical magazines and argued about Darwinism; we were vaguely preparing, and also waiting. What was it in particular that impelled us to start the revolutionary propaganda? It is difficult to say. The impulse originated within us. In the intellectual circles in which I moved, nobody did any actual revolutionary work. We realized that between our endless tea-table discussions and revolutionary organization there was a vast gulf. We knew that any contacts with workers demanded secret, highly "conspiratory" methods. And we pronounced the word solemnly, with a reverence that was almost mystic. We had no doubt that in the end we would go from the discussions at the tea-table to "*conspiratia*"; but nobody was definite as to how and when the change would take place. In excusing our delay, we usually told each other that we must prepare; and we weren't so far wrong, after all. But apparently there had been some change in the air which brought us abruptly onto the road of revolutionary propaganda.

> We called our organization the South Russian Workers' Union, intending to include workers from other towns. I drafted our constitution along Social Democratic lines. The mill authorities tried to offset our influence through speakers of their own. We would answer them the next day with new proclamations. This duel of words aroused not only the workers but a great many of the citizens as well. The whole town was alive with talk about revolutionaries who were flooding the mills with their handbills. Our names were on every tongue. http://marxists.anu.edu.au/archive/trotsky/1930/mylife/ch07.htm

The authorities cited are Marx, Engels, the Italian Hegelian-Marxist Antonio Labriola, Plekhanov, and to a certain extent Kautsky. Above all though, he tends to show that he was drawn to Marxism, as opposed to populism, through participation in working class struggles: "I found no one about me to offer sure guidance". He talks about his own attempt to write a history of freemasonry: "I made no new discoveries .... But I groped my way to the methods somewhat independently. In the writings of Marx, Engels, Plekhanov and Mehring I later found confirmation...".

Likewise, when he wrote about his joining the Bolsheviks only in 1917, there was little that was apologetic:

> Whatever I may say about it, however, the second congress [of the RSDRP – KC] was a landmark in my life, if only because it separated me from Lenin for several years. As I look back now on the past, I am not sorry. I came to Lenin for the second time later than many others, but I came in my own way, after I had gone through and had weighed the experience of the revolution, the counter-revolution and the Imperialist war. I came, as a result, more surely and seriously than those "disciples" who, during the master's life, repeated his words and gestures – not always at the right moment – but, after his death, proved to be nothing but helpless epigones and unconscious tools in the hands of hostile forces. http://marxists.anu.edu.au/archive/trotsky/1930/mylife/ch12.htm

Thus, Trotsky presents his path to Marxism as one he had to work out for himself, and suggests that this is the best path, for if one begins by declaring oneself the subordinate or student of another person, then one will be less able to apply Marxism creatively and accurately in accordance with changing times. He did present a narrative where he acknowledged that Lenin had been right in the organizational struggle against the Mensheviks and he himself wrong. But he stressed, even while writing his autobiography in 1929, that Lenin had been wrong against Trotsky over the nature of the revolution. He called as his witnesses Luacharskii, Joffe, and others. He also did this by stressing that in 1917, Lenin had to take a stand against those who called themselves Old Bolsheviks in order to call for a socialist revolution. He underscored that "In March 1917 Stalin was advocating union" with the Mensheviks, and that Kamenev had accused Lenin of "Trotskyism".

Concerning the insurrection and the civil war, Trotsky attacked the wholesale historical revisionism undertaken by the Stalinist historians showing that he, Trotsky, had been the actual organizer of the insurrection, a claim modern historiography generally accepts, and that he was the overall in charge of the civil war operation on the Soviet side. By 1929, the official discourse was that Trotsky's treason had all but lost the civil war, and it was Stalin who saved the revolution. Trotsky has four chapters on the civil war, where he presents Stalin as the oppositionist who was responsible for the fall of Tsaritsyn and the defeat of the Red Army before Warsaw.

> One must note that one of the reasons for the extraordinary proportions which the catastrophe before Warsaw assumed was the conduct of the command of the southern group of the Soviet armies, operating in the direction of Lvov (Lemberg). The chief political figure in the Revolutionary Military Council of this group was Stalin. Stalin wanted, at whatever cost, to enter Lvov at the same time that Smilga and Tukhachevsky entered Warsaw. Some people are capable of having even such ambitions. When the danger to the armies under Tukhachevsky was fully revealed, and the high command ordered the southwestern armies to change the direction of their advance so as to strike at the flank of the Polish armies before Warsaw, the southwestern command, encouraged by Stalin, continued advancing due west; for was it not more important that they should themselves capture Lvov than that they should help "others" to take Warsaw? Only after repeated orders and threats did the southwestern command change the direction of its advance. But the few days of delay had already had their fatal effect. http://marxists.anu.edu.au/archive/trotsky/1930/mylife/ch37.htm

Whether this was because Stalin wanted to enter Lvov or not, later historians have also concurred [Davies; Higham & Kagan; Lawrynowicz] that the South-Western front failed to assist the thrust to Warsaw, and this was a major factor in the Soviet defeat and the consequent, quite unfavourable Treaty of Riga. Thus, Trotsky's narrative, even when it contained possibly speculative elements, was close enough to actual events for him to be able to say that he was merely telling the truth.

He presented two chapters, one from 1917 and another from the post-1917 affairs, where he elaborates on his relationship with Lenin. A careful historian, combining his book with archival material, would find areas where he steps gingerly. But unlike the official discourse, he takes pains to tell the truth, even if he underplays his differences with Lenin.

> In most cases, the decisions that Lenin and I arrived at independently of each other were identical in all essentials. A few words would bring about a mutual understanding. When I thought the decision of the Politbureau or of the Soviet of People's Commissaries might turn out wrong, I would send Lenin a brief note on a slip of paper. He would answer: "Absolutely right. Submit your proposal." Sometimes he would send me an inquiry whether I agreed with his proposal, and a demand that I speak in his support. Time and again he would arrange with me by telephone the manner in which some matter was to be handled, and if it was important he would insist: "Please come without fall." In cases where we worked hand in hand – the usual thing with us on questions of principle – those who were dissatisfied with the decision, among them the present epigones, remained silent. Many a time Stalin, Zinoviev, or Kamenev disagreed with me on some question of great importance, but as soon as they learned that Lenin shared my opinion they lapsed into silence. We may regard the readiness of the "disciples" to renounce their own ideas in favor of Lenin's in any way we choose, but this readiness clearly contained no guarantee that without Lenin they were capable of arriving at the same conclusions. In this book my disagreements with Lenin assume an importance that they never actually had. There are two reasons for this: our disagreements were the exception and as such attracted attention; after Lenin's death they were magnified by the epigones to astronomic proportions and became an independent political factor in no way connected with either of us". http://marxists.anu.edu.au/archive/trotsky/1930/mylife/ch38.htm

This is followed by his relating his version of the trade union controversy. Independent Marxist scholarship has often held, in recent decades, that both of them actually held bad positions on this issue. (Marik 2008; Chattopadhyay 2006). Trotsky does not really address that. His focus is more on the relationship between him and Lenin.

> A few weeks after the congress, Lenin was assured that I was as anxious as he to do away with the temporary factions, which no longer had any basis in principle. Lenin felt as if a weight had been lifted from his chest. He took advantage of some impudent remark that Molotov, who had just been elected to the Central Committee, aimed at me, to charge him with more zeal than reason, and to add then and there: 'Comrade Trotsky's loyalty in the inter-party relations is absolutely irreproachable'.

So, while it would be dubious to argue that Trotsky's autobiography should be taken as the last word in anything, it is certainly a case that Trotsky tries to make it much more authentic, far closer to actual events, and thereby to challenge the official discourse.

For him, a major problem was how to write and publish in the West and yet proclaim that he remained a Bolshevik, a revolutionary Marxist and anti-imperialist. This is done through two strategies. *First*, he highlights that the struggle of the Left Opposition was not just a national struggle, but the struggle of Marxist (proletarian) internationalism against the bureaucratic messianic nationalism of Stalin and the faction behind him. This is done by arguing that the theory of building Socialism in One Country was a bureaucratic nationalist ploy and a betrayal of the world revolution. The Left Opposition is shown to have fought, not only for the revitalization of socialist democracy in the USSR but also for the revolution in Europe and in China. His *second* strategy is to be found in the final chapter of the book. He develops the theme that though thrown out of the Soviet Union he was still hated by imperialism. In this chapter, titled "The Planet Without a Visa", he explains that he had been refused political asylum by all the democratic countries that pretended that political asylum was the democratic right of people hounded by dictatorships. He concludes:

> Since my exile, I have more than once read musings in the newspapers on the subject of the "tragedy" that has befallen me. I know no *personal* tragedy. I know the change of two chapters of the revolution.

> One American paper which published an article of mine accompanied it with a profound note to the effect that in spite of the blows the author had suffered, he had, as evidenced by his article, preserved his clarity of reason. I can only express my astonishment at the philistine attempt to establish a connection between the power of reasoning and a government post, between mental balance and the present situation. I do not know, and I never have, of any such connection. In prison, with a book or a pen in my hand, I experienced the same sense of deep satisfaction that I did at the mass-meetings of the revolution. I felt the mechanics of power as an inescapable burden, rather than as a spiritual satisfaction. http://marxists.anu.edu.au/archive/trotsky/1930/mylife/ch38.htm

By showing imperialism and Stalinism to be in some kind of collusion, he turns the charges against him back to the rulers of Moscow. It is not surprising that smuggling *Moya Zhizn*, the Russian edition, became a crime, and as late as the 1970s, the Italian publisher Einaudi found their edition, intended for a book fair, blocked under a law that banned pornography, violence, and anti-Soviet propaganda!!

In the officially sponsored autobiographies, the aim was to prove that the authors had elevated themselves to the level of communist consciousness. The move to communist universalism through party membership meant that the author had made a soul searching and had rejected the darkness of capitalism. To critique the party, to even hold any reservation about the line of the party, was an impossible task. To portray Lenin or Stalin and a negative light was a damning heresy. Eventually, even old communists who tried to fight or minimize the damages done by the bureaucratic dictatorship from within, found that they could not resist. Whether Krupskaia's memoirs, or Bukharin's autobiography, had to try to operate within the interstices of the official discourse. Kollontai and Trotsky stand out. Kollontai refused to write what was patently false, but, living in the USSR (or working as a Soviet diplomat) she had to chop out close to a fifth of the text. Trotsky's autobiography stands out as the one work, written after the official discourse had been constructed, that consciously opposed this entire mode.

REFERENCES

Abrams, Robert. "Political Recruitment and Local Government: The Local Soviets of the RSFSR: 1918–21". *Soviet Studies,* 19, No. 4 (April 1968): 573–600.

Andreyev, A. *The Soviets of Workers' and Soldiers' Deputies on the Eve of the October Revolution.* Moscow: Progress, 1971.

Bruce Lincoln, W. *Red Victory: A History of the Russian Civil War.* New York: Simon and Schuster, 1989.

Bruce Lockhart, R. H. *British Agent.* New York and London: G. P. Putnam's Sons, 1933.

Chattopadhyay, Kunal. "Class Struggle among the Molecules: The Rise of 'Proletarian Science'". *Jadavpur University Journal of History,* Vol. XV, (1996–97): 35–46.

Chattopadhyay, Kunal. *The Marxism of Leon Trotsky.* Kolkata: Progressive Publishers, 2006.

Daniels, Robert Vincent. *The Conscience of the Revolution: Communist Opposition in Soviet Russia.* Cambridge, MA: Harvard University Press, 1960.

Farber, Samuel. *Before Stalinism: The Rise and Fall of Soviet Democracy.* Verso: London, 1990.

Figes, Orlando. *A People's Tragedy: The Russian Revolution, 1891-1924.* London: Jonathan Cape, 1996.

Halfin, Igal. *Stalinist Confessions: Messianism and Terror at the Leningrad Communist University.* Pittsburgh: University of Pittsburgh Press, 2009.

Halfin, Igal. *Terror in My Soul.* Cambridge, Mass.: Harvard University Press, 2003.

Kutuzov, V. V. ed. *Velikaia Oktiabrskaia Sotsialisticheskaia Revoliutsiia – Khronika Sobytii.* Moscow: Institut istorii (Akademii'a'nauk SSSR), 1957.

Lowy, Michael. "Stalinist Ideology and Science." Pp. 168–85 in *The Stalinist Legacy,* edited by Tariq Ali. Boulder, Colorado: Lynne Rienner Publishers Inc. 1984.

Vladimirsky, M., ed. *Sovety ispolkomy i s'ezdy Sovetov: Materialy k izucheniiu srtoeniya i devatelrosti organov mestriogo upravleniya,* tom. 1. Moscow: Gosizdat, 1920.

Mandel, David. *The Petrograd Workers and the Fall of the Old Regime: From the February Revolution to the July Days, 1917.* London: MacMillan, 1983.

Mandel, David. *Petrograd Workers and the Soviet Seizure of Power: From the July Days, 1917 to July 1918.* London: MacMillan, 1984.

Mandel, Ernest. *October 1917; coup d'etat or Social Revolution.* Montreuil, France: International Institute of Research and Education, 1992.

Marik, Soma. *Reinterrogating the Classical Marxist Discourses of Revolutionary Democracy.* New Delhi: Aakar Books, 2008.

Nahaylo, Bohdan. "The Case of Nikolai Bukharin: An Old Bolshevik 'Rehabilitated'". *Encounter* 72 (January, 1989): 54–60.

Pipes, Richard. *The Russian Revolution.* New York: Knopff, 1990.

Pirani, Simon. *The Russian Revolution in Retreat, 1920-24. Soviet Workers and the New Communist Elite.* Routledge: London, 2008.

Radzinsky, Edward. *Stalin.* New York: Random House, 1997.

Schapiro, Leonard. *The Origin of the Communist Autocracy.* Cambridge, MA: Harvard University Press, 1966.

Serge, Victor. *Year One of the Russian Revolution.* London and New York: Bookmarks, Pluto and Readers and Writers, 1992.

Stalin, Joseph. *History of the Communist Party of the Soviet Union (Bolsheviks) Short Course.* New York: International Publishers, 1939.

Trotsky, Leon. *History of the Russian Revolution* (with an introduction for the Indian edition by Kunal Chattopadhyay and Soma Marik). New Delhi: Aakar Books, 2013.

Tucker, Robert C. "On the 'Letter of an Old Bolshevik' as an Historical Document". *Slavic Review* 51, no. 4 (Winter, 1992): 782–85.

White, Hayden. *The Content of the Form: Narrative Discourse and Historical Representation.* Baltimore: Johns Hopkins University Press, 1987.

WEB REFERENCES

Kollontai, Alexandra. *The Autobiography of a Sexually Emancipated Communist Woman,* (translated by Salvator Attansio). London: Herder and Herder, 1971. http://www.marxists.org/archive/kollonta/1926/autobiography.htm (last accessed 21.12.2013)

Trotsky, Leon. *My Life.* New York: Charles Scribner's Sons, 1930. http://marxists.anu.edu.au/archive/trotsky/1930/mylife/index.htm (last accessed 17.12.2013)

20

Disabled but Beautiful and Proudly Resistant: Applied Theatre for the Disabled as Minority Discourse

Nehemiah Chivandikwa and Owen Seda

INTRODUCTION

There is an apparent lacuna with regards to scholarly discourses on the politics of the body within the hegemonic and subordinated discourses in the Zimbabwean context, in particular, and Africa, in general. This lacuna may be traceable to the fact that Africa has been largely preoccupied with the "grand" political issues of capitalism, globalization, imperialism, racism, and classism among others. With the exception of the apparent increase in gender-based research, there is evidently very limited academic attention that has been paid to issues related to disability and disabled bodies.[1] While developments in gender-based research are encouraging, it is curious that discourses on disability have not been accorded sufficient space in both the academe and the mainstream media. This is regrettable because we live in a historical epoch that espouses tantalizingly lofty terms, such as human rights for minority groups, democracy, equity, and inclusivity.

In the Zimbabwean context, which is the focus of this study, academic as well as socio-cultural constructions and representations of disabled bodies seem to be largely influenced by hegemonic and normalizing discourses emanating from traditional cultural practices, Western Christianity and the field of medicine. It is in the light of the above that our focus in this collaborative paper is to recognize and analyse applied theatre as a practice that offers emancipatory space for subordinated discourses, such as disability and its related pedagogies. Our interest in applied theatre derives from the recognition that applied theatre is by nature an embodied discourse. In other words, the body is central to the marginalization and subordination of disability. Disabled people are often ridiculed, pitied, patronized, romanticized, and excluded precisely because of their bodies (Peterson and Hughes 1997). Michel Foucault's (1995) notion that bodies are a battlefield for power fits neatly into disability discourse because the body is a target for discipline (Foucault 1980), and also because the disabled body is the most marginalized of the marginalized (Davis 2010).

This study makes an effort to analyse applied theatre as an embodied minority discourse that challenges, contextualizes, and subverts normalizing and subjugating discourses on disability with specific reference to an applied theatre project on albinism, curiously entitled, *The White Man from Buhera* (2011) that was undertaken by undergraduate students at the University of Zimbabwe. Our major interest in this project is that the majority of participant-researchers, actors, dancers, and devisors of the play were themselves disabled students. In that way, the project was able to approximate an ideal in applied theatre, which characterizes applied theatre as a theatre of struggle. As Augusto Boal observes, applied theatre

> Is the theatre OF the oppressed, ABOUT the oppressed and BY the oppressed, whether they be workers, peasants, unemployed people, women, black people, young people, old people, people with mental or physical disabilities in the end, all those on whom silence is imposed and from whom is taken the right to a full existence. (36)

The White Man from Buhera may, therefore, be viewed as a project of the [disabled] minority, about the minority, and by the oppressed minority. This is because disabled people are a minority social group with common and specific forms of group consciousness, which like any other social group, is not necessarily always homogeneous (Peterson and Hughes 1999). Our central concern throughout the paper is that emancipatory applied theatre projects on disability such as *The White Man from Buhera* can serve as formidable minority counter discourses which unmask and subvert subjugating and normalizing discourses in ways that not only affirm the disabled body as a site of oppression, but also as a site for liberation. We view such embodied discourses as necessary in the quest for an inclusive redefinition of aesthetic and physical beauty.

The project which we analyse here was undertaken by twelve students at the University of Zimbabwe. Three of them were participating in this project as part of their course in applied theatre, while other disabled students participated out of their interest in response to an open public invitation. The students were given a choice to target specific forms of disability and this is how *The White Man from Buhera,* targeting albinism, became one of the four projects that were undertaken by the students within a broad aspiration to explore the discrimination and marginalization of disabled university students. The other projects focused on visually and physically challenged students. Themes in the other three projects included unemployment, sexuality, and participation in sport.

In this collaborative study, we bring different but convergent experiences. Nehemiah Chivandikwa teaches the applied theatre course at the University of Zimbabwe[2] under which the university students undertook the project, while Owen Seda has been teaching theatre studies since 1992 and has been involved in numerous applied theatre projects in and outside Zimbabwe. We therefore approach this project as participant observers and critics.

CONCEPTUAL AND THEORETICAL FRAMEWORKS

Our analysis of *The White Man from Buhera* is guided by the recognition that disability is an embodied discourse. As a result, the study is underpinned by three theoretical frameworks, namely; applied theatre discourse, Michel Foucault's bio-politics, and the African philosophical concept of *Ukama/ubuntu* (Shona and Ndebele language for "Humanness"). We make an effort to focus on these theoretical concepts in order to highlight their relevance to the human body as a site of struggle and liberation.

APPLIED THEATRE AND THE BODY

The White Man from Buhera project was undertaken within the broader ambits of applied theatre at the University of Zimbabwe. There are a number of consistent features which define this broad category. *First*, applied theatre is a pro-social practice which functions as an agent for social change. It has a specific focus on ameliorating psycho-social and socio-political oppression (Nicholson 2005). *Second*, applied theatre transcends surface aesthetic ornamentation or sensual appeal which is often conceptualized as the "entertainment" function of art theatre (Ackroyd 2000) that is associated with mainstream, or so-called conventional (and usually), Western theatre practices (Nicholson 2005). It is thus that applied theatre is a discourse of engagement. As a result, applied theatre is usually associated with "non theatrical" environments such as prisons, rehabilitation centres, hospitals, schools, universities, children's homes, and community centres (Taylor 2002).

The focus in the present study is on how dominant discourses on disabled bodies were unmasked, decentred, and destabilised through an applied theatre practice carried out by a group of university students with disabilities. We perceive applied theatre as a discourse which integrates words, actions, values, attitudes, gestures, postures, and other visual images (Weisket and Ociepka 2011). Therefore, the play under analysis is read as a form of performed minority counter discourse.

Applied theatre does not merely reveal discourses; it also deconstructs and constructs alternative discourses. The *White Man from Buhera* adopted the documentary theatre form, which is a form that combines autobiographical, visual, and verbal images that; "foreground the body as an object to be viewed and to be explained" (Thompson 2000: 334). The disabled body thus becomes the medium as well as context of performance discourse (Weistek and Ociepka 2011). The documentary theatre form is relevant because it challenges "master narratives of history and discourse" (Zvi 2006: 45). We are concerned here with dominant narratives on albinism, as a form of disability. The intention is to examine the extent to which applied theatre can "challenge negative perceptions of physicality" (Nicholson 102) so as to recognize and acknowledge the positive contributions of disabled bodies. This aspiration is anchored on the thesis that oppression is also embodied (Boal 1979). This suggests that participating in applied theatre can liberate restricted bodies from the "embodiment of oppression" (Nicholson 102).

MICHEL FOUCAULT'S BIO-POLITICS

Michel Foucault's seminal writings on the politics of the body view the body as central to issues that have to do with the problematic of discourse and representation (Bill and Peterson 1997). Foucault sees the body as an object of knowledge and a target for the exercise of power. This is something which increases the capacities and skills of the body for production, while simultaneously making the body docile, that is, passive in the political sense (Lunn 1997, Bill and Peterson 1997). Foucault writes that institutions such as schools, hospitals, rehabilitation centres, and prisons manage and control the human body not through crude physical power, but through forms of discourse. In this way, individuals become effects of power (Foucault 1980). It is through forms of discourse that disabled bodies have been classified, ranked, and assessed (Lunn 1997). In other words, bodies are constructed as either inferior and/or superior on the basis of normalizing discourses, norms, and ideals that are based on certain skills and abilities. To that extent, disability activists and researchers have theorized the disabled body as the most marginalized of marginalized bodies (Davis 2010). While Foucault's early writings have been heavily criticized for suggesting that the oppressed or "docile" body cannot escape the effects of power (Lunn 1997), our interest is in his latter submissions (Foucault 1980) when he says that marginalized groups can minimize and resist domination through what he calls "practices of freedom and liberty". We appropriate Foucault's latter acknowledgement to posit that applied theatre projects on disability such as the one we analyse can be potent practices for freedom and liberty.

UKAMA/UBUNTU AND DISABILITY

Ukama or *ubuntu* (Shona and Ndebele, respectively) constitutes a body of knowledge that is rooted and embedded in an African philosophy which emphasizes inclusivity, respect, dignity, tolerance, altruism, and empathy within the context of human relatedness (Mhaka 2010; Shava 2010; Mpofu 1999). The emphasis in *ukama/ubuntu* is on respect and shunning selfishness and individualism. *Munhu/Umuntu* (person/humanity) consists of the body, the spirit, strength, vitality, and the mind in non-binary conceptions (Shava 2008). Our interest is in the fact that the discourse of *ukama/ubuntu* rejects human suffering, especially socially constructed human suffering. Socially induced suffering is viewed as an affront to the ideals of *ukama/ubuntu* which encapsulate communitarian relatedness among all people. More specifically, "there was nothing precluding someone who might appear different from the rest of the Shona such as *musope* (albino) from being socialised as *munhu*" (human) (Chimuka 2001, 9).

It is significant to note, however, that this idyllic practice was nevertheless complicated by a combination of factors. *First*, it would seem as if all societies have failed to account for and negotiate bodily differences relating to disability. Superstitious beliefs have often been invoked in order to substitute the absence of rational or scientific explanations for disability, and Africa is not an exception in this regard (Mpofu 1999). However, in Africa, in general, and in Zimbabwe, in particular, the construction of disabled bodies may have been largely shaped by colonialism and Westernization. The combined effect of the above forces is that there has been an apparent tendency to exaggerate traditional conceptions of disability in Africa out of context (Shava 2008). *Secondly*, non-progressive Western models of disability which emphasize lack, deficiency, charity, and rehabilitation have been imposed on Zimbabwe (Shava 2008). It is no wonder then that some African researchers have begun to appropriate progressive local discourses such as the African philosophical concept of *ukama/ubuntu* to partner progressive Western discourses in order to counter traditional hegemonic ideologies on disability (Murove 1999 quoted in Shava 2008).

CONTEXT AND BACKGROUND OF THE PLAY

In this section, we analyse the way an applied theatre project attempts to subvert the effects of hegemonic discourses on albinism. Scientifically, albinism is explained as a lack of, or low levels of melanin, which is a bodily substance that is responsible for pigmentation which functions to "thicken" and protect the skin from the sun's ultra-violet radiation (Lund 2001). Albinism has serious effects on the skin, eyes, and hair. People with albinism have sensitive skin which is vulnerable to cancer. Albinism can also cause a high sensitivity to light and it also triggers involuntary eye movement and "reduced visual acquit" (Baker, Lund, Nyathi, and Taylor 2010, 169). These physical conditions normally lead to stigmatization and ostracism that is also fuelled by hegemonic and retrogressive discourses on disability, in general, and albinism, in particular. For instance, there are several myths surrounding people with albinism in Zimbabwe and South Africa. One is that people with albinism are products of infidelity. The other one is that children with albinism are born when a woman sleeps with a *tokoloshi* (malevolent male spirit that causes trouble) (*ibid*).

In general, albinism in Zimbabwe has been viewed as a curse (Masuku 2011). These beliefs and attitudes have brought several challenges to people with albinism. They have faced discrimination at work. Of the 4,000 people with albinism that are in Zimbabwe today, about less than ten percent are formally employed (Baker, Lund, Nyathi, and Taylor 2010). One of the reasons for this low employment rate among people with albinism is the perception that they have a short life span. Socially, it is difficult for some people to accept people with albinism. There is a belief that people with albinism have evil spirits, while others do not want to get in contact with a person with albinism because they believe that albinism is contagious (Masuku 2011). At the same time, some beliefs make it difficult for people with albinism to find a marriage partner. Even if one manages to get a marriage partner, there is usually the added challenge that relatives might not accept him/her. People with albinism also face the challenge of mistaken identities. For example, some people mistake albinos for whites. The title of the applied theatre project under consideration derives from this context.

The participants and creators of the play under consideration are cognizant of the fact that there have been significant improvements in terms of the attitudes surrounding people with albinism. However, subtle and complex forms of discrimination and prejudice still remain (Sibanda 2011). *The White Man from Buhera* was conceived and devised to expose and challenge the various manifestations of such forms. Our present focus is on how the play confronts discourses relating to bodies of people with albinism. The play itself is a product of intense research through readings, interviews, and discussions involving about twelve undergraduate students from the University of Zimbabwe. The students carried out interviews with several people in and outside the campus. They also read a variety of material from academic and media sources (Mugumira 2011). However, the final play was largely based on two major sources. The first source was the combined narratives of four students with albinism – one female and two males. The second source was personal and media narratives of Professor John Makumbe – an accomplished academic, popular political scientist, as well as a social critic based at the University of Zimbabwe. Representatives of the group held interviews with Professor Makumbe (Sibanda 2011).

Professor John Makumbe was born in Buhera, a rural district located in central South Eastern Zimbabwe. At birth, he was almost killed by a midwife but he was eventually saved by his mother. According to Professor Makumbe, "When the midwife saw me so white and so pale, she wanted to kill me on the spot" (Professor John Makumbe quoted in Baker, Lund, Nyathi, and Taylor 2010:173). At school, fellow students used to shun him. They did not want to share books, desks, and food with him because they had been fed on the myth that albinism is both a curse and contagion (Mugumira 2011 and Sibanda 2011). However, John Makumbe was a fierce fighter against ostracism and stigmatization (Masuku 2011). He has managed to challenge both the government and the public on the need to recognize the rights of people with albinism through influencing the formulation of policies that ameliorate the suffering among people with albinism (Mugumira 2011). He is known internationally as a robust critic of the Zimbabwean government. During the liberation struggle, he faced serious dilemmas which were a threat to his life. On the one hand, white people labelled him a sell out, while on the other, black people almost killed him perceiving that he was white (Machipisa 2003). Since he was intelligent, he was awarded a scholarship to study in Australia where he was awarded a DPhil in Political Science and Administration (Sibanda 2011).

The second source of material that went into the creation of the play was the narratives of three students with albinism. Two of them were twins; a male and a female, while the other was a male. The narratives of the twins revolve around struggles for recognition, academic fairness, ostracism, and academic challenges and constraints. Although they were born at a time when crude forms of ostracism were almost non-existent, they contend that it is a long way before society can fully accept people with albinism without prejudice (Sibanda 2011). The narrative from the other young man also revolves around the similar issues such as romance and the insensitivity of teachers and instructors in schools and tertiary institutions. For example, he revealed that one of his teachers once remarked, "Do you want me to bring the chalkboard to you", after he had told the teacher that he could not see what was written on the chalkboard clearly (Mugumira 2011).

These stories were amalgamated and fictionalized to form the core of the storyline of the play. All the students were collectively involved in playmaking, directing, and critiquing the play. However, the central and key aspects of the play were undertaken by students with albinism. After the play had been devised, six more students with different forms of disabilities were incorporated to take up acting roles in the production.

THE WHITE MAN FROM BUHERA: SYNOPSIS, STRUCTURE, STYLE

Structurally, the play is a combination of realistic and non-realistic features. The basic story begins sometime in the early 1950s and runs through the present. The story unfolds through a flashback technique which revolves around the structure of a television talk show in which the talk-show hostess and her guest reflect on past events, as they simultaneously engage the audience on a number of contemporary issues. The story is told through a combination of dialogue, dance, music, movement, and audience participation through frame breaking and frame expansion.

The basic storyline is as follows: Mrs Sibanda gives birth to a set of twins (a boy and a girl) with albinism. The midwife and the children's aunt are both stunned and the fate of the twins hangs in the balance. Fortunately, however, the determination of the mother saves the lives of the two children who grow up to have different but complementary characters. The girl named Shamiso (Shona for Wonderful) is outspoken and courageous while the boy named Shingirai (Shona for Perseverance or Determination) is tolerant, as well as intelligent. Shamiso becomes a nurse while Shingirai becomes a university professor. The play starts with a popular Zimbabwean television talk show signature tune[3] which is played live by the actors, using their bodies without instruments. The dancers disappear backstage at the appearance of Mai Diego who is the "talk show" hostess as she begins to interview Professor Sibanda (Shingirai). Professor Sibanda is requested to narrate his struggles as a person with albinism and he decides to "show" the viewers his struggles on the "screen" (main stage) where the audience sees a midwife congratulating Mrs Sibanda (his mother) for giving birth to a set of twins. The midwife and the aunt who has just come in are both shocked to discover that the twins are "white," sparking a heated discussion. The midwife and the aunt exit, making serious threats to Mrs Sibanda who is left on the stage "talking" to her children in a ritual that is meant to secure their lives. In Scene Three, the audience watches a group of high school students dancing in a classroom. The teacher comes in to give out end-of-year reports and it turns out that Shamiso and Shingirai are at the top of the class. This infuriates other classmates who start to jeer and ridicule them using derogatory and pejorative terms. Overcome by anger, Shamiso grabs one student by the neck and "floors" him. The young man is saved by the intervention of the teacher who is evidently shocked that an albino girl with such "fragile" skin could be so violent. Mai Diego tries to advise the "viewers" to be sympathetic towards the "less privileged among us", but she is immediately stopped by Professor Sibanda who advises her that people with albinism do not need anyone's sympathy. What they need instead is respect, dignity, and equal opportunity. From there, the focus shifts to the main stage (Scene Five) where a lady manager is on the phone as she waits to conduct an interview with a candidate who has an impressive Curriculum Vitae. Shingirai soon enters and on realizing that the CV belongs to Shingirai (an albino), the lady manager lies that the interview has been postponed to a later date. In Scene Six, David, a medical doctor, is attending to a "patient" with a physical disability (Mrs Nyoni). The doctor is giving his "patient" (Mrs Nyoni) a series of medical instructions and he is visibly agitated that she does not seem to be listening. A female nurse (Shamiso) soon enters and the doctor insults and humiliates her in front of the "patient". Mrs Nyoni is shocked by the doctor's strange behaviour and after a few minutes of discussion, Mrs Nyoni gets to realize that contrary to his outward posturing, the doctor actually loves the nurse, but has failed to woo her. Mrs Nyoni comes to the doctor's aid, giving him useful tips on how to approach the young and attractive nurse. Following Mrs Nyoni's advice, David the medical doctor eventually proposes to Shamiso with success. In Scene Seven, David struggles to convince his mother to accept Shamiso (an albino) as a future daughter-in-law. In the last scene, Mai Diego and Professor Sibanda reflect on all these events as the debate is extended to the audience through an expanded and in-depth post performance discussion and analysis.

In the following sections, we analyse the discourses that are embedded in the above narrative. The central thesis guiding our analysis is that "Discourses are implicit wherever the different languages of communication are used. As we talk, write, move, draw, interact, think, and act, we are doing so through discourse" (Weitsek and Ociepka 2011, 120). Consequently, the movements, gestures, and verbal images that are discussed in the next sections are constructed as implicit minority counter discourse.

CONFRONTING GIVEN DISCOURSES

In this section, we examine *The White Man from Buhera* in terms of how the play reflects on, and critiques some of the ways by which human behaviour and conduct is shaped by hegemonic and normative values on bodily appearance within the context of albinism. We attempt to show how Traditional, Charity and Medical Models (or discourses) on disability are implicit in the way "able-bodied" characters relate to disabled people in society and in the play. In addition, we also attempt to explore the intersection between the medical model and dominant masculine discourses.

The Traditional and Charity models view people with disabilities as victims of impairment arising from misfortune or curse. These models construct disabled people using images of tragic suffering and pity. As a result, able-bodied people are viewed as potential messiahs or good Samaritans towards the disabled. Thus, the Charity model constructs people with disabilities as objects of pity and who are in need of grace as they are minimally involved in policies and practices that shape their lives. It is precisely these ideologies which *The White Man from Buhera* contextualizes and confronts. The project suggests that Traditional and Charity models of disability have gradually moved from overt to subtle forms of manifestation. Whereas in the past, babies with albinism could be killed, modern society allows them to live while covertly denying them opportunities and erecting barriers for their inclusion in social, economic, and educational spaces. We have noted above that Mrs Sibanda (mother to the twins) embodies forms of resistance against crude manifestations of traditional views on albinism. In the second scene, Mrs Sibanda emotionally and vigorously defends her two babies. She speaks to them in a moving, poetic, and defiant voice. She advises Shamiso to desist from adopting a "feminine" timidity if ever confronted with brutal and chauvinist males. Mrs Sibanda continues to counsel Shingirai to brave intimidation and strive against fear and ignorance. Mrs Sibanda fondly kisses the twins thereby affirming their bodily beauty as she says; "*Laze laba bahle bantwabami*" (*Ndebele* for: How beautiful you look my sweet children). These words and gestures are powerful forms of resistance against normative values and prejudices often directed towards people with disabilities. They serve as an embodied and symbolic contestation of the tyranny of perfection as well as the modernist trend of standardizing bodily physicality and appearance.

In Scene Three, the discrimination towards the disabled is not as crude as it is in preceding scenes. However, the children and the school teacher still exhibit a tendency towards "othering". While the name-calling from the students is bad enough, the attitude displayed by the teacher is tragic. The teacher disregards the fact that the boy who has been "floored" by Shamiso has been calling her (i.e. Shamiso) *murungudunhu* (fake white person) and instead worries that a girl with a "fragile" skin could challenge boys, wondering whether Shamiso could be possessed by evil spirits. In a subsequent scene, the prejudice becomes even more sophisticated. Shingirai (now Professor Sibanda) is looking for a job. The female manager pretends to be progressive yet in reality she does not think that someone with albinism would present an "ideal" corporate image for the organization. Of course, Shingirai is not easily fooled as the following excerpt reveals;

Lady Manager: (*With feigned politeness and a professional voice*) I am really sorry my dear. The interview has been postponed.

Shingirai: (*Surprised and touching his skin*) I hope it has nothing to do with this.

Lady Manager: (*Exaggerated and patronising*) No. No my darling. It's not that. *(Trying to accompany him out, she is about to touch him and then realising her 'mistake' quickly and tactfully withdraws her hand*). Ok sweetie!

The hypocrisy of this empty ritual of politeness is further exposed by the fact that as soon as Shingirai moves out, the lady manager picks up her phone and chides the secretary for allowing *inkau* (Ndebele for *albino*) into her office. She reminds the secretary that her office is not a welfare centre. The events described above suggest that while there still exists residual elements of crude forms of prejudice, modern society tries to hide this prejudice under the cover of political correctness in speech and decorum. What inspired the creators of this particular applied theatre project as a form of minority discourse is the hope that human beings can be enlightened and influenced through counter discourse in order to shun discrimination. They can also be persuaded to recognize the imperative that such transformation can only be realized when disabled people take the initiative to craft and shape embodied pedagogies on their own terms (Boal 2006).

We may now attempt and link hyper masculine discourses with the ideology of the Medical model following bell hooks (1989) who theorizes the interconnectedness of domineering discourses. We recognize that both discourses have "ablest" tendencies, which value physical agility and perfection of appearance, albeit with different emphases. The Medical model views disabled bodies as deficient, sick, weak, and essentially abnormal. It emphasizes normalcy and conformity (Kraus 2008). Disability is largely perceived as a "disease", or a "deformity" which leads to individual tragedies that call for medical "correction" or rehabilitation (Mitra 2011). What is particularly relevant to our present focus is the observation that the Medical model is essentially normative, that is, "people are considered disabled on the basis of being unable to function as "normal" persons" *(ibid*: 2). This attempt to correct the "illness" of people with disabilities can result in the allotment of excessive authority to the medical practitioner, leading to the control and devaluation of persons with disabilities. It is thus that hegemonic values of physical normality are perpetuated (Kraus 2008). As a result, modernity has ushered in the standardization of physicality and an obsession with physical perfection which has been theorized as the "tyranny of perfection" (Hughes and Peterson 1997).

The play under consideration symbolically but robustly confronts medical discourse on disability. David, the medical doctor, gives Mrs Nyoni long and authoritative medical instructions and commands. The purpose of his commands is to convince Mrs Nyoni that if the doctor's instructions are followed religiously they will "fix" her body in order that it becomes "normal". He is critical of her diet, her apparent lack of adherence to the exercises she has been given, as well as a host of other medical instructions. However, David's authoritative discourse is symbolically subverted when Mrs Nyoni the "patient" transforms into David's "doctor" for love. Realizing that David is struggling to win the love of Shamiso, Mrs Nyoni engages him and gives him some useful tips and advice which eventually makes him succeed in winning the love of Shamiso. This role reversal is significantly instructive in terms of its symbolic critique of medical discourses. While David is domineering, patronizing, and authoritative if not autocratic, Mrs Nyoni the "doctor of love" is dialogic, sensitive, encouraging, though at times firm and critical. She suggests rather than commands. She has a listening ear, while David has an open mouth and "listens" only in order to find ways of correcting and rebuking his "patient". The language of the medical doctor makes communication difficult while the "doctor of love" uses language which is persuasive and accessible.

What is significant here is that the play unmasks the tendency in medical discourse to overemphasize certain bodily capacities and skills such as agility, productivity, and competitiveness at the expense of other skills, capacities and abilities such as social interaction, politeness, kindness, and humour (Worlbring 2008). The creators of the play deliberately constructed David as a "less" able person in regard to emotional and everyday human interaction. This construction is deliberately complicated by the fact that he finds himself falling in love with a person (an albino) who has an "impaired" body. This becomes the source of the doctor's crisis of consciousness. While he is in love with Shamiso, David is cognizant of the fact society will judge him harshly for falling in love with someone who is "deficient" (i.e. an albino woman). Mrs Nyoni's response to David's crisis is both humorous and powerful. She reminds David that the fact that Shamiso has albinism, "is no big deal", because, "women are the same anyway – especially where it matters the most". This is a light-hearted but powerful invitation for David and the audience to value variation and common humanity within the spirit of acceptance and accommodation. This is significant because we know that:

> "Ableism" has long been used to justify hierarchies of rights and discrimination between other social groups and to exclude people not classified as "able people" (Worlbring 252).

By focusing exclusively on Mrs Nyoni's single bodily limitation, David fails to appreciate her other skills, competences, and abilities, which construct her as a complex being. This serves as a reminder that society's overemphasis on conformity and normative values risks losing sight of the complexity and richness of humanity. Our reading is that beyond offering a critique of medical discourse, the play also embraces communitarianism as a progressive philosophy of human existence which emphasizes diversity and reciprocity. David embodies two subordinating and subjugating discourses, namely, medical discourse and masculinity, the latter of which has been likened to imperialism. Masculinity like imperialism is a phallocentric, supremacist ideology that subjugates and dominates its subalterns (Zenenga 2007: 127).

In the context of this study, we recognize that there are also interesting similarities between medical discourse on disability and masculinity, at least as implied by the theatre text under consideration. Masculinity values physical performance of the body, authority, and perfection. Both discourses value competitiveness and a "narrow" rationality. In the same way as medical discourse, masculinity tends to seek control rather than reciprocal engagement. Lastly, both the medical model and masculinity privilege individualism.

David epitomizes the major ideals of masculinity which have been identified as toughness, authority, self-mastery, handsomeness, hard work, articulation, emotional stability, and arrogance (Kraus 2008; Zenenga 2007; Atree 2007). David also has an agile and athletic body which performs all masculine rituals to expectation – giving the impression of a "perfectly" masculine body – physically, mentally, and emotionally. His masculine arrogance is at its most evident when he rebukes Shamiso in the presence of Mrs Nyoni, making chauvinist remarks to the effect that women are a problem because they always want to pretend that they have a capacity to think rationally. David says, "Not here nurse Shamiso. Your job is to listen. You are not here to think, that is my job" (*The White Man from Buhera*). However, as the play progresses, it becomes evident that all this hyper-masculinity is neither as strong, nor as rooted as it would appear. David's emotional fragility is deftly "diagnosed" by Mrs Nyoni. She correctly realizes that David's verbal outbursts emerge from emotional instability. Mrs Nyoni shatters David's macho image of hyper-masculinity, challenging him until he almost weeps, confessing that while he truly loves Shamiso, he is worried about what people will say if he goes into a relationship with an albino woman. David's emotional vulnerability is in sharp contrast to the rational and self-mastery image of hyper-masculinity. This is at its most vivid when he lies on the floor – helpless and begging for Shamiso's love. In the meanwhile, Mrs Nyoni stoically and calmly watches from a distance while Shamiso defiantly gives her back to him. This image contrasts sharply with the social construct and expectations of this middle class, "rational" and "able-bodied male". Clearly then, the play suggests interesting interconnections between the Medical model of disability and the ideology of hyper-masculinity, which perhaps deserves further interrogation in academic research on body-based discourses.

BEAUTIFUL BODIES, AESTHETICS, AND DISABILITY

For people with disabilities, the body is a site of oppression in terms of both form and what is done to and on it (Abberely 1987: 17). At a general level, the "able" African body has been devalued, restricted, and objectified by colonialism and the excesses of Western capitalism (Gordon 1994). By extension, the disabled African body has been doubly devalued by both colonialism and "ableism". The tyranny of physical perfection can also be extended to the realms of aesthetics and performance. A fundamental question has been raised elsewhere as follows: Can the body of a disabled person be ever considered "beautiful"? (Peterson and Hughes 1999). The above question seeks to explore the extent to which society is able to consider notions of beauty beyond hegemonic and normative approaches. More specifically within the context of applied theatre, Hargrave (2009) wonders if it is possible for a person with cerebral palsy to be considered "eloquent" in vocal delivery. We could also extend the question to kinetic eloquence in movement and gesture for people who are challenged physically and visually.

Issues to do with the degree of artistic excellence in theatre for the disabled are further complicated and affected by environmental and structural limitations since the "devices of theatre are disabling rather than the impairment of the body" (Alica 17). What all this means is that assessing aesthetic beauty is inevitably, a political issue especially within the context of disability. Conceptualizing notions of artistic beauty is generally a highly subjective enterprise (Conroy 2009). For our current purposes, it is critical then to realize that perceptions of artistic excellence are coloured and implicated by normative values of physicality and appearance. The majority of participants in the project under analysis were a mix of students with varying types and degrees of physical and visual challenges who were complemented by a few able-bodied students. Our particular focus, however, is on performances by the disabled students.

The controversies and complications noted above notwithstanding, we posit that *The White Man from Buhera* was generally a well-crafted play that was performed in interesting ways which expanded and challenged the audience's understanding of notions of aesthetic excellence with regard to people with disabilities. We posit this on the basis of our analysis of movement, gesture, and aspects of dialogue, and dance in the play. We contend that all in all, *The White Man from Buhera* achieved a commendable standard of artistic merit, notwithstanding a number of problematic elements pertaining to the performance that were raised by some members of the audience. We view the following as some of the high points emanating from the performance.

In Scene One, the audience is confronted with a group of actors made up of able-bodied students and students with different forms of disability. Their bodies move in unison, in a rhythmical pattern of movements, gestures, and sounds, which rise to a captivating crescendo. All the actors and actresses appear in this scene, some in glasses and some on crutches, including a few others who are able-bodied. These actors create the sound of the signature tune for ZTV's popular Mai Chisamba show which is played without instruments. They replace the instruments with their voices and their bodies in ways that are reminiscent of Jerzy Grotowski's Poor Theatre. The actors and actresses' rendition of Mai Chisamba's signature tune is rich in its vocal texture and its melody. The actors dance in a free but well-coordinated style much to the audience's amusement and approval. In any case, this "strange" mix of able and variously disabled bodies is a spectacle which is in itself beautiful in ways that challenge society to embrace variety and diversity in bodily appearance and physicality. We posit that the mere physical appearance on stage of these differently able and disabled bodies served as a powerful symbol for the dynamics of dependence and independence, autonomy, and communitarianism, all of which pointed to the wealth of diversity in the physicality of human existence. In our view, it is this beauty that enhanced the socio-political potency of the minority counter discourse represented by the play as it unmasked everyday issues relating to the politics of the body that are often taken for granted.

While the performance robustly engages normative discourses on disability, there are several humorous elements which add to its aesthetic beauty. There were several moments of humour which ignited laughter among the audience. These humorous moments were necessary in order to prevent the play from engendering afore-mentioned negative emotions of patronage, pity, and compassion that are often generated whenever "able-bodied" people see or listen to disabled people (Mlilo 2011). For example, in Scene Six, Professor Sibanda is asked the pertinent question on whether or not albinism is a form of disability in Zimbabwe. In his response, he refers to the fact it (albinism) is a permanent condition that limits and affects several bodily functions such as visual acquit. He then reminds the audience that "There is no way I will ever wake up as black as Robert ..." The humour in this dialogue is obviously embedded in its ambiguity and incompleteness, it being a veiled or oblique reference to [President] Robert Mugabe (who is very dark in complexion) and for whom Professor John Makumbe is a fierce critic. It is thus an "edited" version of Professor Makumbe's remarks in a personal interview (Sibanda 2011). Thus, the audience is tempted to link this remark with Professor Makumbe who usually begins his political comments by making scathing political attacks in which he often mentions President Mugabe by his full name. What is also crucial within the context of disability politics is the fact that the statement mentioned above is an explicit affirmation of, and pride in the bodily identity of albinism. This affirmation of albinism counters normative discourses which largely seek to view, fix, or mystify the bodies of people with albinism. In yet another humorous body-affirmation remark, Professor Sibanda dismisses all the myths about men with albinism as false and superstitious. He says only one myth is "authentic":

Professor Sibanda: Mai Diego, all the myths about albino men and women are hopelessly false and they are based on superstition. There is only one that is true.

Mai Diego: Which one Professor?

Professor Sibanda: That all men with albinism are extremely charming and romantic.

Mai Diego: That's not for you to say Prof. Let's leave it to the women to confirm.

Lastly, Shamiso rebukes David's patronizing reference to her "condition" in an attempt to impress her when he says that he loves her as "she is";

David: (*Desperate and begging*) Shamiso please, I love you as you are, in your condition.

Shamiso: (*Turning angrily to look at David*) David I do not want to hear that nonsense (*Pointing at the audience*) *Ndizvo zvaunoita here kana uchinyenga vasikana vako ava vese, vakasviba kuti tsvaa – sepoto*) (Is that what you do when you are proposing to dark skinned girls – literally girls who are as dark as black pots).

The last line quoted above drew a mixture of responses from the audience which included laughter, protest, surprise, and anger. This is because the reference to dark skinned people as "black pots" is usually associated with self-deprecating remarks by blacks who have internalized colonial oppression to the extent that they contend that in comparison with the "white" skin the "black" skin is inferior and "less beautiful". Shamiso's remarks are therefore meant to provoke as well as generate discussion on the troubled concept of beauty.

The above performative, as well as other humorous elements in the play enhanced its aesthetic quality in such a way as to suggest that applied theatre for and by people with disabilities, need not be necessarily aesthetically "dull" and animate sentiments of pity. While the issues in question were extremely serious and sensitive, they were raised in a context and in such a way that left space for debate, laughter, amusement, as well as entertainment. What rendered the performance captivating was the level of sincerity in the portrayal of character, including other aspects of performance such as vocal and tonal variation, emotion, movement, and gesture.

CONCLUSION

Although we do not wish to suggest that the *The White Man from Buhera* was flawless, or that it necessarily reached the "high" sensual and technical standards of conventional or mainstream theatre, we nevertheless wish to contend that *The White Man from Buhera* constitutes a credible intellectual challenge to hegemonic and normative discourses on disability that was able to assert the socio-political, bodily, and aesthetic agency of disabled people. We also hope that our study has been able to demonstrate that applied theatre can be strategically deployed to unmask and subvert normalizing and subordinating discourses. Consequently, we encourage more research into the opportunities, constraints, and complications surrounding the project of liberating the disabled body from discourse- imposed docility.

NOTES

1 Cognizance of controversies on disability terminology, we define disabled bodies as both a product or construct of social political processes as well as an embedded experience (Kraus 2008).
2 The course is titled Theatre and Development Communication. It is a practical course in which students initiate and facilitate an applied theatre project for an identified marginalized community.
3 The actors appropriated the signature tune for the Zimbabwe Television popular Mai Chisamba Talk Show after which all the talk show scenes are modelled.

REFERENCES

Abberely, P. "The Concept of Oppression and the Development of a Social Theory of Disability". *Disability, Handicap and Society*, 5 (2), 1987: 5–19.

Ackroyd, J. "Applied Theatre: Problems and Possibilities." *Applied Theatre Research 3(1)* 2000: 16–32.

Baker, C. "Representing the Tribes of Ghosts: Stereotypes of Albinism emerging from reports or recent attacks in Tanzania and Bhurundi" <http://www.inter-disciplinary.net/ws-conent/upload/2011/07 cbakerrepaperspdf accessed 19/11/11>.

Baker, C., Lund D., Nyathi R., and Taylor J. 'The Myths Surrounding People with Albinism in South Africa and Zimbabwe: *Journal of African Culture Studies*, 22 (2) 2010: 169–81.

Boal, A. *Theatre of the Oppressed*. London: Pluto Press, 1979.

Boal, A. *The Aesthetics of the Oppressed*., London: Routledge, 2006.

Chimuka, T. A. "Ethics among the Shona", *Zambezia, XX11(1)* 2001: 23–42.

Conroy, C. 'Disability: Creative tensions between drama, theatre and disability arts. *RIDE. The Journal of Applied Theatre and Performance*, 14 (1) 2009: 1–19.

Davis, C. L. "The Disability of Thinking. The 'Disabled' Body". *Broadreach Training and Resources* 2010 *http://www.normemma.com/advocacy/artcreal.htm accessed 26/12/2011.*

Foucault, M. *The History of Sexuality, Vol. 1: An Introduction*, Harmondsworth London 1980.

Foucault, M. *Discipline and Punish: The Birth of the Prison*, New York: Vintage Press, 1995.

Gordon, G. E. "Motion Arrested" Body Politics and the Struggle for Physical Theatre, Unpublished Inaugural Lecture, Rhodes University, South Africa, 1994.

Hargrave, M. "Pure Products Go Crazy" RIDE. *The Journal of Applied Theatre and Performance, 14(1)* 2009: 37–59.

Hughes, B. and K. Peterson. "The Social Model and Disability and the Disappearing Body: Towards a Sociology of Impairments", *Disability and Society, 12 (3)* 1997: *325–40.*

Kraus, A. "The Socio Political Construction of Identity: A Multidimensional Model of Disability", PhD Thesis, USA: University of Arizona, 2008.

hooks, b. *Talking Back: Thinking Feminist Thinking Black*, London: Sheba, 1989.

Lunn, M. "What am I for Her? Feminism and Disability within the Post-Modern," Unpublished DPhil Thesis, Massey University, 1997.

Machipisa, L. "Rights Zimbabwe: The Last Minority Group to Find a Voice" Inter-Press Service News Agency, Harare, 2002.

Machipisa, L. "Albinism hit by Zimbabwe Race Divide" BBC News Edition 2003 available http://news.bbc.em.uk/2/hl/Africa 2646967. stm accessed 16/01/2012.

Masuku, J. 'Masuku Speaks to John Makumbe' Radio Netherland Worldwide-Africa available on http://www.rnw.n/affrica/a accessed 20/06/2012

Mhaka, V. "Becoming a Christ for your Neighbour": Exploring Lutheran' Notion of Neighbourliness in light of *Ukama/ubuntu* in the Zimbabwean Lutheran Church, MA, thesis, Kwazulu-Natal University, South Africa.

Mlilo, T. Personal Interview, 22 May 2011.

Mpofu, "Social acceptance of Zimbabwean early adolescence with physical disabilities" Unpublished PhD thesis, University of Wisconsin, 1999.

Mugumira, N. *Theatre for Development Communication Journal*, University of Zimbabwe, Harare, 2011.

Peterson, K. and B. Hughes. "Disability Studies and Phenomenology. The Carnal Politics of Everyday Lives" *Disability and Society, 14 (5)* 1999: 579–610.

Shava, K. "How and in what ways can models of disability inform and promote the empowerment of disabled people and their participation in mainstream Zimbabwean society?" MA thesis, UK: Leeds University, 2008.

Sibanda, P. *Theatre and Development Communication Journal*, University of Zimbabwe, Harare, 2011.

Taylor, P. "Applied Theatre": Building Stronger Communities. *Youth Theatre Journal 16 (1)* 2002: 88–95.

Thompson, R. G. "Staring Back: Self-Representations of Disabled Performance Artists," *American Quarterly, 52 (2)* 2000: 334–35.

Weitsek, G. L. and K. Ociepka. "Reading the Maps of Meaning within Drama: Visible Discourses, Multimodal Semiotics and Analogous Reflections in Applied Theatre Inquiry" *Youth Theatre Journal 25(2)* 2011: 120–35.

Worlbring, G. "The Politics of Albinism", Society for International Development, 2008: 525–28.

Zenenga, P. "Performing Boys: Masculinity in Zimbabwean Drama" in Muponde R. and Muchemwa K. (Eds.) *Fathers of the Nation: Masculinity and Nationalism in Zimbabwe*, Harare: Weaver Press, 2007.

Zvi, L. B. "Staging the Other Israel: The Documentary Theatre of Nola Chiton" *The Drama Review* Vol. 50 (3) 2006: 42–55.

21

Blurring the Boundaries of the Canon: Place and Performance as Alternative Practice in the Townships of Colonial Rhodesia

Owen Seda

INTRODUCTION

A thoroughgoing analysis of the discursive significance of place and performance as alternative practice in the townships of colonial Rhodesia (present day Zimbabwe) has to begin with a close examination of the formative years of early settler white theatre in the colony of Southern Rhodesia. This has to go with a summary of salient discursive practices which characterized this theatre, as well as the ideological underpinnings which played a prominent role in pushing the majority indigenous people into a marginalized cultural minority.

This study proceeds from the premise that colonialist power relations have the capacity to convert majority populations into a cultural minority through systematic marginalization and political subjugation. I would argue that to the extent the indigenous black people were marginalized both socially and economically by the politics of the colonial state, township arts as performed by colonized blacks, became a form of minority discourse which nevertheless sought to destabilize so-called mainstream colonialist (Western) practices at two levels. *First*, these arts deliberately blurred the strictly observed discursive genres separating theatre, music, and dance, and *second*, these arts were able to challenge colonialist spatial practices by performing not in professional theatre spaces but in conveniently found space(s). The paper uses Roman Jakobson's (1971) and Jinrich Honzl's (1976) concepts of dramatic devices and dominants to foreground the way by which township arts in colonial Rhodesia may be theorized as a nascent form of resistance, or minority discourse, as well as alternative practice within the post-colony.

IDEOLOGY AND SETTLER WHITE THEATRE

The ideological underpinnings of Rhodesian settler white theatre are to be found in the framework of European cultural hegemony which took root in the colony with the arrival of Cecil John Rhodes' British South Africa Company's (BSA Co.) 187 member-strong Pioneer Column in September 1890. The arrival of Cecil Rhodes' Pioneer Column at Fort Salisbury is generally considered to mark the beginning of the effective occupation of the colony of Southern Rhodesia (see Taylor 1968; Gann 1965). It also marks the beginning of a significant shift in the practice of, and attitudes towards, cultural life in the British colony of Southern Rhodesia. As Stephen Williams observes:

> A people's history is reflected in its culture. Art and its institutions are the material embodiment of that culture, the visual arts symbolizing life experience and being a means of communicating and bequeathing cultural ideas and values (1991: 61).

Williams' observation is corroborated by Charles Taylor, who in his outline of the early history of Rhodesian entertainment states:

> Accompanied by 300 police... the Pioneer Corps numbered a mere 187 men – men who had been specially picked, by order of Cecil Rhodes, not only for their ability to live in the bush, but as a cross-section of modern civilization: miners, agriculturalists, merchants, and men from the various professions. This was a wise provision, for the land they were about to enter and civilize... was virtually an unoccupied wilderness. At that time it contained no more than half a million Bantu... and the life they lived

> was primitive, both in its working methods and the nature of its infrequent amusements. The pioneers, by contrast, came for the most from environments which had all the sophistications of the nineteenth century, environments which, for their relaxation, required entertainment of the standard civilized type – theatre, music, variety (1968: 13).

It is on the basis of views such as the ones outlined above that the choice of cultural practices by Europeans in the colony was itself ultimately driven by ideologies of cultural supremacy.

As the colonial economy expanded, it was accompanied by the growth and establishment of several major towns, cities and agricultural, as well as mining settlements. The demographics of most of these colonial settlements was characterised by sizeable European populations whose control of local cultural life was instrumental in the establishment of small- to medium-sized theatre buildings which have been referred to as the "little theatres" (Chifunyise 1997; Seda 2004). The establishment of little theatres was also linked to a desire by these settler European populations to maintain metropolitan values and traditions. It is thus that a group of white colonialists came together in 1930 to establish a cultural organization which they called White Rhodesia Movement. The main purpose in establishing White Rhodesia Movement was to promote white interests and culture (Taylor 1968; Cary 1977). It was supposed to lead to the founding of the Salisbury Dramatic Society which brought together a group of white middle class citizens in the then city of Salisbury (capital city of the colony of Rhodesia). The Salisbury Dramatic Society was to become the fore-runner of the Salisbury Repertory Players (or Salisbury REPS) which came to epitomize the growth, development, ideological, and aesthetic orientation of European settler theatre in colonial Rhodesia. Other European theatres in the smaller centres all seem to have taken their cue from Salisbury Reps.

A standard feature for nearly all these European style little theatres was the proscenium arch stage, or box set, set in front of raked seating for perspective scenery in the style of Renaissance and late nineteenth century realism and naturalism. These little theatres were located in the urban and peri-urban centres of Salisbury (REPS Theatre), Kadoma (Campbell Theatre), Umtali (Courtauld Theatre), Bulawayo

(Bulawayo Theatre), Gwelo (Gwelo Theatre), Fort Victoria (Charles Austin Theatre), Wankie (The Little Theatre), Banket (Banket Club), and Raffingora (Ayrshire Theatre). Except for Salisbury's REPS Theatre which was a privately owned space, most of these little theatres were built by urban and rural district local government councils, and they were run on a private long-lease basis by amateur European theatre societies. According to Susan Hains, these theatres were also "operated on club lines that were basically Eurocentric" (Hains 1994: 1).

The repertoire in these theatre venues was dominated by Western canonical playwrights such as Harold Pinter, Arthur Miller, Samuel Beckett, Eugene Ionesco, George Bernard Shaw, Oscar Wilde, and William Shakespeare, as well as a variety of musicals drawn from South Africa, London's West End and New York's Broadway, such as Andrew Lloyd Weber's hit musical *Jesus Christ Superstar* among others (Cary 1975). A characteristic feature of these performances was that of strict differentiation on the basis of genre, along the lines of straight dialogue plays, pantomimes, musicals, and the opera.

PERFORMANCE CULTURE IN THE TOWNSHIPS OF COLONIAL RHODESIA

Writing on South Africa's black city music and theatre, David Coplan observes that "studies of popular culture provide an important means of understanding the experience, attitudes, and reactions of the mass of otherwise inarticulate people, those who vitally affect the course of urban development but who do not read or write about it" (Coplan 1985: 3). More importantly, Coplan goes further to say that urban performing arts, (such as those analysed in this study) represent not the disintegration but the creation of a culture. Following Coplan (1985), I would like to argue that the arts of the colonized, and politically and economically marginalized black people of Rhodesia represent a form of minority discourse that was produced by a mass of otherwise inarticulate people. I would also posit that the practice of popular theatre in the townships of colonial Rhodesia constitutes a significant attempt to depart from Western canonical practices, which were largely and strictly differentiated along the discursive genres of theatre, music, and dance as commonly manifest in the colonial settler white theatres. I would argue further that popular township theatres in colonial Rhodesia represented a spontaneous art form that was able to decentre the afore-mentioned colonialist theatre practices through a process of dominant shifts. I borrow the concept of dominant shifts from Roman Jakobson (1971) who uses it to refer to the various ways by which different performance genres such as music, dance, opera, and theatre are structured and characterized in such a way as to establish their essential characteristics and their difference. Jakobson (1971) further makes the point that one of the characteristics of theatre which is produced in syncretic, or intercultural contexts, is that as it operates within the context of diverse cultural influences, as it begins to display substantial shifts in what Jinrich Honzl refers to as "the hierarchy of dramatic devices" (Honzl 1976: 118). This hierarchy of dramatic devices presupposes the existence of dominants or codes of signification which enable the spectator, listener, or reader to make sense of dramatic structure in a meaningful way. To this end, Western canonical theatre practices consist of a hierarchy of dominants which is principally organized according to genre. These operate in the way that dialogue emerges as the dominant for drama, while music emerges as the dominant for opera and musicals, and kinesics as the dominant for ballet and dance (Balme 1999).

A significant feature of colonial township theatre was among other things, its ability to resist colonialist practices through the blurring of the discursive boundaries outlined above. This was achieved through the transgression of strictly observed discursive genres drawn along the lines of theatre, music, and dance. In other words, as practised in colonial Rhodesia, township arts were able to challenge canonical Western theatre practices through the interplay of dominant shifts wherein it was not possible to differentiate shows on the basis of genre. Although he writes in the strikingly similar context of South Africa, Coplan rightly observes:

> The social history of urban black performing arts is therefore an account of the development and relationship of styles. The phrase 'performing arts' may in turn require explanation. I use it because it best reflects the nature of black expression in South Africa, which cannot be

> divided realistically into Western categories of music, dance, or drama. These categories are not only foreign to Africa: they fail to recognise the close integration of song, lyric, tone, rhythm, movement, rhetoric, and drama in African performance. I use the term 'performance culture' as well, to represent a crucial conjunction between performance and everything that immediately supports it – a social crossroads of performers, participants, styles, categories, materials, and occasions of performance (1985: 4).

In the following section, I attempt to foreground ways in which popular performing arts in colonial Rhodesia were able to infuse music, song, dance, and dialogue within a single act as part and parcel of the afore-mentioned process of the intermingling of discursive dominants.

BLURRING THE BOUNDARIES OF THE CANON: PLACE AND PERFORMANCE

Some of the researches that have been conducted on urban colonial culture seem to reflect the somewhat erroneous view that the life of black workers in southern Africa was nothing more than "a dreary struggle for survival" (Hellman 1948: 22) and a "giddy variety of existential experience" (Ranger 1975: 2). Such researches espouse the view that colonial, racial, and economic prejudice tended to place the welfare of urbanized Africans on the periphery. As Kaarsholm observes:

> The only public concern was to prevent various nuisances attributed to the 'kaffirs" such as noise, dirt, prostitution, tom toms, idleness, thieving, and it was left to the missionaries to look after African welfare and recreation (1999: 230).

While it may be true that the dynamics of colonialist power relations largely pushed Africans on the periphery of urban social and cultural life, the townships of colonial Rhodesia nevertheless provide an interesting site of discursive resistance in which colonial cultural hegemony was challenged and resisted in a number of ways, including the blurring of generic boundaries.

The townships of colonial Rhodesia attracted black people not only from the Rhodesian countryside but also from Zambia, Malawi, Mozambique, and South Africa. As Richard Parry notes in his research on culture, class, and social organization in the then city of Salisbury:

> Any examination of black cultural patterns [in colonial Rhodesia]... must begin with the obvious point that they were shaped fundamentally by the forces which brought the town into existence... Numbers of blacks, like many of their white counterparts, were uprooted and dragged along by the complex of forces that produced Rhodesia (1999: 55).

Writing on the sociology of the city in colonial Rhodesia, Tsuneo Yoshikuni similarly observes:

> Plainly, in origin, functions, form, and power structure the southern African town was thoroughly "European". Yet it did have some interactions with African societies from the beginning, as these societies came under colonial rule and provided labour for the colonial economy. Before long large numbers of Africans congregated in the town, a few even making the town a permanent home, and created a new type of society there. This society had many rural connections, in the form of movements of people... and circulation of ideas and values, which greatly influenced the urban social environment (1999: 113).

It may thus be posited that the forces of cultural uprooting, migration, and interaction between black and black as well as black and white rendered the townships of colonial Rhodesia something of a melting pot for a variety of cultures in which European cultural hegemony was significantly challenged and/or negated. African immigrants brought into the colonial cities and towns more than just their labour; they also brought with them a complex array of cultural baggage (Parry 1999). Parry also notes the presence in Southern Rhodesia at that time of immigrant South African males who were known as "Cape Boys". Like their local and Northern Rhodesian counterparts, the so-called Cape Boys brought the most portable aspects of their culture and performance traditions into the newly established urban social milieu of Southern Rhodesia. Coplan views the process by which urbanized Africans coming from diverse backgrounds transported their performing arts into the colonial cities as part and parcel of this cultural baggage, or a form of "creative syncretism in which performers combine (d) materials from cultures in contact into qualitatively new forms in response to changing conditions, needs, self-images, and aspirations" (Coplan 1985: 236).

Because of a number of socio-political and economic reasons which brought together black African immigrants to reside in racially segregated townships, African performance culture became the product of a fusion of diverse traditional performing arts and elements of Western discursive practices in which the usual Western canonical insistence on classifying performance on the basis of specific genre was significantly challenged. It is also against the larger background of economic, cultural, and racial deprivation that urbanized Africans were able to forge an alternative performing arts tradition for their own entertainment. This was a tradition that was largely informed by the black people's own discursive practices in which the usual boundaries between specific discursive genres was largely blurred. As a result, performances by Southern Rhodesia's urbanized blacks were highly eclectic. They were able to destabilize colonialist notions of art that is based on the separation of specific discursive genres.

The then city of Salisbury (capital of colonial Rhodesia) provides several examples of these performing companies. Among the very first companies to be established in the townships of colonial Rhodesia was the Bantu Actors which started out as a choir under the direction of Kenneth Mataka, a famous musician, actor, and comedian. In addition to choral music, the Bantu Actors also toured the Central African Federation (CAF) of Southern Rhodesia (present day Zimbabwe), Northern Rhodesia (present day Zambia) and Nyasaland (present day Malawi), presenting a mixture of plays, music, and stand-up comedies. Other groups which were based in Salisbury included the De Black Evening Follies (established in 1943), the City Quads, The Gay Gaities (an all-female ensemble established in 1950), the City Slickers, the Milton Brothers, the Golden Rhythm Crooners, the Arcadia Rhythm Lights and the Epworth Theatrical Strutters. In Bulawayo, the colony's second largest city, there were groups such as The Merry Makers and the Cool Four. These groups similarly defied the colonialist notion of performances based on strict adherence to genre, presenting non-stop shows of up to four hours on an average, covering jazz music, traditional song, and dance, *marabi* (a fusion or assimilation of various African musical and dance styles) and what was then referred to as sketches (i.e. drama). Originating from South Africa where it developed in Johannesburg during the 1920s and 1930s, and from which it was transported back to Southern Rhodesia by the so-called Cape Boys and returning immigrants, *marabi* was a pan-ethnic fusion of urban African music and dance (Coplan 1985). According to Coplan, *marabi* was more than just a musical and dance style, it became "a social occasion... a convivial, neighbourhood gathering for drinking, dancing, coupling, friendship and other forms of interaction" (Coplan 1985: 94) that was strongly influenced by the social and economic conditions of working class life where the boundary between work, fun, and leisure was blurred in as much as the division between performance categories was blurred.

The tendency by urbanized Africans to destabilize strictly compartmentalized performance genres is nowhere more evident than in the work of the late Safirio Madzikatire, better known by his stage name of '*Mukadota*'. Safirio Madzikatire, affectionately known by his stage names *Mukadota* or *Baba VaRwizi,* may forever remain Zimbabwe's most popular dramatist and entertainer of all times if the language, form, content, and patronage of his work are anything to go by. Safirio Madzikatire's career in township performing arts spans a period lasting between 1961 and 1986. As a township artist, Madzikatire's work did not belong to any one specific genre. He was a comedian, a dramatist, and a musician all rolled into one. There always existed a close and symbiotic relationship between his work as a touring musician and his work as a dramatist. Like other township artists of his era, Madzikatire's work was first and foremost a popular art form whose appeal cut across social groupings and classes that may have been differentiated on the basis of wealth, privilege, and power (see Jeyifo 1984, Seda 1999). Madzikatire's work as a township artist in colonial Rhodesia compares favourably with that of the tradition of the Travelling Theatres of West Africa (see Jeyifo 1981, 1984, 1988; Barber, Collins, and Ricard 1997). Madzikatire's incorporation of different discursive genres within the framework of his performances destabilized the notion of performing arts based on the strict adherence to specific genres. His work was a form of popular cultural expression where as a general rule, improvization, variety, innovation, and mixing marked the nature of a typical evening's programme that was also often remarkably open to varied styles and influences within the cultural mix of the colonial townships.

The afore-mentioned blurring of generic boundaries was also played out in terms of spaces of performance. In the absence of specialized facilities clearly marked out as performance space for urbanized Africans (as was the case with European style "little theatres"), performance spaces that were used by colonized blacks included ordinary people's homes in the townships. Domestic space in the townships became performance space through the agency of shebeens, or illegal drinking houses in which liquor was sold to the working classes. Shebeens developed into key centres of urban social life where beside the availability of beer in more convivial, domestic, and social neighbourhood settings, patrons could enjoy their leisure time to the accompaniment of music and dance, bidding for performers, refreshments, and musical items.

As the population of urbanized Africans grew, colonial town councils began to make an effort to provide basic social amenities and recreational facilities in African communities across the colony. Landmark facilities for the entertainment of urbanized blacks in Southern Rhodesia include Mai Musodzi Hall in Salisbury's Harare Township (built in 1935), Stanley Hall in Bulawayo's Makokoba Township (built in 1937) and McDonald Hall in Mzilikazi Township in Bulawayo (built in 1957). Although all these community centres were constructed to include stages roughly approximating representational proscenium arch spaces, these venues provided spaces for a variety of cultural entertainments that were not tied to any specific performance genre. In other words, these spaces lent themselves to an eclectic mix of performance genres ranging from musical bands, choral music, film shows, traditional dance and drama. In some cases, as in the case of the then city of Salisbury (present day Harare), these facilities were also complemented by less formal, privately owned venues such as Karimapondo Restaurant which was located along Charter Road on the western part of Salisbury's central business district (CBD). Popular in the 1950s and 1960s, Karimapondo Restaurant was a privately owned family property belonging to the Bhika Brothers, a family of Asian businessmen based in the then city of Salisbury. Because of its liminal existence on the edge of the city centre at the boundary between white and black areas, Karimapondo Restaurant was something of a multi-racial venue that was able to destabilize colonial spatial boundaries based on race, class, and culture, affording township performing artists to present variety shows that included drama, song, and dance.

CONCLUSION

Although the area of performing arts in the townships of colonial Rhodesia is a dynamic force which in its own way enabled colonized black people to endure and to survive the economic and socio-political vagaries of the colonial experience, they still remain a largely under researched aspect of Zimbabwean cultural history. In that sense, David Coplan's observation in the context of apartheid South Africa when he writes that "Lack of interest in these forms may be explained by the widespread perception that they are not authentically African, but rather the diluted, bastardized, commercial stepchildren of Western cultural colonization" (Coplan 1985: 3) perhaps also applies to colonial Rhodesia.

In that event, this study has attempted to present a broad view of these arts with an intention to expose in particular how township arts served as important avenues through which we can understand the experience, attitude, and reaction of colonized blacks to the whole notion of performing arts and discursive genres following the colonial encounter. This study acknowledges the necessary fact that more research still needs to be done into this potentially fascinating area. What has been outlined in this study is no more than an overview which may nevertheless provide exciting pointers for further research. Principally, this study has attempted to demonstrate how urban performing arts by colonized blacks were characterized by an enduring effort to create a performing arts culture based not on a divergence between discursive genres but their amalgamation through the integration of music, song, dance, and drama. This was a blurring of discursive boundaries which was occasioned at the social cross-roads of performers, styles, categories, and the occasion of performance.

REFERENCES

Balme, Christopher. *Decolonizing the Stage: Theatrical Syncretism and Post-colonial Drama*. Oxford: Clarendon Press, 1999.

Barber, Karin, Collins John, and Ricard Alain. *West African Popular Theatre*. Bloomington, Indiana: James Currey, 1997.

Cary, Robert. *The Story of Reps: The History of Salisbury Repertory Players 1931 to 1975*. Salisbury: Galaxie Press, 1975.

Chifunyise, Stephen. *World Encyclopedia of Contemporary Theatre* edited by D. Rubin. Vol. 3, London: Routledge, 1997.

Coplan, David B. *In Township Tonight! South Africa's Black City Music and Theatre*. Johannesburg: Ravan Press, 1985.

Gann, Lewis H. *A History of Southern Rhodesia: Early Days to 1934*. London: Chatto & Windus, 1965.

Hains, Susan. "The Potted History of the National Theatre Organisation" NTO, Harare (Unpublished Monograph), 1994.

Hellman, Ellen. *Rooiyard: A Sociological Survey of an Urban Native Slumyard.* Cape Town: Oxford University Press, 1948.

Honzl, Jindrich. "The Hierarchy of Dramatic Devices." Pp 118–27 in *Semiotics of Art: Prague School Contributions*, edited by Ladislav Matejka and Irwin R. Titunik. Cambridge, Massachusetts & London: MIT Press, 1976.

Jakobson, Roman. "The Dominant." Pp 82-87 in *Readings in Russian Poetics: Formalist and Structuralist Views*, edited by Ladislav Matejka and K. Pomorska. Cambridge, Massachusetts: MIT Press, 1971.

Kaarsholm, Preben. "Si Ye Pambili: Which Way Forward? Urban Development, Culture and Politics in Bulawayo." Pp 227–56 in *Sites of Struggle: Essays in Zimbabwe's Urban History*, edited by Brian Raftopoulos and Yoshikuni Tsuneo. Harare: Weaver Press, 1999.

Parry, Richard. "Culture, Organization and Class: The African Experience in Salisbury 1892-1935." Pp 53-94 in *Sites of Struggle: Essays in Zimbabwe's Urban History* edited by Brian Raftopoulos and Tsuneo Yoshikuni. Harare: Weaver Press, 1999.

Ranger, Terence O. *Dance and Society in Eastern Africa*. London: Heinemann, 1975.

Seda, Owen. "Transculturalism in Post-colonial Zimbabwean Drama: Projections of Zimbabwean Theatre at the Onset of the New Millennium." *ZAMBEZIA* Vol. 31 i/ii 2004: 136–47.

Taylor, Charles T. C. *A History of Rhodesian Entertainment: 1890–1930.* Salisbury: Collins, 1968.

Williams, Stephen. "Art in Zimbabwe: From Colonialism to Independence." Pp 61–74 in *Cultural Struggle and Development in Southern Africa* edited by Pereben Kaarsholm. London: James Currey & Heinemann Educational Books, 1991.

Yoshikuni, Tsuneo. "Notes on the Influence of Town: Country Relations on African Urban History Before 1957: Experience of Salisbury and Bulawayo." Pp 113–28 in *Sites of Struggle: Essays in Zimbabwe's Urban History* edited by Brian Raftpoulos and Yoshikuni Tsuneo. Harare: Weaver Press, 1999.

22

Re-claiming the Mammy: Racial, Sexual, and Class Politics Behind "Mammification" of Black Women

Shaweta Nanda

Black women writers and visual artists seek to redefine "canon" as they represent a distinct voice that chooses to distance itself not only from half the members of their race (black men) but also from half the members of their sex (white feminists), apart from rebelling against the dominant white patriarchal capitalist discourse as they are oppressed on multiple grounds of race, sex, and class. The dominant representations of black women in the popular American cultural discourse, constructed by everybody but themselves, were centred on their bodies. The cultural and visual imagination that is dominated by the white male capitalist discourse constructs black women either as asexual and highly maternal mammies, or as highly eroticized Venus Hottentots, apart from being ugly and inferior.

To begin with, an effort has been made here to define the contours of the "Mammy myth". This leads to unraveling the role that different cultural forces play in generating and then sustaining these stereotypes in the popular imagination. Due the immense popularity of the slave narratives, one tends to focus on the sexual exploitation of the house slaves. While not denying the sexual exploitation that was hidden due to the construction of the Mammy figure, the third part of this study intends to bring to the fore the entire economic and commercial politics behind the white world's popularization of such straightjacket stereotypes and hierarchies. I wish to explore how the stereotype of Aunt Jemima was deployed to present slavery as an enriching institution in antebellum South, thereby, hiding the truth about sexual and economic exploitation of black women. Later, in post-bellum America, she was upheld as an icon of both idealized domesticity and racial harmony. Black intellectuals during the Black Power movement realized the pernicious potential of such stereotypes to regulate black women, both externally and internally: externally because the stereotype became the social anticipations and internally because these stereotypes percolated through black women's consciousness so completely that they appeared to be their inherent and natural virtues. Black woman's life was predetermined by the politically instigated stereotypes. Therefore, one of the primary concerns of feminism along with that of the Black Arts movement at this point of time was to dismantle these negative stereotypes about blacks and underscore their damaging consequences on the black psyche. In response to the constricting and demeaning images, black intellectuals seek to re-read race not in biological terms but in social terms, thereby, highlighting the role of dominant ideology in constructing the identity, image, and role of the subservient group. The last part of the study explores the manner in which writers like Toni Morrison and Sapphire engage with the figure of Mammy, and visual artists like Betye Saar, Jackie Ormes, and Renne Cox deploy their art as means of political protest by resisting, challenging, and subverting such stereotypes in order to create new parameters by which to judge and carve out new identities for the black female subject.

One of the most popular stereotypes about black women is that of the Mammy/Aunt Jemima which is created and then entrenched in the popular American imagination by different cultural expressions/forces, such as novels, films (*Gone with the Wind*), advertisements, and quotidian household objects like salt shakers. In the visual and literary imagination, Mammy/ Jemima[1] figure has been enshrined as a pitch black, fat woman, dressed in a red kerchief and oversized, long dress and has a characteristic expression of a wide grin on her face. The fact that she is shown as an "ideal", that is, loyal, loving, and servile servant in the white household, taking care, ironically, of white children, and never of her own children, adds to her image of a selfless, asexual, maternal figure. She is never placed in a setting, such as in front of a dressing table or a bedroom that underscores her sexuality and material desires. She is rather depicted in highly domesticated sites like the kitchen or the nursery. Acceptance of her inferiority, devotion to the whites, and grin pointing to her non-existent self-esteem are some of the other key characteristics of this stereotype.

The image of Aunt Jemima on the Aunt Jemima pancake mixes and syrup has been rated as top ten advertising icons of the century. The presence and popularity of the image of Mammy even in the contemporary world deflates the claim that racism is a thing of the past. One needs to unearth the economic, cultural, racial, class, and sexual politics lying embedded in these deceptively simple advertisements. The stereotype of the Aunt Jemima was created to redeem slavery as a benign institution where slaves were a happy and intrinsic part of the family. It serves to mask the truth about sexual and economic exploitation of black women in ante- and post-bellum America where they were exploited in a similar fashion.

The construction of Aunt Jemima as a highly expert cook of the renowned Southern households, known for their wealth and hospitality, significantly connects this stereotype with nostalgia associated with the "charm" of the old Southern plantation life. One of the marketing strategies adopted by the whites in the post-Civil War era was to cash in on the sense of longing, nostalgia, grandeur, and quality that was associated with the old South. The pan cake advertisements, thus, strategically deployed terms like "Old South," "Old Time," "Old South Supper," and "Plantation Home" in order to capitalize on the charm of the pre-Civil War South instead of harping upon the nutritional value of the product. "Aunt Jemima offered northerners the southern antebellum experience of having a mammy, without actually participating in slavery. In this way, her popularity bolstered the romantic mythology of the southern plantation" (Wallace-Sanders 2008: 5). Analysing an advertisement that depicts Aunt Jemima helping Mrs. America to produce best quality pancakes that are made using the "secret" recipe of the old South, Wallace-Sanders observes that this fulfills the fantasy of the North to have access to the relics associated with the glory of the South delivered into their kitchens. Such advertisements propelled women to think products like these would given women an access to the special "secret" knowledge that would transform them into exceptional housewives. In the politics behind such campaigns that promote plantation domesticity there seems to be "a sophisticated plan to confirm the alleged positive aspects of slavery, capitalize on the appeal of the brown hand service" (Wallace-Sanders 68). Many narratives presented her as the heroine of the Civil War since she is emblematic of the loyal servant who supports the master's family and does not run away. Apart from upholding Aunt Jemima as an icon of both idealized domesticity and racial harmony, these advertisements also disseminated constricting images about black women by circulating messages about black female body, sexuality, and the socio-economic role that was allotted to her by the dominant culture.

The stereotypes about black women that were deeply engrained in the American psyche continue to have a strong hold on the contemporary popular imagination. For instance, Oliviero Toscani's breast feeding advertisement (1989) created for a famous apparel company, United Colours of Benetton, can be cited as another instance to underscore the continued power of this stereotype on the cultural imagination. This campaign not only created a furor but also won many awards. The advertisement showed a bare-breasted black woman nursing a newborn white infant. Toscani's claim of raising awareness and problematizing the received stereotypes seems questionable to many intellectuals as the advertisement appears to reinforce the stereotype without any constructive criticism or interrogation of the same. However, an analysis of the poster enables one to zero in on the dynamics of the race relations and the precise role that a black female has been accorded in it. The advertisement has all the classic features of the Mammy stereotype. *First*, it depicts a black woman feeding a white baby and not a black one. *Second*, the fact that it depicts a headless and faceless black woman holding a white child asserts the fact that it is not the personal identity and self of the black woman that is important but it is her body, especially her arms, that hold the white child and the breast that feed him are significant. It is disheartening to notice that these racist, classist, and sexist attitudes of the white world that are visible in Aunt Jemima advertisements, continue to exist in the Post-Emancipation Era also.

Furthermore, when one critically analyses a pancake advertisement featuring Mrs. America and a conventional Mammy, one realizes what is *deemed* to be beautiful in a particular socio-political and economic setup, although seems to be apolitical on the surface, is in fact deeply fraught with issues of power and politics. The ideal white femininity defined by and for the male gaze is constructed in opposition to the obese, soot black Jemima, whose poor working class status is reinforced by her rural black dialect that she speaks. Mrs. America, described as "lovely", is a fair skinned, slender bodied, middle class or upper middle class white woman, who is accentuating her appeal by combining her abilities to cook with the charm of the "Old flavour of the South". Aunt Jemima with her shining white teeth and stark red lips also evokes another stereotype of a picaninny with a watermelon. Moreover, one cannot help but notice that the people who are shown enjoying these food products are always white. Black families are conspicuous by their absence. Even when blacks are depicted in such advertisements there is no mention of the rising black bourgeoisie, or black working class families as the depiction of Aunt Jemima along with her husband, Uncle Mose and two children seems to further affirm the existing stereotypes for they are shown to be barefoot, dressed in rags and grinning foolishly. For instance, in a 1890s advertisement Aunt Jemima rag doll family is used as a marketing strategy to boost the sales of the product. It seems all the more ironical as a recipe prepared by the black woman is actually for the consumption of the whites as most black families could not even afford to buy such readymade food packs. Pauline, the "ideal servant" in Morrison's *The Bluest Eye*, is renowned for her special dish called blueberry cobblers. As shown in the pancake advertisements, the special recipe by this woman of the South, Pauline, is prepared for the white master and not for her own family.

From the 1960s to the 1990s, such representations, thus, served to popularize the stereotype of the matriarch[2] which denounced black woman as a domineering, unloving, and uncaring mother to her own children. She was blamed for the breakdown of the black families. Like Mammy, she is portrayed as dark in skin tone, fat, unattractive, and possessing masculine features. It later gives rise to another stereotype called the "Welfare Queen". Welfare Queen is described as a poor working class black woman, most often unwed mother, who is lazy, shuns work, and has no qualms in sitting idle and using the precious State funds. The hold of these stereotypes on the popular imagination can be gauged from the fact that the contemporary feminist author, Ramona Lofton, who has written *Push* using the pen name Sapphire, as an act of appropriating another negative stereotype about the garrulous black woman, ends up denigrating Precious's mother as the stereotypical bad Matriarch and also a Welfare Queen. Precious's mother, Mary, is presented as a single unwed mother who lives with her daughter and grandson on welfare money. She fits the stereotype as she is immensely obese, black, ugly, and evil. She abuses her daughter physically and sexually. Furthermore, she has been completely vilified as she feels sexually jealous of Precious when her boyfriend and Precious's father rapes Precious instead of saving her from the ordeal. She is also lazy and depends on the welfare money allotted for Precious and her first child despite the fact that the baby lives with Precious's grandmother.

It is my contention that black literary and visual artists have responded to the stereotype of Mammy/Aunt Jemima the most because the trope of the Mammy/Aunt Jemima continued to pervade the post-bellum American society. These stereotypes continued to have destructive effect on the lives of black women in the PostEmancipation Era also, as they restricted the opportunities of growth that were available to black women. Accurate representation of black women is subsumed by these controlling images that were omnipresent in American society. These stereotypes further naturalized the racialized notions about their inherent servility, thereby, deeming them fit for the jobs of domestic servants, nannies, washerwomen, seamstresses, and cooks. This reading is further strengthened by the proposal to construct a "Black Mammy Memorial Institute" which would serve as a training school meant to train the next generation of African-Americans for domestic service in order to meet the shortage of domestic servants that was created due to the migration of the black population to the Northern states.[3] Post-World War II, the black civil society underwent significant changes due the black activism of the 1950s and 1970s, which was aimed at dismantling the racial segregation in fact and in law. The fore mentioned shifts were not without inherent contradictions. On the one hand, many blacks gained formal political rights, access to education, housing, and jobs. On the other hand, many blacks plummeted from the working class centre. The growing group of the black underclass along with gender specific pattern of growth and employment were the outcomes of this period. Work for black men in manufacturing vanished, and most of them failed to acquire new jobs. Black women could find jobs but they were often low paid part-time jobs that too in the domestic setup where there was neither a job security nor any benefits attached. Thus, apart from pre-existing "racial segregation," "class stratification" of the black civil society, cropped up as an additional malaise (Collins 2002: 58). Like the antebellum South where the stereotype of the Mammy was created to justify the exploitation of domestic servants, Collins argues that "portraying African American women as stereotypical mammies, matriarchs, welfare recipients and hot mamas helped the U.S. justify Black women's oppression" in the present society also (69). These "controlling images", thus, were constructed with the aim of maintaining their subjugation. According to Hazel Carby, the objective of stereotypes is not to reflect or represent a reality but to function as a disguise, or mystification of objective social relations. Racist ideology, thus, negates the reality of the black intellectualism, aspirations for upward mobility and competence to excel in other jobs.

Due to the reasons mentioned above, dismantling negative stereotypes about the black womanhood became one of the cardinal concerns of the black women intellectuals as they realized the pernicious potential of these "controlling images to make racism, sexism, poverty,... appear to be natural and inevitable parts of everyday life" (Collins: 69). Cartoonist Jackie Ormes in her single panel black and white cartoon series called *Candy* (March 1945–July 1945) overturns the set hierarchies regarding the moral and physical superiority of the whites, especially the white women. She ruptures the dichotomy where the white feminine beauty is constructed in opposition to the unattractiveness and asexuality of the black Mammy figure. Ormes dismantles the mammy myth as Candy is young, beautiful, and curvaceous instead of being soot black, unattractive, and obese. Ormes also frees her of the trademark kerchief and long dresses. Candy, instead, sports a fashionable hairstyle which seems closer to that of Ormes herself. Candy appears to flaunt her buxom body and shapely legs in short stylish dresses and high heel sandals. Ormes reverses the prevalent stereotype by showing a slender black woman worrying about her white mistress gaining weight. Candy exclaims "Gee I hope Mrs. Goldrocks doesn't gain any more weight. I can't possibly wear a size larger" (75). Candy comes across as an empowered woman who successfully upholds her positive self-image in the face of the demeaning dominant portrayals about blacks. In *Candy*, Ormes tries to seize back and assert the "voice" that has been denied to the black women. Candy is radical and subversive as she establishes her moral superiority over her self-interested and uncaring white mistress who ignores her children while it is Candy who takes care of the children. Candy also undoes the image of an ideal house servant who is unconditionally happy and content to serve the master. She says: "I am getting fed up with rolling her cigarette" (75). Moreover, unlike other cartoonists, Ormes avoids "pigmentocracy" in sketching her characters as everyone from masters to servants has the same skin tone. She fills the body of the character artistically with shading or dotting. Thus, Ormes's work is path breaking for her technique, stereotype squashing, and presentation of the alternative positive models for blacks to emulate.

Black artists like Betye Saar and Renée Cox continued to engage with the stereotype of Aunt Jemima and Mammy. However, unlike Ormes in Chicago Renaissance, the tone of their work is more militant and revolutionary. During the American Civil Rights movement and the Black Power movement, Saar produced one of her most politically barbed and radical works named *The Liberation of Aunt Jemima* (1972). The work registers a strong critique of the racist stereotypes about the African-Americans that are perpetuated and normalized through the advertisements. She gives a clarion call for the revolutionary action to combat it. As opposed to the non-violent approach that was taken by the contemporary Civil Rights movements, Saar's work expresses the overt, militant confrontation of racism which is reminiscent of the methods of the Black Nationalist groups like the Black Panther Party, who believed that the non-violent methods were ineffective, especially after Martin Luther King Jr.'s assassination in 1968 (Dallow 2005: 12). This is a mixed media assemblage work which is multilayered as it is made of different objects like advertisement posters, figurine, broom, rifle, and black fist image. The background of the assemblage work is made up of the image of grinning Aunt Jemima drawn from popular pancake advertisements. On this background, Saar places a huge figurine of stereotypical Aunt Jemima that has all the characteristics like ebony skin colour, obese body, red kerchief, and round dress. However, Saar registers her rebellion primarily in three ways. *First*, she depicts Aunt Jemima in a militant pose as she is holding a broom in one hand and a rifle in the other. *Second*, in the foreground of the figurine, Saar depicts a smiling black mammy holding a mulatto baby, thereby, exposing the oft hidden fact of sexual exploitation of the black women by their white masters. *Third*, this image is partially covered by a raised black fist which is symbolic of the Black Power movement and announces Saar's intention of combating racism in a militant fashion. Saar clarifies her intent in creation of the piece "was to transform a negative, demeaning figure into a positive, empowered woman who stands confrontationally with one hand holding a broom and the other armed for battle....a warrior ready to combat servitude and racism" (Saar Saltzman 2006: 58).

Saar's *Liberation of Aunt Jemima* continued to exert considerable influence on Jamaican American artist and photographer Renée Cox (1960–). Like Saar's work that gives a clarion call for action, Cox takes the issue of black empowerment to the next level by creating her two alter-egos, Raje and Yo Mama. Raje is the reincarnation of herself as an "African American super hero who gets back into history and changes things around…She takes on the issues that plague African Americans and other minorities" (Guillory 58). Rage teaches black children about their culture with the aim of countering the damage caused by mainstream media and inculcates confidence in them to fight racism and other forms of oppression.

Cox in her photo creation named *The Liberation of Lady J and U.B.* (1998) subverts the two iconic stereotypes about blacks, namely that of Aunt Jemima and Uncle Ben. Aunt Jemima Pancakes and Uncle Ben's Brown Rice advertisements form the backdrop of her *The Liberation of Lady J and U.B.* The foreground depicts Raje liberating Aunt Jemima and Uncle Ben from their boxes. Instead of the perpetually grinning, servile house servants, one encounters svelte figures that look athletic, strong, virile, and exude confidence in their body and identity which is stressed by their African-American braids. Thus, Cox not only liberates Aunt Jemima but also recasts black woman as an empowered super heroine of the fantasy genre who exercises agency and acts instead of passively accepting her marginalization. Furthermore, black women artists also dismantle the stereotype of the "bad matriarch" and reclaim and celebrate black motherhood as a source of empowerment. Saar's *Lullaby* (1999) asserts the need to reclaim the black female body and maternity back for the black child who is deprived of her mother's care, affection, and milk as black women were deployed as mammies and wet nurses for the white kids. Saar uses serving tray as a background for this work. A framed studio photograph, depicting a mammy with her three charges, is placed inside the tray. The conventional photograph is made to yield new interpretations when it is placed inside a tray, which is symbolic of servitude, with the black child teetering on the far edge of the tray. This work propels one to analyse mammy as a multi-dimensional figure who has different, often hidden and unexplored, aspects to her personality. Saar brings into light the often invisible and neglected children of mammy. Saar also gives voice to the unexpressed desires and longings of a woman who has been forced to take care of someone else's child while her own is forlorn and cries somewhere for the want of love and care.

This radical intervention on Saar's part is rendered more forceful when seen in conjunction with the text that accompanies the work as the conventional lullaby that a mammy sings for the white child is ruptured by another lullaby that she sings for her own child. Two different lullabies are engraved on the two ends of the serving tray. The one meant for the white children reads:

Hushaby, don't you cry
Go to sleepy little baby.
When you wake, you'll have a cake
And all the little pony.

The other engraved at the lower end of the tray, near the picture of the black child, gives voice to mammy's hidden pain due to this enforced separation with her child:

Way down yonder in the meadow
There's a poor lil' lambie
The bees and the butterflies
Pickin' out his eyes
The poor lil' thing cries
"Mammy"

The work asserts the need to reclaim the black female body and maternity back for the black child who is deprived not only of the care, attention, and affection of her mother but also of her milk as black women, deployed as wet nurses for the white kids, were forced to feed their mistresses' children instead of their own. This work challenges the reader to revisit the past in order to uncover hidden histories that have got lost or subsumed by the dominant narrative that declared black women's exceptional love for the white kids. Furthermore, the exclusion of mammy's children from the discourse also served to hide the fact of their sexual exploitation by their white masters.

The theme of self-empowerment in relation to motherhood is further explored by Cox in one of her most famous series, *Yo Mama* (1993). Yo Mama is another alter ego of Cox, apart from Raje.

Cox's own pregnancy inspired her to create this work. In this photograph, she is standing tall and upright, wearing nothing, but black high heel stilettos while holding her two-year old second son. In this seven-feet towering self-portrait, she looks regal and dignified. Cox is determined to assert the dignity and identity that has been denied to the blacks since the days of slavery. She comes across as a woman who owns her body and sexuality. She is confident about posing nude in her work. Moreover, she looks erotic and sensual despite the presence of the child. This picture seeks to overturn not only the stereotypes about the black women but also re-visualizes a (black) mother as someone who is empowered and not passive or victimized. The series has a universal appeal for women of all races. Most women are conditioned to believe that their own lives end once their child is born. Cox, however, visualizes motherhood in terms of empowerment and agency. She argues that it is her way of saying "Girl you can put your pumps on, give your body a good line, pick up you child with pride and move forward" (Wallace-Sanders 60). Cox believes that if one can continue to pursue what motivates one in life even after becoming a mother. To conclude, it, it might be posited that the black female body that is raped, objectified, denigrated, ugly, and stereotyped actually becomes the source of empowerment as black women artists dismantle negative stereotypes, reclaim their body, create alternate positive models who are empowered and have agency and celebrate motherhood as a source of their power.

NOTES

1 Aunt Jemima and Mammy are two distinct stereotypes. While is one is associated with the kitchen, the other is associated with the nursery. Despite this both the terms, most often, are used interchangeably in the popular imagination.

2 Apart from the image of the Mammy, a closely related image of the Matriarch was also systematically circulated in which Like Mammy, she is portrayed as dark in skin tone, fat, unattractive, and possessing masculine features.

3 Thomas Page and Moses Ezekiel planned to build this institute in 1911. Brown argued that "black women educated at Parmer, would learn to become fine clean mothers and good homemakers for themselves and for others" (qtd in Wallace-Sanders: 114). Later, for unknown reasons this institute was never built.

REFERENCES

Collins, Lisa Gail. *The Art of History: African American Women Artists Engage the Past.* London: Rutgers, 2002.

Collins, Patricia Hill. *Black Feminist Thought: Knowledge, Consciousness and the Politics of Empowerment.* New York: Routledge, 2000.

Dallow, Jessica and Barbara C. Matilsky. *Family Legacies: The Art of Betye, Lezley and Alison Saar*. London: Washington Press, 2005.

Goldstein, Nancy and Jackie Ormes. *The First African American Woman Cartoonist.* New York: University of Michigan Press, 2008.

Morrison, Toni. *The Bluest Eye*. New York: Holt Rinhert, 1970.

Lofton, Ramona(Sapphire). *Push.* New York: Vintage, 1997.

Saltzman, Lisa. *Making Memory Matter: Strategies of Remembrance in Contemporary Art.* Chicago: The University of Chicago Press, 2006.

Wallace-Sanders, Kimberley. *Mammy: A Century of Race, Gender, and Southern Memory*. Ann Arbor: University of Michigan Press, 2008.

VISUALS/ADVERTISEMENTS

Aunt Jemima Pancake Mix. Advertisement. Web. 8 December 2010. <http://www.syracusenandow.org>

Aunt Jemima Pancake Mix. Advertisement. Jim Crow Museum of Racist Memorabilia.

Ferris State University, Michigan. Web. http://www.ferris.edu/jimcrow/

Cox, Renee. *Liberation of Aunty Jemima and Uncle Ben.* Photograph. 1998. Web. 30 May 2010. <http://reneecox.org>

——— *Yo Mamma.* Photograph. 1993. Web. 30 May 2010 http://reneecox.org

"Pancake Queen tells Mrs. America about her Newest Pancake Success." Advertisement. *Mammy: A Century of Race,*

Gender, and Southern Memory. By Kimberley Wallace-Sanders. Ann Arbor: University of Michigan Press, 2008:55. Print.

Ormes, Jackie. "Candy." Cartoon. *Chicago Defender*. 31 March 1945. Print.

——— "Candy." Cartoon. *Chicago Defender*. 2 June 1945. Print.

Saar, Betye. *Liberation of Aunt Jemima.* Mixed Media Assemblage.1972. Collection of University of California, Berkley Museum, Los Angeles.

——— *Lullaby.* Mixed –Media Assemblage on Serving Tray. 1999. Mary Anne Mott, Santa Barbara, C.A.

Toscani, Olivero. *United Colours of Benetton.* Advertisement. 1989. Web. 7 December 2010. <http://lawrenceberry.wordpress.com/>

23

Voices of Silence: The Case of Women Musicians

Bandana Chakrabarty

> The woman artiste shares a sense of exile and of discontinuity with all women. Like all women, she is acknowledged but not inscribed in history of musical traditions. But learning, teaching and performing music provide her a space where she can experience and express a self, separate from the given familial roles. (Meegan Jordan, 204)[1]

Members of minority groups are prone to discrimination in their own societies. Creativity in the field of music has ever been the prerogative of men, and it has always been associated with masculinity. As far as women's creativity in this field is concerned, women have never been taken seriously. They have not been regarded as capable of making a space for themselves as singers, performers, and instrumentalists. To put precisely, women musicians have been concealed from history because they have been seen from a perspective of *Otherness*. As for men, the conditions have been different. They have not been traditionally bound to the home and the children, as women have been. As opposed to men, if women indulged in the world outside, they were supposed to be doing so by neglecting their duties as wives and mothers. As such, many women, in spite of possessing creative talent had to subject themselves to self-censorship. They were content to practice music only as a hobby, and were not supposed to nurture it as a full time occupation because the emphasis on home, hearth, and domesticity had been ingrained in their psyche since childhood. They were made to feel guilty for having such interests. Thus, women who defied conventions by attempting to pursue music, or any other creative art, were considered *unwomanly*. Meegan Jordan appropriately marked: "Though music itself is neither masculine nor feminine, those who create music are of predominantly one sex…"[2]

This study takes up Shashi Deshpande's *Small Remedies* (2000), Ameen Merchant's *The Silent Raga* (2008), and Mitra Phukan's *A Monsoon of Music* (2011) to illustrate the points made above. It analyses the lives of the women protagonists who are musicians and demonstrates how they negotiated with the challenges thrown by the male-dominated society and how, in spite of that, they made a mark for themselves. An effort is made here to address the questions in relation to gender and music. In this course, some of the implications of the so-called category of "women musicians" will also be considered. This would be done through examining how the three women musicians in the three texts faced problems in the process of becoming artistes.

To begin with, let me present the brief summaries of the texts chosen for study. *Small Remedies* by Shashi Deshpande uses the story of Savitribai Indorekar, a talented vocalist and a living legend in the world of music, whose passion for music makes her defy the established conventions of time. A daughter-in-law of an orthodox Brahmin family, she gets the facilities to learn music due to the generosity of her father-in-law, but she chooses to abandon a secure married life in a Brahmin household, and elopes to live with Ghulam Saab, a Muslim tabla accompanist. In *The Silent Raga* by Ameen Merchant, we have the case of Janaki, the protagonist, who belongs to a middle-class Tamil Brahmin family. Within two weeks of her mother's death, all family forces act together to bring her out of school and take on her mother's responsibilities. She is a talented musician on the veena and her father magnanimously allows her to continue with her veena lessons. But Janaki too chooses to escape her predicament at the age of twenty-three and elopes with Asgar, a Muslim movie star to become his second wife and settle down to a life of luxury in Bombay. The third novel *A Monsoon of Music* by an Assamese writer-cum-vocalist, Mitra Phukan, is once again set in the world of Hindustani classical music in and around Assam and Bengal. Nomita Sharma, the twenty-six year old vocalist, living in the small town of Tamulbari, studies classical music from Guruma, Sandhya Senapati, and also teaches music to school children. Soon she receives a marriage proposal from the mother of Kaushik Kashyap, an internationally renowned sitar maestro from Kolkata who travels the world over for his concerts. Who will she marry, and whether marriage is necessary for a woman musician, are the questions that are dealt with in the text.

A common feature in the three texts is that they project the dichotomy of music and women musicians belonging to middle-class families. The question that looms large is: what do we intend to suggest/state when we speak of women as musicians? To answer, one might posit that when we refer to women musicians, we seem to potentially separate them from the mainstream tradition of music. This might also imply that the quality of her work could be inferior to that of men. This would, however, be a prejudiced statement, if that had to be made. According to Anderson and Zinsser, "Gender has been the most important factor in shaping the lives of women" (1990: xii). In this respect, it could be suggested that women musicians had no option but to cope with limitations placed upon them by society. Professional activities were seen as improper. Also, there existed the widespread belief that women were incapable of creating art. In the case of the three musicians in question, Savitribai and Nomita are vocalists pursuing Hindustani classical music, whereas Janaki pursues Carnatic music on the veena. To differentiate between the two forms of music, I would briefly mention their features. Indian classical music has been the site of a remarkable confluence of Hindu and Islamic ideologies and traditions. Namita Devidayal in the *Music Room* says, "Like a tumultuous river, this music has gathered different influences along the way and merged them into the flow" (97). Around the fourteenth century, Indian music got divided. Hindustani classical music seems to be greatly influenced by the music of Persia and Arabia. It emphasizes on the musical structure and the possibilities of improvization. Carnatic music, on the other hand, is "kriti", based and "saahitya" (lyric), with spiritualism as its significant marker. Even Carnatic instrumental music is meant to be performed in "gayaki" (singing) style. This musical form has not lost its traditional character even today.

In both *Small Remedies* and *The Silent Raga,* the narrative unfolds "leisurely like a raga". The narrative in *Small Remedies* begins with "an *alaap* continuing with *vistaar,* gradually gaining momentum in a quickening spiral of suspense eventually to achieve a cathartic calm."[3] On the other hand, Ameen Merchant's prose resembles the rhythms and progression of a Carnatic raga. The different sections in his book have been named *Varnam, Alaapna, Krithi, Ragam Thaanam Pallavi, Padham, Thillana,* and *Mangalam,* which demonstrates his knowledge as well as admiration for the nuances of Carnatic music. An *alaapna* is the exposition of a *raga,* a slow improvization with no rhythm, whereas the *raga* acts as the basis of embellishment.

It would be in place to mention that classical performances on the stage have always been a male domain. Prior to the 1930s, virtually all women musicians and dancers belonged to communities of courtesans known as *tawaifs* or *baijis* in the northern, and *devdasis* in the southern part of India. As such, there was no respectability associated with them. With the advent of the British, however, there was a certain change of attitude towards these women. They believed that music and dance practices were immoral and were fit to be abolished. With Acts and legislation such as the Anti-Nautch Act around the 1920s which was discriminatory, woman's position became ambivalent. It must be noted here that it is within the realm of culture that women exist and feminist identities are sought to be constructed. Adrienne Rich constructs a case when she says that patriarchy is symbolized by the father who represents a set of values in all domains of life, and it is patriarchy that exerts pressure on all aspects of life, and decides the parts women may or may not play. Till about 1950, life for women was governed mostly by male dictates, and by the consideration as to what people might think. For women musicians, there was always a possibility of their exploitation. When Savitribai in *Small Remedies* elopes with Ghulam Saab, she gives up all her respectability of being a dutiful Brahmin daughter-in-law in order to gain her love and happiness. People said about her, "A woman who has left her husband's home—what morals would she have anyway?" (222). A woman's identity cannot be disassociated from the religious, national, ethnic, and cultural context of her existence. For most women in patriarchal societies, says Vidya Rao, "Life is a series of discontinuities, shifts, adjustments ... She belongs nowhere and nothing belongs to her. She may be loved and acknowledged as daughter, sister, mother but she herself is absent from the pages of history" (76).

Savitribai who has a daughter is not even recognized as a mother by Munni. Madhu, who is writing Bai's biography, is at a loss to know the real Bai. Savitribai had lived the life she wanted, "steady in the pursuit of her goal, pure of purpose" (170). Deshpande writes that Bai may not have been aware of the term "gender discrimination" but she very well knew "how much longer it takes for a woman to reach the top, how difficult it is for her to break through the barrier to get there" (224). But she was magnanimous enough never to complain about the problems she had to face in her professional life. To her, "these were part of the road she had chosen, they just had to be endured" (224). But as Hasina, the granddaughter of Ghulam Saab confides in Madhu, "Ghulam Saab was the one who made Bai known. He met people on her behalf, he arranged her programmes, he made the contacts for her" (274). Madhu, the biographer, says that Savitribai was one of those women who "reached beyond their grasp" (284) but they had to pay a price for their attempts to break out. In a conversation, Shashi Deshpande aptly underlined the organizing principle that lay behind *Small Remedies*: "What interested me was the situation of the women artistes. Music is something given to them and yet they were in a way barred into it because they were not allowed to take it up seriously. So for me, it was choosing your life that was important."[4]

In *The Silent Raga*, Ameen Merchant's question "Where do middle-class Tamil Brahmin girls go when they turn eighteen?" is a very pertinent one. Janaki is exhibited for marriage to nearly a dozen men—shipping clerks, tea-estate accountants, LIC agents, and even a mathematics teacher from Dubai. All of them have one thing in common: "Arrogance with a price tag" (33). She was reminded of her fate at least twice a month till she was twenty-three. An invisible boundary that defined the space between the back well and the temple bell was all that could be allowed to the middle-class Tamil Brahmin girls when they turned eighteen. After her mother's death, Janaki "washed endless dishes … drew oceans of water in a metal bucket from the well" (46). Andal N. is of the view, "Maternal responsibilities is often used as an alibi to exclude a woman from power, authority, decision-making and a participatory role in public life" (92). Janaki is pulled out of school to do the daily chores of the house, and act as a surrogate mother for her younger sister, Mallika. An early adulthood is thrust upon her. At the same time, she is allowed to continue with her veena lessons, not to be accomplished in that art and become an artiste, but to possess knowledge of music to be used as an asset in the marriage market. The roots of discrimination can often be traced to home and an anti-female bias can be seen in many family practices.

In *A Monsoon of Music*, unlike Janaki of *The Silent Raga*, Nomita Sharma, the protagonist, is neither under parental pressure nor suffers any unreasonable demands from her in-laws to be. She agrees to the marriage proposal acting like a docile daughter. She is given ample space and time to ponder over this business of an arranged marriage. Only after a series of musical concerts does she realize the depth of classical music and the special relationship between the *guru* and *shishya*, in her case, her relationship with Guruma, Sandhya Senapati. Nomita's mother tells her that it was not perceived "proper" for women belonging to good families to perform on stage since music was essentially about performance, and performance was only to be gazed at. The implication is that women who sing in public are usually from the courtesan community. It was unheard of for a Brahmin girl to be associated with the performing arts. Even women who were educated were taught to be better cooks, better homemakers, and better companions. The ulterior motive behind this was to discourage them from entering into public sphere and lead an active life. Although Nomita's mother agrees that "those days" have more or less gone, though "there are vestiges of that disapproval still around … women being allowed to sing in public" (213). Daughters were never taught music in traditional homes because they would get married and would be disclosing this wealth to a rival home after marriage. In Nomita's case, her mother feels that since both Nomita and Kaushik Kashyap have the "same passion, the same interest in music," (213) they would be able to relate to each other. But immediately Nomita reminds her mother of those women musicians who married other musicians and ultimately "had to put their own musical careers on the back burner" (213). Women musicians operate in a sexist environment that socially controls every movement of theirs.

Vidya Rao, in *Heart to Heart: Remembering Nainaji*, writes about Zohra Begum who gave up the life of an artiste in exchange of the "stolid security of marriage" (60). This implied that a woman artiste's life had to be defined only in terms of childbirth, illness, and old age. These bring her career to an end. Devidayal in *The Music Room* has a similar view about marriage between two artistes and its repercussions. She writes, "Marriages were strategically arranged in those days so that music did not go out of known territory" (146). She also says that daughters in the house learnt music by default. They were never officially trained but picked up knowledge by "being a fly on the wall or a wife in the next room" (146).The stigma that surrounded these marginalized women singers was not to disappear so quickly. A patriarchal society which enjoyed the spectacle of women entertainers did not want to see them mingling with their daughters. Society's attitude towards these women has been ambivalent and full of double standards. While these women artistes were young, attractive, and worthy of performance, they sang to please their patrons. But when they were no longer young, they died in deprivation.

Even after India attained Independence and entered an era of modernity, prejudice against women artistes prevailed. Kesarbai Kerkar was a legendary singer of Hindustani classical music. When her granddaughter, Ila, was getting married in 1970, she faced murmurs of outrage because of her lineage. The people were hardly bothered that Ila's grandmother was one of the doyens of classical music in India. She was after all a "bai" from the courtesan community. Because of the stigma attached to women artistes, Kesarbai's daughter did not learn her mother's art. Rather, she became a doctor. When she married a doctor from Surat, the boy's family disowned him because of his mother-in-law's profession. Such was the discrimination that women musicians in India faced at that time.

In *A Monsoon of Music*, Nomita's Guruma, Sandhya Senapati, tells her that when she was a young performer lighting up the stage with her music, none of the established tabla players of the day "wanted to sit with her on stage" (231). It was demeaning for senior men to accompany a woman musician on the tabla, that is, sharing the same space with a woman was unthinkable for men. Women musicians have faced a lot of discrimination. *First*, their music has always been considered inferior to that of men's music. *Second*, men who manage their performances, or stage shows, control women's space and artistic freedom, and finally their femininity. Furthermore, their sexuality and age are always under scrutiny. Thus, Meegan Jordan rightly believes that female musicians have mere token value, and are inappropriate for the profession they aspire to pursue.

In *The Silent Raga*, the locale and setting are culture-specific. Janaki and her sister, Mallika, live in a closed colony called *agraharam* outside the city of Madras in South India but their story is universal. Ameen Merchant has retained many Tamil words in the novel. The concept of family still remains traditional in India as the two sisters, bound by caste, religion, and their female identity, are left with little opportunity to escape from their claustrophobic world. Even while Janaki dares to flee from her conventional household, the younger sister, Mallika gets chained to her home, taking care of her father. Indian culture demands that specific duties be fulfilled by women and a high level of morality be observed. As is the case of many such girls in India, Janaki too must live a life of servitude, first in her father's house, and then in her husband's house, without asking any questions. However, she realizes that tradition will ensnare her which makes her flee from home. She does this even at the cost being the second wife of Asgar, the famous movie star. Yet, at the same time, she is popular in her own way with a successful music academy, whose students are at the point of universal renown.

In *The Music Room*, Dhondutai Kulkarni, a legend of Hindustani classical music, confesses to her disciple, Namita Devidayal, why she never married: "You cannot have two masters. It has to be music or a man. Both demand too much from one" (279). She believes that there was no end to family issues. Husband, in-laws, children, sickness, etc., make great demands upon a woman, whereas Indian classical music requires years of rigorous practice, learning, and dedication. Hence, many a time music has to take a back seat for many women musicians. In Nomita's case, she gives up the idea of marrying Kaushik Kashyap, the living legend of sitar, and settles down to marrying Rahul, her childhood friend, an engineer. Her focus in life would thus be on "teaching the children music ... but it would take a back seat" (419).

Indian classical music is an art nearest to life. All the three protagonists satiate their passion for music in different ways. Their circumstances may vary but their sensibilities remain the same. Linked by the common trajectory of being a part of the same society and culture, Savitribai, Janaki, and Nomita emerge as performers who evolved in different ways, as they encountered several similar as well as dissimilar conditions in their lives. To conclude, I would use Nomita's final word in an argument with Rahul over women tabla players and gharanas: "Of course things have changed now, at least from the gender perspective. But only changed. They haven't got rid of that mentality totally" (232).

NOTES

1 Meegan Jordan.*10X The Talent=1/3 of the Credit. How Female Musicians are treated differently in Music*. Orlando: University of Central Florida 204.n.d.Web19 Feb.2012

2 *ibid.*

3 'On Her Own Term'. *The Hindu*. Web http://hindu/2000/05/07/stories/13070781.html/ Viewed19/2/2012.

4 Interview of Shashi Deshpande by T. Vijay Kumar, Web http://www.musicindia.com/viewarticleas?myr=2007&issid=112id. Viewed 19/5/2012

REFERENCES

Andal, N. *Women and Indian Society. Options and Constraints.* Jaipur and New Delhi: Rawat Publications, 2002.

Anderson, B. and Judith Zinsser. *A History of Their Own* 2nd edition 2 vols. London: Penguin, 1990.

Deshpande, Shashi. *Small Remedies.* New Delhi: Penguin, 2000.

Devidayal, Namita. *The Music Room.* Noida: Random House, 2008.

Merchant, Ameen. *The Silent Raga.* Noida: Harper Collins, 2008.

Phukan, Mitra. *A Monsoon of Music.* New Delhi: Penguin, 2011.

Rao, Vidya. *Heart to Heart: Remembering Nainaji.* Noida: Harper Collins, 2011.

Rich, Adrienne. *Of Woman Born: Motherhood as Experience and Institution.* 1976.

WEB REFERENCE

Jordan, Meegan.*10X The Talent=1/3 of the Credit. How Female Musicians are Treated Differently in Music.* Orlando; University of Florida, 204.n.d. Web 19 Feb. 2012

24

Minority Discourse through Bioscope: *Fire* and *Between Two Women*

Pragati Sobti and Amit Joshi

"There is no word in our language for what we are," says Sita in *Fire.* This loss of word leading to silence reflects the condition of sexual minorities both in and outside India. Scholars working in various areas of literature and culture are now finding people receptive to serious analysis and evaluation of queer and non-heteronormative representations in art forms. Homosexuality, widely maligned as deviant or sinful behaviour in most cultures, is being interrogated, and attitudes stemming from religious and philosophical ideas about what amounts to right behaviour, in terms of nature and natural law, is widely debated upon. In the given context, I have selected to develop a comparative perspective on two movies – Deepa Mehta's *Fire* and Steven Woodcock's *Between Two Women* – hailing from two different locations. A single thematic thread that binds these representations together concerns the problematic of "pulling" and "pushing" between the mutually inclusive and mutually informing cultures of the East and the West. Sexual minorities are universal, but their interpretations, and moreso their politicizations, are not. So, if this recognition of "pulling and pushing" is not always explicit, it is surely implicit in the shared and common English language in which queer politics and theory have been most encoded and disseminated worldwide.

The image that these movies carry takes us to queer theory which intervenes between the alternately sexual films themselves and their reception, distribution, and interpretation. Not necessarily originating from Western or Asian concepts of sexual identity as a political phenomenon, the supposed meaning of these films should also not be freighted with chimerical notions of a truth found in indigenousness. They are not only pure Platonic representations, but they also are the products rooted in their own local, social, economic, artistic, and sexual relativisms. We must, therefore, navigate the visual media through two systems of compounded imagery and interpretation. My analysis of both the movies will be an attempt to highlight the role of cinema in raising the problems, issues, and matters of a social community considered to be a type of sexual minority. It will connect these films to the discourses surrounding identities in the post-colonial environment and it will also consider how these communities interact with class domestic family dynamics.

One of the main doctrines of postmodern theory lays stress on the fact that all identities are constructed on social level. History holds ample proof that dominant groups not only possess the power to construct their own identities, but they also have the power to construct the identities of the groups they dominate which is a matter of serving their own vested interest. The postmodern theory appeals to create methods of deconstruction to demolish the power relationship inherent in the construction of identity, so that it becomes possible to articulate a counter ideology, which has as its aim, the liberation and de-objectification of marginalized groups.

Although homosexual acts were legally decriminalized in some parts of the Western world, such as Denmark, Sweden, and Canada, and even in India in 2009, the issues of sexual minorities have never been seriously articulated.[1] Denial and rejection by society under various pretexts backed by an enforced invisibility, exposes sexual minorities to constant abuse and discrimination. Social discrimination against sexual minorities manifests itself in the production of the ideology of heterosexism which establishes the male–female sexual relationship as the only valid possible lifestyle and renders invalid the lives and cultures of those who do not fit into it. The ideology of heterosexism pervades all dominant social institution, such as family, public spaces, popular culture, and such others. Life in such communities is a matter of constant struggle to acquire social and personal identity. In his critique of the globalization of lesbian and gay politics and identity, the anthropologist Martin F. Manalansan notes that within the rhetoric of certain international gay and lesbian organization, "lesbian gains meaning according to a developmental narrative that begins with an un-liberated, pre-political, homosexual practice that culminates in a liberated 'out' , 'politicized', 'modern', 'gay and lesbian' subjectivity" (46).

For the last two decades, the main aim of the feminist discourse is to "liberate" lesbian identity from the shackles of patriarchal control and to scum up the real "individual self" as a woman. Women identity has great use-value in the scheme of gendered society but possesses very little exchange-value since gender can never fully be exchanged, or reach a point where it may establish an equivalence with another facet of identity, rooted deeply within both the self and society. Any exchange that occurs within the gendered subject, who scrambles to compromise her own identity; the bartering of gender roles and other facets of identity is thus an individual, internal, symbolic act never accepted by the surrounding society. In Raunch's words, "Self-consciousness exists in and for itself by virtue of the fact that is in and itself for another. That is, it exists only in being 'recognized'" (20). As such, a woman locates her internal and social agency in relation to the gaze of the man, whose eyes reflect those religious ideals that paradoxically produce her both as a subject and as a commodity. The leading characters in both the movies try to change their socially assigned roles and decide to stay together, rather than with their husbands, in order to get, not only physical satisfaction, but also an emotional and physiological satisfaction, which ranks much higher than the merely physical. Media, whether in visual or print format, is like a metaphorical image for human beings and it has gained momentum especially in the post-colonial and postmodern era. We, as viewers, learn more about self and identities by watching movies and assimilating the social, cultural, and political issues embedded in their visual narratives. Films, therefore, are the mirrors after which viewers pattern themselves. Both the movies articulate racialized, classed, sexualized, religious, and gendered forms of social regulation and normalization. In the contemporary scenario, many feminist institutions supporting lesbianism are against the concept of role playing and heterosexuality, as according to them it totally depends upon sexual difference, which they regard as oppressive, hierarchical, and polarizing. They argue that heterosexual roles are based on grounds of sexual difference, and thus distribute the power unequally. Many writers believe that heterosexuality exists to spread male dominance, which is not a natural phenomenon but is reflected in the institutionalization of male–female roles.

Lewis Hyde once said that "fear of sexuality is the new, disease sponsored register of the universe of fear in which everyone now lives" (19). In India, this fear is buttressed by social conservatism and hypocrisy and our films, for the most part, are a reflection of this. Burdened by archaic censorship laws and the pressure of playing to the gallery, most Indian films approach sex and its attendant concerns only gingerly, if at all. Deepa Mehta's 1996 film *Fire* both adheres to and challenges the developmental narrative of lesbian identity, which underlies dominant Euro-American discourses. Mehta's heroines are subaltern, who are re-repressed for being lesbians, as well as Indian women, engrossed in the mesh of familial foundations and image of *pativratas*, wholly devoted to their partners in marriage. The movie embodies the shame of a lesbian desire that empowers the female protagonists, enabling them to narrowly escape and complacently accept the patriarchal culture of post-colonial India. Likewise, lesbians and other minority groups can measure themselves against these images and deconstruct what they have always known as the ostensible roots of their desires. Mehta's film is a metaphorical mirror that renders to subaltern women a visual agency with the potential to confirm their existences in a world dominated by film and media images. The film opens with a scene of the adult protagonist Radha's fantasy of herself as a young girl, sitting beside her parents in a wide open field of yellow flowers. Her mother urges the young Radha to "see the ocean" lying just beyond the landlocked field: "what you cannot see you can see, you just have to see without looking". This scene with its exhortation to "see" without looking, to "see' differently, recurs and resonates throughout the film, and suggests an analogy with the ways in which *Fire* interrogates the notion that the proper location of lesbianism is within a politics of invisibility in public sphere. *Fire* takes place in the middle-class neighbourhood of Lajpat Nagar, in New Delhi and tells the story of burgeoning love and desire that emerge between Radha and her new sister-in-law Sita, in a joint family household. Mehta quickly establishes the familiar familial violence and compulsions that inhabit the household: the women do most of the labour for the family business, while their husbands ignore or abuse them. Radha's husband, Ashok, is tender and attentive not to Radha but to his Guru with whom he spends all his free time, and who preaches sexual abstinence, while Sita's husband, Jatin, is too preoccupied with his "Westernized" Chinese girlfriend to attend to Sita. The two women eventually turn to each other for sex and emotional sustenance.

The problematic that the two women represent in their drifting towards lesbianism because of the callous attitude of their husbands, becomes the hard core of the film and imparts it a controversial character at the larger levels of response by the common viewers and the press. The violence that followed the screening of *Fire* brought lesbianism into public and media attention. Activists fought for the movie not because they agreed with it in totality but because they felt it was high time people realized that lesbianism did exist in India. Homosexuality, in this film, is projected both as the last resort and also a kind of consolation prize but not as a message that should make that the queer community is happy about.

Steven Woodcock's *Between Two Women* charts the difficulties of nuclear family life. Ellen who is not able to get physical as well as emotional support from her husband Jeff clings to her son's teacher Miss Kathi Thomson for her fulfillments. The movie, though set in a particular western setting of kitchen-sink-drama, has no patriarchal limitations as we have in *Fire*, but still the indifferent attitude of Hardy towards Ellen forces her to seek the support from Miss Thomson. Ellen is burdened not only due to her family responsibility and proper upbringing of her son, but because she is unable to give vent to her emotions as Hardy is too busy with his factory work for most of the time. The character of Hardy is only a partial onscreen representation of Osborne's Jimmy porter who shares dissatisfaction with life. Hardy has no specific cause for indifference towards his family, but his attitude hurts Ellen. The movie depicts the growing intimacy between two women which underpins the larger theme with motifs of escape, freedom, and hope. It probes the dynamics of a relationship between an idle adult housewife and an aspiring young talented teacher. Woodcock uses a gentle and breezy tone to portray the parity of homosexual and heterosexual relations.

Both the directors depict queer female desire at the interstices of rigidly heterosexual structure in their movies. In *Fire*, men in the family access pleasure and fantasy through, "escape hatches" from the strictures of the conjugal heterosexual domesticity. Ashok, for instance, emerges through the homosexuality of religious discipleship and Jatin trades in porn videos and escapes into sex with his exotically "other" Chinese girlfriend. Similarly, in Woodcock's movie, Hardy engages himself in his work, strolling and playing cards with his friend Joe. Male desire is gratified in these movies but female characters are shut out of such economies of desire; they mutually witness men's pleasures, fantasies, and desires, while being denied their own. For the women whether she be Radha, Sita, or Ellen, queer desire becomes a means of extricating oneself from patriarchal heteronormativity by creating alternative circuits of pleasure and fantasy.

The reaction against such movies, specially in India underlines the fact that historically speaking, sexuality secures the grounds for the production of gendered colonial, bourgeois, nationalist, and religious nationalist subjects. It is somewhat surprising that even such recent attempts to specifically consider the imbrications of discourses of nationalism and women's sexuality still presume the heterosexuality of the female subject. For the procurators of social and cultural codes, women's sexual autonomy never extends beyond the boundaries of heterosexuality; indeed, the possibility that these may exist in other forms of non-heteronormative subjectivities that challenge the logic of such nationalisms is never addressed. Both the movies go beyond depicting queer sexuality or drumming messages home to a fuller exploration of the relationships and their implications. The mainstream cinema, whether in India or anywhere else, has traditionally adopted an attitude of denial, or mockery, towards queer sexuality. Representations of gays, lesbians, and transsexuals have veered between the comic and the criminal. Especially in India, many halls and auditoria that screen serious or provocative issues of some other kind, shy away from homosexuality and view it as a potential law and order problem. The representation of queer people as deviant, victim, or criminal cuts to the heart of what is wrong here which highlights an unwillingness to understand and a deep seated denial that may be multiple forms of sexuality in a society.

In her influential essay, "Can the Subaltern Speak", Gayatri C. Spivak has raised specific issues that concern women, their existence, and the agency that these women secure in the perpetual resurrection of their very roles that construct their gendered domination. The term "subaltern" can be replaced with "sexual subaltern" in this context to refer to the broad theoretical category that brings together a range of sexual minorities within wider perspective. Analysis of these movies suggests that minorities are made to speak on a global level through the medium of cinema as cinema is believed to perpetuate hegemonic discourses in its narrative, and create a new confrontational genre. With the passing of years the horizons of speaking for the subalterns have expanded with the growing economic exchange. According to Frederic Jameson, "it is technology and the media which are the true bearers of the epistemological function; whence a mutation in cultural production in which traditional forms give way to mixed-media experiments and photography, film and television all begin to seep into the visual work of art (and the other arts as well)" (110).

Issues relating to identity and self within the sexual minorities have remained unchanged over the years in spite of all interrogations and deliberations in the recent past. The media, however, has facilitated exchange of ideas in the wake of global capitalism. In this context, Quayson rightly observes that mere highlighting of issues does not constitute the social freedom for sexual minorities that "such proliferations must be understood in their hegemonic or counter-hegemonic implications before they can be aligned potentially to questions of freedom" (147).

The minority issues have been treated on different plans by the Western and non-Western countries. Culture is also being hysterically debated in India. A wide ranging concern regarding Indian cultural values being in danger is quite noticeable and every time it is sex and sexuality that is being interrogated as the threat, the risk, and the perpetual enemy of age-old cultural values. It is in this context that the release of *Fire* in November 1998 in India became a subject of yet another moral and cultural panic. Many U.S. critics commented on this occasion by entitling India as a site of regressive gender oppression, against which the "West" stands for enlightened egalitarianism. Though, the West stands for the so-called modernity, but still the existence of Third World citizens is beleaguered and besieged. According to Gayle Rubin, "the ideology of compulsory heterosexuality may be a powerful force in social construction of lesbianism as 'deviant', but the supposedly feminist insistence on regulated sexuality even between women is equally powerful, and no less oppressive"(24). She states that the transgression should occur both at social and sexual levels in stating the idea of "sexual correctness" under the cover of institutionalized heterosexuality.

Comment by an official on BBC News Online, "if women's physical needs get fulfilled through lesbian acts, the institution of marriage will collapse, and the reproduction of human beings will stop", amply demonstrates the extreme anxiety of sociologists all over the world regarding queer issues. The movies like *Fire* and *Between Two Women*, as also the intellectual interventions through verbal and visual media addressing the issue of the queer/sexual minority, both in India and abroad, have extended the scope of representation and taken the debate in two directions, *first* by viewing heterosexuality and contemporary religious nationalisms as overlapping structures of domination, and *second*, moving beyond the nation-state in order to account for the transnational circuits that both prop up and challenge contemporary nationalisms. Broadly speaking, discourses of normatively, like those in the films, expose negotiations not only between the subject and the nation-state but also between the politics and economics of globalization and post-coloniality. Queer studies offer a useful framework and methodology for interrogating the hetero-normatively of cultural citizenship in the post-colonial scenario.

If we come to analyse the emergence of sexuality and sexual identity, we would agree with David Halperin who makes the statement that "homosexuality has a history and should not be treated as a foundational category" (111). Jonathan Ned Katz forcefully suggests that "homosexuality and heterosexuality are social historical constructions emerging recently in western discourses" (12). He adds that transhistorical references and arguments regarding lesbianism and homosexuality can, therefore, be seen as political and problematic projects often highlighted by visual and print media. In this scenario, homosexuals have to fight for their freedom, respect, and cultural autonomy. Much of the lesbian and gay studies are concerned with issues of representation, media accessibility, and the shaping of discourse about lesbian and gay images. Lesbian and gay studies originated in various domains of knowledge and activity. This may be seen in how the lesbian and gay writers and filmmakers broke liberationist-feminist way of looking at art and culture. We may notice these manifestations in the domains of culture, politics, identity, and power play, and how all these contribute towards creating gay, lesbian, and queer theory.

Globalization has come to signify a whole new set of practices and trends. It is held responsible for some of the major transformations in the structures of media production, representation, and audience reception. Where cinema is believed to perpetuate hegemonic discourses in its narrative, global productions, on the other hand, are believed to contest those points of view and create thereby a new confrontational genre. The advancement in this domain of contestation is well borne out by the fact that it reveals complex political positions and discontinuous process of identifications encountered by sexual minorities. In the words of Mark Chiang, "the politics of sexuality in the global system cannot be directly extrapolated from within the nation" (66). Homosexuality has thus become a sign of the global. In her work on Foucalt's theories of sexuality, Laura Ann Stoler, argues that "Foucalt linked class and race to sexuality" (39). Similarly, it is very true that post-coloniality, globalization, and modernity remain central to our feminist and queer politics in all prevalent cultures. Attempts at global gay movements, like global feminism, lesbian layouts, are plagued with teleological logic that employs Western-centric models coupled with assumptions of the oppressive Third World cultural difference. Similarly, other paradigms and politics that assume simple global and local binaries require reconsideration to encompass the multivalenced and discontinuous transnationality of sexualities engendered by post-coloniality, modernity, and globalization. As Yukio Hanawa writes:

> It is not simply a matter of locating indigenous or local sexuality, whether in Asia or in Asian American cinema and identifying an appropriate lexicon of sexualities. Perhaps and even more so than in other areas of inquiry, the terms by which the sexual-political economy gets defined in both local and global at the same time, widening its horizons with aid and assistance of media. (96)

Despite the glocalizing of this issue, queer sexuality still remains a much maligned and misunderstood area. Of all the art forms, it is the cinema that has the potential to go a long way. There are not enough affirmative representatives that anyone in the queer community can identify with directly, without looking for subtext, or underlying meaning. Other forms of relationship and other forms of "being" have to be explored. As such, it is necessary to create transnational studies of sexualities through print and visual media that vary in discussions about Western hegemony, and indigenous identities and practices, instead of imagining sexualities as complex and contradictory practices located in multiple fields of power.

NOTE

1 Recent intervention by the Supreme Court of India may be referred to that has once again criminalized homosexuality. The judgment has raised considerable amount of controversy in the public domain.

REFERENCES

BBC News Online, 9 Dec 1996.

Chiang, Mark. 'Coming Out Into the Global System: Postmodern Patriarchies and Transnational Sexualities' in *The Wedding Banquet, in*

Q & A: Queer in Asian America, ed. David L. Eng and Alice Y. Hom. Philadelphia: Temple University Press, 1998.

Halperin, David. *One Hundred Years of Sexuality and Other Essays on Greek Love.* New York: Routledge. 1990.

Hanawa, Yukio. *Dangerous Crossroads.* London: Zed Books, 1984.

Hyde, Lewis. *The Gift: Imagination and the Erotic Life of Property.* N. York: Vintage, 1979.

Jameson, Frederic. *The Cultural Turn: Selected Writings on the Postmodern 1983–98.* London: Verso, 1998.

Katz, Jonathan Ned. "Homosexual and Heterosexual Questioning the Terms" in *A Queer World: The Centre for Lesbian and Queer Studies Reader,* ed. Martin Dubermen. New York: New York University Press. 1997.

Martin F. Manalansan, "In the Shadows of Stonewall: Examining Gay Transnational Politics and the Diasporic Dilemma", *The Politics of Culture in the Shadow of Capital.* Ed. Lisa Lowe and David Lloyd. Durham: Duke University Press, 1997.

Quayson, Ato. *Postcolonialism: Theory. Practice or Process?* Malden, MA: Polity 2000.

Rubin, Gayle, "The Traffic in Women: Notes on the 'Political Economy' of Sex". *Toward an Anthropology of Women.* Ed. Rayna R. Reiter. New York: Monthly Review Press, 1975.

Spivak, Gayatri Chakravorti. "Can the Subaltern Speak?" *Colonial Discourse and Postcolonial Theory: A Reader.* Patrick Williams and Laura Chrismen. New York: Columbia University Press. 1994.

Stoler, Laura Ann. *Race and Education of Desire: Foucalt's History of Sexuality and Colonial Order of Things.* Durham, N. C: Duke University Press, 1995.

Contributors

Ameena Kazi Ansari, Professor, Department of English, Jamia Millia Islamia (Central University), New Delhi.

S. Asha, Senior Lecturer, Department of English, Government College, Tonk, Rajasthan.

Rachel Bari, Professor, Department of PG Studies and Research in English, Jnanasahyadri, Kuvempu University, Shankarghatta, Karnataka.

Assumpta Camps, Professor, Department of Roman Philology, University of Barcelona, Spain.

Bandana Chakrabarty, Principal, Rajasthan School of Art, Jaipur.

Ipshita Chanda, Professor, Department of Comparative Literature, Jadavpur University, Kolkata.

Kunal Chattopadhyay, Professor, Department of Comparative Literature, Jadavpur University, Kolkata.

Nehemiah Chivandikwa, Lecturer, Department of Theatre Arts, University of Zimbabwe, Harare, Zimbabwe.

Keki N. Daruwalla, eminent Indian English poet and fiction writer.

Sayantan Dasgupta, Assistant Professor, Department of Comparative Literature, Jadavpur University, Kolkata.

Dorothy Figueira, Professor, Department of Comparative Literature, University of Georgia, Atlanta, USA.

John Burt Foster, Jr, Professor, George Mason University, USA.

Mashrur Shahid Hossain, Associate Professor, Department of English, Jahangirnagar University, Savar, Dhaka, Bangladesh.

Amit Joshi, Assistant Professor, Department of English, Manda Institute of Technology, Bikaner.

Laxmi Kannan, eminent poet, fiction writer, translator in Tamil and English.

Charu Mathur, Associate Professor, Department of English, University of Rajasthan, Jaipur.

Rashmi Mathur, Assistant Professor, National Law University, Jodhpur.

Christi A. Merrill, Assistant Professor of South Asian Literature, University of Michigan, USA.

Shaweta Nanda, Assistant Professor, Department of English, Central University of Himachal Pradesh, Dharamshala.

Anisur Rahman, Professor, Department of English, Jamia Millia Islamia (Central University), New Delhi.

E. V. Ramakrishna, Professor, School of Language, Literature and Culture Studies, Central University of Gujarat, Gandhinagar.

Owen Seda, Senior Lecturer, Department of Entertainment Technology, University of Botswana, Botswana.

Maninder Pal Kaur Sidhu, Associate Professor, Department of English, PG Government College, Chandigarh.

Gurbhagat Singh, Formerly Professor of English, Punjabi University, Patiala, Punjab.

Pragati Sobti, Assistant Professor, Department of English, Maharaja Ganga Singh University, Bikaner.

Kazi Asraf Uddin, Assistant Professor, Department of English, Jahangirnagar University, Savar, Dhaka, Bangladesh.

Index

"A Cow in Aligarh," 123
Abberely, P., 271
Abhimanyu, 95–96
Abrams, Robert, 235
Ackroyd, J., 258
Aesthetic regime, 29
African–American, 28, 36
Agraharam, 312
Akal Ustat, 51
Akhanda Bharat, 63
Akhil Bharatiya Hindu Mahasabha, 58
Alawis, 6
Almaguer, Tomás, 84
Ambedkar, Bhimrao, 20, 36, 39, 116, 158
American Blacks, 21
American slave narratives, 34
Amin, Shahid, 118
Anatta-Moral Law doctrine, 47
Andal, N., 310
Anderson, B., 307
Andreyev, A., 235
Anglo-Indians, 203, 207
Anglophone culture, 14
Anna Karenina, 220–221, 223–225
Ansari, M. T., 118
Anthony, Frank, 204, 207–208
Anti-racism statement, 36
Applied theatre for disabled, 255–275
Ariku, 123
Article 378, removal of, 62
Asad, Talal, 116–117
Ashtapadi, 140
Atma-Brahman, 46–47, 49
Atwood, Margaret, 139
Autobiography
  distinct pattern, 240
  function of party, 237–240
  minority and oppositional, 241–252
  structure for, 237
Autobiography of a Sexually Emancipated Communist Woman, 242
Avant-garde, 29
Azad, Abul Kalam, 57, 65–67

Baamani, 29–30
Badrinath, Tulsi, 127–140
Baisantri, Kausalya, 34
Baker, C., 261–262
Bala, Jatin, 154, 156–157
Balme, Christopher, 282
Bangla Dalit literature, 153–154
Barah Mah, 51
Barber, Karin, 286
Barthes, Roland, 162–163
Basheer, Vaikom Muhammad, 119–121

Beauvoir, Simone De, 79, 91
Begumpura, sign of, 50
Bene Isreal community, 212
Berman, Antoine, 109
Beteille, Andre, 36–39
Between Two Women, 315–324
Bhabha, Homi K., 106, 195
Bharat Mata, 8
Biswas, Mahitosh, 158
Black Liberation struggle, 19
Black Mammy Memorial Institute, 297
Black Panther Movement, 19, 36,
  see also Dalit
Black Power movement, 292
Black women, 291–303
Blasphemy Law, 7
Blue Mutiny (Bengal), 208
The Bluest Eye, 164–165, 295
Boal, A., 256, 259, 267
Book of Esther, 204, 209–210
Borderland, 106
Brahman, 48
Brahmanical system of four castes, 46
Brahmsutrabhashya, 48
British East India Company, 63, 205
British South Africa Company, 279
Bruce Lincoln, W., 236
Bruce Lockhart, R, 235
Building socialist man, concept of,
  239–240
Butler, Judith, 82, 87–88, 91, 95

Caliban strategy, 103
Candy, 298
Cape Boys, 284
Cary, Robert, 280–281
Caste-based discrimination, 34
Caste practices, 25
Caste and race, 37–39
Central African Federation (CAF), 285
Chakravarty, Radha, 129–130, 136, 139
Chandra, Bipan, 173
Chatterjee, Partha, 117
Chattopadhyay, Kunal, 233–252
"Chhobol", 154–156, 158
Chiang, Mark, 323
Chicano literature, 105–109
Chifunyise, Stephen, 280
Chilman, 140
Chimuka, T., 260
Chow, Rey, 14
Cisneros, Sandra, 105–107
Citizenship status, 5
Cixous, Helene, 162
Closing the Sea, 164, 167
The Collaborator, 145, 147, 149
Communist autobiographies, 233–252
The Comparatist, 12
Comparative Literature, 32
Connell, R. W., 89–90
Conroy, C., 271
Coplan, David B., 281–282, 284–286
Cruel Muhammadan, 118
Cuban-American critic, 12
Curfew King, 150

Daiken, Leslie H., 10
Dalit, *see also* African–American
  autobiographies, 34
  literature, 18, 26, 34–43, 153,
    158–159
  movement, 36, 40, 116–117
  panthers, 36
  studies, 18–19
Dallow, Jessica, 299
Damrosch, David, 16
Daniels, Robert Vincent, 236
Dasam Granth, 49–50
Dasgupta, Sashibhushan, 49, 153–159
Dasgupta, Sayantan, 153–159
"Death of God," 46
The Death of Ivan Ilych, 223–225, 227
Deleuze, Gilles, 45, 80, 84, 98
Deleuze's theory, 45
Delman, Carmit, 208
"The Delusion of Truth," 30

Deshpande, Shashi, 306, 309
The Development of Capitalism in Russia, 243
Devidayal, Namita, 307, 311
Devi, Mahasweta, 19–20, 109
Devy, G. N., 101
Dhammapada, 46–47
The Difficulty of Being Good, 183
Disabled people, 255–275
 applied theatre for disabled, 255–275
 beautiful bodies, aesthetics, and disability, 271–275
 The White Man from Buhera, 256–258, 262–266, 270, 272, 275
Discourse of convergence, 55
Discourse of divergence, 55
Discursive regime, 86
Divakaruni, Chitra Banerji, 185–187, 190
Dombs, 199
Dominant minorities, 81
Draupadi, 187
Duravasta, 118

Ecriture feminine, 162, 168
Egan, David R., 227
Empowerment, 6
The Evidence of Experience, 39
Exclusivist discourse, 55, 58–63

The Fallacy of Race, 38
Farber, Samuel, 233
Feminism, 132
Feminism and Contemporary Women Writers: Rethinking Subjectivity, 129–130, 139
Figes, Orlando, 234
Fire, 315–324
Foucault, M., 50, 84, 86, 91, 96, 171, 256–257, 259
Freud's theory of sexuality, 84

Ganda, 140
Gandhi, M. K., 7, 20, 57, 59–60, 64–65, 68, 73, 174, 200, 208, 216
Gann, Lewis H., 279
Gender-transformation, 91–92
German Social Democratic Party (SDP), 233
Ghalib, Mirza Asadullah Khan, 53–54, 74
Gharana, 140
Ghetu Putro Kamala (2020), 85
Ghurye, G. S., 209
The God of Small Things, 164, 166–167
Golwalkar, M., 60–62, 66, 74–75
Gone with the Wind, 292
Gordon, G. E., 271
The Great Golden Sacrifice of the Mahabharata, 183
Guha, Ramachandra, 57, 68, 174
Gupta, Dipanker, 177
Guru Granth, 49, 51

Habermas, J., 121
Hadji Murad, 229–230
Hains, Susan, 281
Haldar, Bimalendu, 154–155
Halfin, Igal, 237–240
Halperin, David, 323
Hanawa, Yukio, 324
Hargrave, M., 271
Harry A., 10
Heart to Heart: Remembering Nainaji, 127–128, 311
Hedgewar, K. B., 56, 60, 74
Hellman, Ellen, 283
Hellweg, John, 184
Heretics, 9
Heterosexual matrix, 88
Hijra community, 85–86, 91–93
Hinduization of names, 199
Hindu–Muslim riot in India, 61–62
Hindu–Muslim unity, 63, 66

Hindu *Rashtra*, 60–62, 64
Hindus, 56–57, 59
in Bangladesh, 81
Hindutva, 59–60
ideologues, 56
Holmstrom, Lakshmi, 42–43
Homosexual, 79–80, 84–85, 89, 94–97, 315–317, 320–321, 323
Honzl, Jindrich, 279, 282
Hossain, Mashrur Shahid, 78–98
Hosseini, Khaled, 79, 86, 90, 145–150
The House on Mango Street, 107
Huggan, Graham, 18
Hutcheon, Linda, 204

I Am, 79, 86, 94
l'ecriture feminine, 162
Inclusivist discourse, 55, 63–70
India After Gandhi, 174
India: A Million Mutinies Now, 171, 175, 179
Indian epic recitals, subaltern voices in, 182–191
Indian Muslim, 53–74
Indigenous Roots of Feminism: Culture, Subjectivity and Agency, 132
Ini Njan Urangatte, 183
Irigaray, Luce, 79

Jaatiya, 29–30
Jain, Jasbir, 20, 46, 132
Jakobson, Roman, 279, 282
Jap Sahib, 51
Jinnah, Mohammad Ali, 57, 60, 63–65
Joothan, 35

Kaarsholm, Preben, 283
Kabir, Humayun, 49, 66–67
Karukku, 42
Kashmir, 147
Kellman, Steven, 103
Khair, Tabish, 69
Kichaka-Vadha, 183
The Kite Runner, 79, 86–87, 90, 145, 148
Kocharethi: The Araya Woman, 193–202
Kollontai, Alexandra, 233–252
Kothari, Rajni, 178
Kraus, A., 268, 270
Kundalini, 48
Kutuzov, V., 234

Lacan, Jacques, 79
Lahore Resolution, March, 64, 1948
Laugh with Leacock, 8
Lawall, Sarah, 223
Le Degre'Zero'de l'ecriture, 162
Leninist dictatorship, 6
Lesbian, 317–319, 321–324
Lewis, C.S., 190
The Liberation of Aunt Jemima, 299
The Liberation of Lady J and U.B., 300
Little theatres, 280
Lopez, Alfred J., 12–13, 19
Lowy, Michael, 240
Lullaby, 300
Lunn, M., 259

MacCormack, Patricia, 83
Machipisa, L., 262
Mack, Maynard, 223
Mahabharata, 182–183, 185, 189
Mahaparinibban Sutta, 49
Mainstream colonialist, 279
Majority, 3, 6, 8, 26–28, 45, 47, 56, 58, 60, 78–83, 90, 97–98, 100, 145, 151, 172–174, 203, 233, 272, 278
Majority–minority binary, 6
Makariev, Plamen, 121
Make Way for Winged Eros, 242
Malik, Harji, 174
Malik, Singh, 174
Mammy myth, 291

Mandal Commission, 18
Mandel, David, 233
Mandel, Ernest, 235
Manning Majority, 79–83
"Man's Most Dangerous Myth: The Fallacy of Race," 36
Mapilla rebellion, 118
Marik, Soma, 233, 251
Master and Man, 221
Masuku, J., 261–262
Maude, Aylmer, 219, 222, 229
Meeting Lives, 127–128, 134
Me Grandad 'ad an Elephant (Me Grand 'ad), 119
Meisami, Julie Scott, 204
Menon, Nivedita, 175
Merchant, Ameen, 306, 308–309, 312
Metaphorical space, 16
Mexican-American frontier, 106
Mhaka, V., 260
Minorities, *see also* Dalit
  in America, 3
  in Bangladesh, 81
  "black," 27–28
  in India, 8–9
  in Kerala, 123
  and majority, 81
  modes of representation, 24
  and sexual abuse, 10, 78–79, 82–86
Minority, 3, 24–27, 30, 45, 54, 80, 98
Minority discourse, 23–33, 121–122, 203, 219–220
  applied theatre for disabled, 255–275
  communist autobiographies and, 233–252
  conference on, 127
  Kollontai, Alexandra Mikhailovna, 241–252
  through bioscope, 315–324
  Trotsky, Lev Davidovich, 241–252
Minority Men, 79, 83–85
Mitra, Chandan, 176
Mlilo, T., 273
Mohanty, Gopinath, 193–202
Mohanty, Paraja, 193–202
A Monsoon of Music, 306, 312
Morrison, Toni, 164–166, 292, 295
Mrityunjay, 183, 185
Mufti of Damascus, 6
Mugumira, N., 262–263
Mujeeb, Mohammad, 57, 67–68
Mulvey, Laura, 79
"Mumbai for Mumbaikars", 61
Mumbai riots of 1992–93, 61
The Music Room, 307, 311, 313
Muslim, 144, 149
  in Bangladesh, 81
  of Delhi against migrating, 66
  in India, 8–9, 54
  Indian discourse, 55
  minoritization of, 116–117
  minority, 53–74
  notions prevalent among Hindus regarding, 68
Muslim-dominated areas, 123

Nabokov, Vladimir, 145, 147, 223–225, 227
Nagaraj, D. R., 116
Nahaylo, Bohdan, 236
Nairatma, 48
Nama, 204
Narayan, Kocharethi, 193–202
The Narrative of the Life of Frederick Douglass, 41
Navakeralam, 125
Nehru, Jawaharlal, 57, 64–65, 211
The New Morality and the Working Class, 242
Nirvana, 46, 91
Nixon, Sean, 82
Nomenclature, transformation in, 4
Noorani, A. G., 174
Norton Anthology of World Masterpieces, 223

Obligatory Transsexual File (OTF), 94
Otherwise Occupied, 15

The Palace of Illusion, 185–186
Paraja, 193–202
Parry, Richard, 283–284
Pashtun tribe, 89
Pattanaik, Devdutt, 185, 187–190
"The Pedestrian Called Badusha," 124
Pérez Firmat, Gustavo, 101
Personal Identity and Gender: A Revised Aristotelian Approach, 137
Peterson, K., 256, 259, 268, 271
Phallogo-centric schema, 79
Philosophy of Hindutva, 55–56
Phukan, Mitra, 306
Pillai, Meena T., 200
Pipes, Richard, 234
Pirani, Simon, 287
The Planet Without a Visa, 251–252
Political Dynamics of Punjab, 173
The Politics of Translation, 109
Poshlust, 147
Pramanik, Shyamal, 154, 158
Prashad, Vijay, 17
Prison Masculinities, 85
Psychosexual anxiety, 88
Punjab, 172–177

Qadianis, 9
Quayson, Ato, 321
Quran, 48, 68–69

"Race and Caste," 36
Race, Language and Culture, 37
Radhakrishnan, S., 46, 49
Rai, Amrit, 222
Ramanujan, A. K., 182, 190
Ramayana, 182
Ranciere, Jacques, 29
Randaamoozham, 183
Ranger, Terence O., 283
Rangila Rasul, 69
Rao, Vidya, 127–140, 309, 311
Rape, 10, 78–79, 82–84, 90
  victim in India, 10
Rashtriya Swayamsevak Sangh (RSS), 58, 199
Reading Lolita in Teheran, 145, 148
Relationality of social existence, 31
Religious minorities in India, 8–9
Revathi, A., 79, 86, 90–93, 97
Revolutionary transformation, 40
Rhodesia, 278–289
  performance culture in the townships, 281–283
  settler white theatre, 279–281
Rich, Adrienne, 308
Rizvi, Fazal, 14
Roy, M. N., 63
Rural life, marginalizing, 219–231
Rushdie, Salman, 8

Saamna, 61
Sahaj-ecstas, 49
Sahajyanis, 46, 48–49
Sahaj-yogini, 49
Sahgal, Nayantara, 171–176, 178–179
Sahlins, Marshal, 196
Said, Edward, 37, 171, 179
Sales, Dora, 102
Salisbury Dramatic Society, 280
Samad, Kunnakkavu, 123
Sanyasi, 81
Sarangi, 140
Sarasanghachalak, 60
Savarkar, V. D., 56, 59–62
Sawant, Shivaji, 183, 185–187, 190
Schapiro, Leonard, 234
Schmitt, Carl, 115
Scholes, Robert, 194–195
Scott, Joan W., 39–40, 43
Sealy, Allan, 204–207
Self-minoritalization, 116
Sen, Amartya, 8
Serge, Victor, 235

The Sexuality of Men, 82
Sexually abused men, 82–83, 97
Sexual violence, 10, 78–79, 82–85
Sex work, 92–93
Shakespeare, William, 281
Shaniwar Telis, 209
Shava, K., 260
Shias, 3, 6
Shiv Sena, 61
Sibanda, P., 262–266, 273–274
Sikh majority state, 173
Sikh minority, 172–173, 178
The Silent Raga, 306, 308–309, 312
Silliman, Jael, 208
Singh, Gurbhagat, 45–52
Slogans of *Shuddhi*, 65
Small Remedies, 306, 308–309
Socialist Revolutionary Party, 235
Solitarist approach, 5
Speak, Memory, 224
Spivak, Gayatri Chakravorty, 19–20, 94, 109, 184, 321
Spokespersonship, 19–21
Sri Guru Granth Sahib, 49
The Stalin School of Falsification, 245
Stoff of "Fatna," 155
Stoffgeschichte, 154
Stoler, Laura Ann, 323
Storm in Chandigarh, 171–172, 175, 179
Strong Democracy, 6
Subaltern School of Historiography, 184
Subaltern Studies XII, 118
Sundarikalum Sundaranmarum, 118
Suras of *Quran*, 48
Swamy, Subramanian, 56, 61–63
Symbol of Brahmanical order, 157

Taboo of literary, 26–27
Tagore, Rabindranath, 133
Tawaif, 130–131
Thackeray, Bal, 61
Thathata, 48
Theories of *ecriture*, 163
Third-World literatures, 109
Thumri-dadra, 140
Tolstoy, Leo, 219–231
  Anna Karenina, 220–221, 223–225
  The Death of Ivan Ilych, 223–225, 227
  Hadji Murad, 229–230
  Master and Man, 221
  and minority discourse, 219–220
  War and Peace, 220–221, 225
  What is Art?, 222–223
Transcultural literatures, 101–104
Transculturation, concept of, 101–102
Transformations: Thinking through Feminism, 134
Travelling Theatres of West Africa, 286
Trotsky, Leon, 233–252
Trotsky, Lev Davidovich, 241–252
Trotter, Justin, 205–207
The Trotter-Nama: A Chronicle, 204, 211
The Truth About Me: A Hijra Life Story, 79, 86, 90, 94
Tucker, Robert C., 234
Tymoczko, Maria, 107–108

Ukama/ubuntu, 257, 259–260
Uncle Tom's Cabin, 41
Un/common Cultures: Racism and the Rearticulation of Cultural Difference, 38
Universal citizenship, 11
UN's Human Rights Council, 36
U.N. World Conference Against Racism (Durban, South Africa), 36

Valmiki, Omprakash, 35–36
  autobiography, 37
Varnam, 140
Vasilisa Malygina, 242
Vedantic, 48
Violated men, 78–79, 85–86
Vishwa Hindu Parishad (VHP), 199
Vismadic capital, idea of, 51
Visweswaran, Kamala, 38

Vladimirsky, M., 235
Vocal minorities, 81
Vulnerable minority, 10

Wahiguru, 49–50
The Walled City, 204, 209–210
War and Peace, 220–221, 225
The Weave of My Life: A Dalit Woman's Memoir, 41
Weber, S., 105
Weitsek, G., 265
Welfare Queen, 296
What is Art?, 222–223
White, Hayden, 238
The White Man from Buhera, 256–258, 262–266, 270, 272, 275
    synopsis, structure, style, 263–265
Whitman, Walt, 12–13
Who are the Jews of India?, 209–210
Wilson, Katherine, 43
Women musicians, case of, 305–313
Worlbring, G., 269
World Literature, 13–14

Yajnaseni, 183
Yo Mama, 301

Zakaria, Rafiq, 57, 62, 68–69
Zenenga, P., 270
Zinsser, Judith, 307
Zvi, L., 258